Mr. Justice Black

Absolutist on the Court

VIRGINIA LEGAL STUDIES are sponsored by the School of Law of the University of Virginia for the publication of meritorious original works, symposia, and reprints in law and related fields. Titles previously published are listed below.

Studies Editors; Carl McFarland, 1967–73
Richard B. Lillich, 1973–

Central Power in the Australian Commonwealth, by the Rt. Hon. Sir Robert Menzies, former Prime Minister of Australia. 1967.

*Administrative Procedure in Government Agencies—*Report by Committee appointed by Attorney General at Request of President to Investigate Need for Procedural Reforms in Administrative Tribunals (1941), reprinted with preface and index 1968.

The Road from Runnymede: Magna Carta and Constitutionalism in America, by A. E. Dick Howard. 1968.

Non-Proliferation Treaty: Framework for Nuclear Arms Control, by Mason Willrich. 1969.

*Mass Production Justice and the Constitutional Ideal—*Papers and proceedings of a conference on problems associated with the misdemeanor, held in April 1969, under the sponsorship of the School of Law, edited by Charles H. Whitebread, II. 1970.

*Education in the Professional Responsibilities of the Lawyer—*Proceedings of the 1968 National Conference on Education in the Professional Responsibilities of the Lawyer, edited by Donald T. Weckstein. 1970.

*The Valuation of Nationalized Property in International Law—*Essays by experts on contemporary practice and suggested approaches, edited by Richard B. Lillich. v. I, 1972; v. II, 1973; v. III, 1975.

Legislative History: Research for the Interpretation of Laws, by Gwendolyn B. Folsom. 1972.

Criminal Appeals: English Practices and American Reforms, by Daniel J. Meador. 1973. Out of print.

*Humanitarian Intervention and the United Nations—*Proceedings of a conference held in March 1972, with appended papers, edited by Richard B. Lillich. 1973.

*The United Nations, a Reassessment: Sanctions, Peacekeeping, and Humanitarian Assistance—*Papers and proceedings of a symposium held in March 1972, edited by John M. Paxman and George T. Boggs. 1973.

*Mr. Justice Black and His Books—*Catalogue of the Justice's personal library, by Daniel J. Meador. 1974.

Legal Transplants, by Alan Watson. 1974.

Limits to National Jurisdiction over the Sea, edited by George T. Yates III and John Hardin Young. 1974.

Commentaries on the Constitution of Virginia (in two volumes), by A. E. Dick Howard. 1974.

*The Future of the United States Multinational Corporation—*Proceedings of a conference held in 1974, edited for the J. B. Moore Society of International Law by Lee D. Unterman and Christine W. Swent. 1975.

Dictionary of Sigla and Abbreviations to and in Law Books before 1607, edited by William Hamilton Bryson. 1975.

An International Rule of Law, by Eberhard Paul Deutsch. 1977. Out of print.

Mr. Justice Black

Absolutist on the Court

JAMES J. MAGEE

University Press of Virginia

Charlottesville

THE UNIVERSITY PRESS OF VIRGINIA

Copyright © 1980 by the Rector and Visitors

of the University of Virginia

First published 1980

Library of Congress Cataloging in Publication Data

Magee, James J.
  Mr. Justice Black, absolutist on the court.
  (Virginia legal studies)
  Bibliography: p. 197.
  Includes index.
  1. Black, Hugo Lafayette, 1886–1971.   2. Judges—
United States—Bibliography.   1. Title.   II. Series.
KF8745.B55M33   347'.73'2634 [B]   79–11555
ISBN 0-8139-0784-5

This volume may be cited as:

J. MAGEE, MR. JUSTICE BLACK: ABSOLUTIST ON THE COURT (1979).

Printed in the United States of America

For Patricia, Jamie, and David

Foreword

A decade ago, on a lovely spring day in Mr. Justice Brennan's home, I summoned every ounce of courage at my command to ask a distinguished octogenarian how he had managed "to get away" with the dedication of his *A Constitutional Faith* to three women: his deceased first wife, his present wife, and his daughter. Mr. Justice Black smiled softly, and responded, "Oh, that was easy: I have loved them all."

There were no doubts; he had few in his long and supremely useful life—be they personal or professional. Principled and determined, he resolutely strived for the right as he saw the right. Whatever some of his friendly or not-so-friendly critics may have concluded then or since, he never failed to offer an explanation—be it of such peaks as his opinion for the unanimous Court in *Gideon* v. *Wainwright* and his dissenting opinion in *Dennis* v. *United States* or of such valleys as his majority opinion in *Korematsu* v. *United States* and his dissenting opinion in *Tinker* v. *Des Moines Independent School District*. Even his very rare silence in a recorded stance in a case portrayed the absence of doubt, once he had determined upon a position, a noted illustration being the cryptic lonely announcement, "Mr. Justice Black dissents," in *Sheppard* v. *Maxwell:* He must have been alive to the media outrages that had informed Judge Blythin's Dayton, Ohio, courtroom in 1954, prompting Mr. Justice Black's eight colleagues to vote for reversal and remand for a new trial. But to the senior United States Supreme Court justice freedom of the press was *absolute*, of course—and thus he had no choice (even if his failure to write an opinion did constitute an embarrassed sheepishness, discountable by consistency).

Professor Magee's superb work identifies, explains, analyzes, and evaluates the Alabaman's articulation of and commitment to "absolutism" with rare objectivity and insight. He sheds significant new bright light on both its genesis and its denouement. He is an ardent admirer, but he is not blind to demonstrable warts. He recognizes the pitfalls of a total embrace of the Black jurisprudential twins of absolutism and literalism. Yet he succeeds admirably in bringing to life the towering role their contemporary creator and guardian played in enhancing not justice at any cost, but equal justice under law. To Mr. Justice Black that law was the literal verbiage of the Constitution of the United States. Period. If it was written there, it was absolute. For the Founding Fathers were literate and intelligent; they knew what words meant! What observer could thus ever forget that marvelous demonstration of the justice's faith and conviction in his memorable December 1968 TV appearance when, time and again, he would respond to the gentle but fervid questioning of veteran CBS correspondents Martin Agronsky and Eric Sevareid by pulling out of his pocket his well-thumbed, omnipresent copy of the Constitution of the United States and pointing to appropriate passages or words, the favorite one inevitably being the word "no" in the First Amendment. "Now, Mr. Agronsky," he would softly but firmly ask, "what does that sentence say? It says 'no,' does it not? 'No' to me means 'no' . . . not 'maybe' or 'occasionally,' or only in certain circumstances or applications." And he would chuckle a bit and lean back, eager for the next quaere—which he would field with conviction and disarming admonitory documentable reference. The bottom line came to be inevitably: "The phrase 'Congress shall make no law' is composed of plain words, easily understood. [And he understood them to be applicable also to the several states, an understanding that, pace his literalist persuasions, he translated into their incorporation through the Fourteenth Amendment.] . . . Neither as offered nor as adopted is the language of this Amendment anything less than absolute. . . ."

Even one week before his death at eighty-five in 1971, Mr. Justice Black, who served longer on the Supreme Court than any other member save Associate Justices Douglas and Field and Mr. Chief Justice Marshall, still argued "absolutism" and "literalism" with his—also then hospitalized and terminally ill—respected colleague, John Marshall Harlan. Friends who called at the funeral home in Washington before Mr. Justice Black's burial in Arlington Cemetery received a poignant parting gift: On a desk bearing a book for visitors' signatures lay a pile of small paperbound copies of the document, a copy of which he had always carried in his pocket and would so often refer to as "my legal bible," the Constitution. He would have approved.

Foreword

Professor Magee, whom it was my privilege to have as a student, has captured admirably, sensitively, and expertly the fascinating jurist's seminal contributions to court, country, and Constitution. Few, if any, have so ably identified and articulated the jurisprudence of that "kindly giant" who will ever live in our history and our hearts.

HENRY J. ABRAHAM
James Hart Professor of
    Government and Foreign Affairs
University of Virginia

Charlottesville, Virginia

Preface

Mr. Justice Hugo Lafayette Black's appointment to the Supreme Court of the United States in 1937 coincided with the end of a constitutional crisis in government and the beginning of what has become a revolution in constitutional development. He was President Franklin D. Roosevelt's first of nine appointees to the Court, and he served that institution and the country with distinction for more than thirty-four years, until his retirement and death in September 1971. It seems to be no exaggeration to say that during his tenure he was the most influential member of the Court in shaping the development of substantive constitutional law, particularly in the realm of civil liberties. Although he did not always succeed in prompting the Court in his direction, many of his dissenting views ultimately became written into law. For example, his persistent belief that the Fourteenth Amendment to the Constitution was designed to make all of the specific guarantees applicable against state power—a position originally outlined in dissent—prodded the Court into incorporating piecemeal almost all of those guarantees. His eloquent and unswerving determination to defend freedom of expression and association made him a hero to many believers in democratic self-government, especially during the darkest days of McCarthyism when a "restrained" Court thought it both expedient and possible to treat the First Amendment's guarantee of freedom of speech as an expendable commodity and still proclaim the strengths and values of freedom and a free society. Justice Black's libertarian defense of this "first freedom" ultimately prevailed, as a changed Court in a calmer time swept aside many of its earlier pronouncements. His defense, as revealed in his opinions in the *United States Reports*, stands as a monument to the meaning of political courage and political freedom.

Not only has the substance of the law been greatly influenced by Justice Black; he was one of the very few members of the Court (past and present) who have sought diligently and conscientiously to develop a constitutional jurisprudence which would serve to limit as well as to justify the exercise of judicial power. Based on his firm conviction that judges ought not to act as the nation's policymakers, and that the Constitution as written establishes real limitations on what the government and the Court can do—a belief nurtured by vivid memories of "government by judiciary" which exploded into the constitutional crisis of 1937, and a belief intensified by the Court's accommodative treatment of the First Amendment during the 1950s—Justice Black expounded and attempted to practice the doctrines of absolutism and literalism, the central pillars of his constitutional jurisprudence.

For obvious reasons, then, Justice Black has justly merited the frequent attention of numerous scholars and commentators seeking to explain and appraise the profound contribution that he made to the growth of constitutional law and to the continuous, often consuming, debate over the proper role of the Supreme Court in the American governmental process. Despite his many statements to the effect that his jurisprudence was rather straightforward and uncomplicated, much of the commentary has been contradictory and somewhat confusing. Some have interpreted his judicial philosophy as an attempt to restrain the exercise of judicial power; others have characterized it as "the philosophical foundations of judicial activism." By some he has been saluted as "that great American," "a kindly giant," "magnificent," "the dean of American judicial liberalism," and a "man . . . meant for the ages." By others he has been dismissed—even derided—as "absurd," "irresponsible," a conservative, "rigid, crotchety, dogmatic old man," and a "liberal without being intelligent."

It is doubtless true that many, if not most, of the conflicting views reflect the extent to which one agrees or disagrees with the values or causes that Justice Black championed or the doctrinaire reasoning to which he sometimes resorted when protecting those values and promoting those causes. In a sense it is good that diverse opinions should proliferate in evaluating the justice who so welcomed freedom of expression; and also, so it has been said, truth is to be discovered in the competition of ideas. But some of these assessments emerge either from a fundamental misunderstanding of his judicial philosophy or from a refusal to believe that it was as important to him as it, in fact, was.

The present volume examines not so much his substantive achievements or contribution to constitutional law as his constitutional jurisprudence (although both are inextricably related), particularly the doctrine of absolutism. The focus is on Justice Black's well-known, but frequently misconstrued, absolutist interpretation of the First Amendment. In the first two chapters I try to explain what he meant by absolutism and to assess the literal and historical support that he offered to sustain his version of the First Amendment. Chapters III, IV, and V trace the evolution of his treatment of that amendment, beginning with his avowed allegiance to the balancing of interests doctrine and ending with his utter rejection of that doctrine as a judicially created distortion of the written Constitution. The latter part of Chapter V and Chapter VI point to the nature of the dilemmas and the difficulties that Justice Black encountered in his attempt to implement what he insisted were "plain words, easily understood."

In different ways many people have contributed to this book. Professor Henry J. Abraham read an earlier draft of the manuscript and provided me with an array of discerning and very helpful suggestions that have made this a better book. He has ever since been a source of encouragement and guidance. Professors Robert J. Harris, G. Edward White, James R. Soles, and Dean Louis H. Pollak (now a federal judge) each also read earlier versions of the manuscript and pointed me toward still other ways to improve the manuscript. Though he has not read the manuscript, Professor Dean Alfange's ideas about the Court and Justice Black are surely infused in various pages of this book, for his courses on these subjects have left their lasting impression and inspiration. Mrs. Dorothy Tyrawski expeditiously and patiently supplied typing assistance. Mr. Gary Lawrence Francione of the University of Virginia law school, who did most of the legwork during the final stages, was indispensable in the completion of this book. Linda Sasser expertly prepared the indexes.

The University of Delaware furnished me with a Faculty Research Grant that made it easier for me to finish the manuscript, and Victor and Catherine Delnore had earlier furnished me with "grants" that made it possible for me to get the project off the ground.

I am sincerely grateful to all of these people for their important contributions and generous support, but, needless to say, any errors or misinterpretations remain the responsibility of the author.

Finally, three special people sacrificed and tolerated far more than I could ask of them while I was preoccupied with this book. The least that I can do in return besides love them is to dedicate this book to them.

Contents

Foreword, by Henry J. Abraham *vii*

Preface *xi*

 I Of Freedom of Expression, Justice Black,
  and Absolutism: Introduction 1

 II Of Absolutism, History, and Freedom of Expression 29

 III Justice Black and the Balancing of Interests 64

 IV Justice Black and the Judicial Process: The Road to
  Absolutism 99

 V Judicial Behavior and Judicial Philosophy: The Dilemmas
  of an Absolutist 144

 VI Conclusion 182

  Bibliography 197

  General Index 203

  Name Index 206

  Case Index 211

Mr. Justice Black

Absolutist on the Court

CHAPTER I

Of Freedom of Expression, Justice Black, and Absolutism: Introduction

THE PROBLEM OF FREEDOM OF EXPRESSION

A free, well-ordered society cherishes and seeks to protect numerous freedoms and interests that are, however, frequently in conflict with each other. The First Amendment's guarantee of freedom of expression, a central pillar supporting the American tradition of democratic liberty, sometimes collides with other, often equally valid, societal interests. A damaging and malicious lie involving discussion of public affairs not only misinforms the public—thereby obstructing the purpose of public comment—but may destroy the good name and livelihood of its intended victim. Unauthorized yet truthful disclosure of military secrets no doubt will inform the people of the affairs of their government but also may cause irreparable injury to the government's effectiveness in conducting the affairs of state; the release of such information may further endanger the security of this better informed society. There are countless other situations in which an unbounded license to speak and publish encroaches on, and inhibits the preservation of, other legitimate values and concerns. Even in a liberty-loving society the right of expression must be harnessed in order to preserve freedom—and perhaps even society itself.

At various points in the interplay of social forces these collisions are

[1]

played out in court cases, most of which are litigated and, even if settled definitively, often forgotten. But some cases, particularly the difficult or great ones, which Mr. Justice Oliver Wendell Holmes said "make bad law," raise the central questions and spawn new legal doctrines designed to resolve at least part of the problem of freedom of expression. Very often the apparent legal resolution or settlement of one dispute serves as the beginning premise of sundry other legal arguments especially as changes in communications technology and public tolerance outdate legal conclusions and outmode the means of expression, thus broadening the dimensions, obscuring the lines, and intensifying the difficulties of the endless free speech debate. The efficacy and fairness of any proposed solution to the problem are usually scrutinized, analyzed, and eventually challenged somewhere by someone as new issues and new directions are added to the domain of an old and recurring problem which society—usually through its courts—must continually attempt to solve.[1]

The problem is not whether the freedom to express diverse ideas, as an end in itself, is desirable,[2] but how that freedom is to be exercised and protected in a pluralistic and changing social system where values other than free speech are deemed essential to liberty and order: How can a society tolerably confine that freedom without destroying it; how does society guarantee the right to expression without enabling it to overtake society? Liberal America has been nearly unanimous in its veneration of that freedom in its ideal, abstract concept. Yet beneath the exaltation lie the seeds of suppression when the test of guaranteeing that freedom in concrete cases arises, that is, when the problem arises. "I believe in free speech for all no matter what their views might be," responded nearly 90 percent of the general electorate surveyed. Yet almost 40 percent would deny a man the right to speak "if he doesn't know what he's talking about," while more than 50 percent would not allow "foreign ideas" to be taught in our schools or permit the publication of books containing the "wrong

---

[1] The literature on this issue is enormous and cannot, for this reason, be cited extensively here. Among the most important is Thomas Emerson's sprawling effort to systematize the freedom of expression. T. EMERSON, THE SYSTEM OF FREEDOM OF EXPRESSION (1970). Professor Emerson's work is perhaps the most comprehensive and contemporary treatment of the subject in that it attempts to present all dimensions of the problem of freedom of expression. *See also* Z. CHAFEE, JR., FREE SPEECH IN THE UNITED STATES (1941); A. MEIKLEJOHN, POLITICAL FREEDOM: THE CONSTITUTIONAL POWER OF THE PEOPLE (1960).

[2] *Cf.* W. BERNS, FREEDOM, VIRTUE, AND THE FIRST AMENDMENT (1957); Marcuse, *Repressive Tolerance*, in A CRITIQUE OF PURE TOLERANCE (Wolff ed. 1965).

political views."[3] But, as Justice Holmes once explained the right, "the only meaning of free speech is that they ['foreign ideas' or the 'wrong political views'] should be given their chance . . . ."[4]

Orthodox or majoritarian ideas seldom require the support of the First Amendment's guarantees. When expression claiming constitutional protection represents dissentient, unorthodox, or "subversive" views (or "the thought we hate," to borrow again from Justice Holmes), the problem of line-drawing may then seem most acute. The difficulty of careful judgment is further accentuated in times of tension and fear of the nonconformist. But that is the time when the very purpose of the First Amendment is put to the task of fulfilling its promise, one which a free society cannot afford frequently, if at all, to hedge. However, it is often necessary to deny constitutional immunity to speech that does not depart from accepted views and ideas if it falsely and recklessly injures someone or if it incites or inflames—even with truthful utterances—an already anxious audience, be it sympathetic or hostile to the speaker. The ramifications of the free speech problem are thus not restricted to the clash of minority and majority beliefs. Indeed, the dimensions and difficulties are infinite, insofar as any number of problems and consequences remain as yet undiscovered. Unfoldings of the future will often demand that the painstaking balances or accommodations struck between conflicting interests by an earlier generation adjust to new situations or else give way.

Sociological innovations and developments shape the context within which arguments about the limits of expression are framed; from social conditions evolves an atmosphere which affects, if it does not establish, the extent to which society and its courts will go to safeguard a dissenting view and its proponent. The Cold War, the product of the unsettled questions of the Second World War and the enormous escalation of the stakes involved on both sides, was in part waged through the confrontation of ideological differences, and in the United States national fear ensued over the potential threat of one such ideology; this fear and concern left the First Amendment liberties in a distressed state. Merely to have been, or only to have been suspected of being, a member of the Communist party was enough to invite upon an otherwise peaceful and law-abiding individual the full wrath of the public hatred and insecurity

---

[3] McCloskey, *Consensus and Ideology in American Politics*, 58 Am. Pol. Sci. Rev. 361, 366–67 (1964).

[4] Gitlow v. New York, 268 U.S. 652, 673 (1925) (Holmes, J., dissenting).

engendered by the intensity of the Cold War and the exaggerations of subversion put forth by congressional inquisitors investigating so-called "un-American activities." The prominence of that issue has since subsided, and the First Amendment freedom of political association has been restored.

From technological discoveries and sociological changes emerge the means of communication and expression. The advent of radio, television, and the electronic amplification of the human voice carries with it an abundance of regulatory considerations that could not have been contemplated by those who wrote and ratified the First Amendment. Moreover, the 1960s stood witness to widespread use of symbolic demonstrations as a way of conveying ideas and expressing ineffable emotions regarding such matters as racial subjugation and the war being waged in Indochina. Wearing black armbands in protest, burning draft cards, holding mass demonstrations in public places, and exhibiting written expletives on one's clothing were among the many measures to which some resorted to publicize their disagreements and frustrations concerning the politics of the established order. Such means may serve as valid instruments of expression, especially for those who conscientiously and peacefully attempt to air their grievances and persuade others to their cause but who have little access to traditional communications media. But such measures also may be exploited by those deliberately bent on violence and destruction. Courts are thus required, if they are "to say what the law is," to discern and delineate a principle which will separate protected symbolic expression from that which should be denied a place under the shelter of the First Amendment. It is not enough simply to hold that such a form of expression falls either within or without the purview of that constitutional guarantee which is so essential to the maintenance of a free and democratic society.

Even if governed by the wisdom of the sages, or what the eminent Judge Learned Hand called "a bevy of Platonic Guardians,"[5] a free social order could still not avoid dealing constantly with the manifest and latent complexities that inhere in the problem of freedom of expression. It could never be assured that the accepted lines around that freedom fashioned, or determined upon, by one generation would even make sense to the next. And if, once more in Holmesian terms, the life of the law has not been

[5] L. HAND, THE BILL OF RIGHTS 73 (1968).

logic but experience, then the future of the First Amendment must depend on, and be nourished by, the pragmatic experiences of the past and present and the uncertain circumstances of the future. The problem is both real and enduring.

JUSTICE BLACK AND THE FIRST AMENDMENT

The name and influence of Mr. Justice Hugo Lafayette Black occupy a preeminent place among those who have sought a viable resolution of the difficult, vexatious, and weighty challenge of setting appropriate limits to the right of expression. Justice Black was appointed to the United States Supreme Court in 1937 by President Franklin D. Roosevelt, and his distinguished and profoundly influential career of more than thirty-four years on that tribunal left a host of contributions to the development of constitutional law, especially on matters relating to individual rights and liberties. Long after various solutions to the problem of free expression are proposed and challenged, one of Justice Black's many legacies will still retain its towering place and no doubt will command a prestigious following, as it did during his service on the Supreme Court: his oft-repeated insistence that the First Amendment to the Constitution is absolute. Because of his vigorous and eloquent defense of freedom of expression, the late Harry Kalven, Jr., could say the First Amendment "now bears his personal trademark."[6]

No member of the Supreme Court, past or present (perhaps excepting Mr. Justice William O. Douglas) has exceeded, in theory at least, the sweep of the First Amendment attributed to it by Justice Black, nor has anyone else of consequence in the annals of constitutional law or history. Regarding the problem of freedom of expression, the First Amendment says that "Congress shall make no law . . . abridging the freedom of speech, or of the press . . . ." Justice Black read these words as evincing a clear and unequivocal command: that the freedoms contained therein are to be absolutely protected against governmental abridgment. In 1962, in a rare public interview, he was asked by his interviewer, the late Edmond Cahn, to explain what appeared to be a doctrinaire and rather cavalier solution to the not so simple problem of free expression. Justice Black

---

[6] Kalven, *Upon Rereading Mr. Justice Black on the First Amendment*, 14 U.C.L.A. L. REV. 428, 429 (1967).

explained: "I believe the words do mean what they say. I have no reason to challenge the intelligence, integrity or honesty of the men who wrote the First Amendment. . . . [T]hese plain few words actually mean what they say."[7] As he saw it, there never was a constitutional problem of freedom of speech in the United States. If the amendment created problems for some, for Justice Black it abolished them. If there existed such a problem which perplexed generations of Americans and the nation's most gifted jurists, it resulted from the unwillingness of courts to enforce the First Amendment's "plain words, easily understood." Moreover, to him it was a dereliction of judicial duty not to enforce the First Amendment absolutely.

Beyond what he deemed the compelling nature of constitutional language, Justice Black conveyed his personal approval of the absolutism he claimed to have found in the First Amendment: "I happen to believe that this was a wise choice" by those who designed the First Amendment.[8] "I have to be honest about it. I confess not only that I think the Amendment means what it says but also that I may be slightly influenced by the fact that I do not think Congress *should* make any law with respect to these subjects," the First Amendment freedoms. Absolute protection for freedom of speech is the only viable means by which to protect that freedom at all. "I realize that there are dangers in freedom of speech," he explained, "but I do not believe that there are any halfway marks." Treated as something less than an absolute, the First Amendment will cease to afford any protection at all, according to his reasoning. "It is a free country; it will remain free only, however, if we recognize that the boundaries of freedom are not so flexible."[9] This precious freedom, "as important to the life of our government as is the heart to the human body,"[10] must be protected "without deviation, without exception, with any ifs, buts, or whereases."[11]

Thus, the difficult, intricate, recurring, and perhaps impossible task of fashioning coherent principles reconciling freedom of expression with other legitimate social values could be performed merely by following the

---

[7] Cahn, *Justice Black and First Amendment "Absolutes": A Public Interview*, 37 N.Y.U. L. Rev. 549, 552–53 (1962).

[8] Carlson v. Landon, 342 U.S. 524, 555 (1952) (Black, J., dissenting).

[9] Cahn, *supra* note 7, at 553, 559, 562.

[10] Drivers Union v. Meadowmoor Dairies, 312 U.S. 287, 302 (1941) (Black, J., dissenting).

[11] H. BLACK, A CONSTITUTIONAL FAITH 45 (1968).

literal command of the Constitution; the multidimensional solution to the problem of free expression and its untold complexities could thus be reduced to a refrain: "Congress shall make no law." When confronted with some of the facets of the problem, Justice Black easily eliminated the difficulties with this absolutist refrain. The problem of distinguishing free speech and press from obscenity and pornography was eliminated by granting absolute constitutional protection to all such expression.[12] Likewise, libel and slander he held absolutely immune from civil damage suits and criminal prosecution, no matter how intentional the lies might be or how ruined the subject of those lies might emerge.[13] Incendiary harangues delivered to incite an angry mob were also to be protected absolutely, despite the importance of the valid social interest in peace and order.[14] He emphasized the reason for his position in a concurring opinion in which he joined the Court's reversal of an obscenity conviction: "I read 'no law . . . abridging' to mean *no law abridging*."[15]

His literal reading of the First Amendment led him to what he conceded might be "a very radical position."[16] Some of his critics have derided his position because, to them, such an interpretation degrades and perverts the principle of freedom of expression. The idea that the First Amendment should be read—or must be read, as Justice Black insisted—as an absolute shield for malicious defamation has been dismissed as an absurdity.[17] "But all I am doing," Justice Black countered in defense, "is following what to me is the clear wording of the First Amendment that 'Congress shall make no law . . . abridging the freedom of speech, or of the press.' . . . As I have said innumerable times before I simply believe that 'Congress shall make no law' means Congress shall make no law."[18]

The results—such as the absolute protection of pornography—provided most of his critics with the evidence needed to ridicule and

[12] *See, e.g.,* Mishkin v. New York, 383 U.S. 502, 515–18 (1966) (Black, J., dissenting).

[13] *See, e.g.,* Curtis Publishing Co. v. Butts, 388 U.S. 130, 170–72 (1967) (Black, J., dissenting).

[14] *See, e.g.,* Yates v. United States, 354 U.S. 298, 340–41 (1957) (Black, J., concurring in part and dissenting in part); Feiner v. New York, 340 U.S. 315, 321–29 (1951) (Black, J., dissenting).

[15] Smith v. California, 361 U.S. 147, 157 (1959) (Black, J., concurring).

[16] H. BLACK, *supra* note 11, at 45.

[17] Hook, *A Philosopher Dissents in the Case of Absolutes* in FREE SPEECH AND POLITICAL PROTEST 79, *passim* (Summers ed. 1967). *See generally* S. HOOK, THE PARADOXES OF FREEDOM (1962).

[18] H. BLACK, *supra* note 11, at 45.

ignore his rendition of the First Amendment. But other observers have focused their criticism on the seemingly simplistic judicial reasoning Justice Black advanced to justify his sweeping construction of the First Amendment. Some have been stirred to challenge the notion of literal absolutes and have concentrated their attack on the doctrines of literalism and absolutism, the two principal components of Justice Black's constitutional jurisprudence. To comprehend his construction of the First Amendment and the reasoning on which it rested, it is important to understand his professed allegiance to these doctrines and what he meant by them. His most vocal critics, however, have misstated the meanings of these doctrines in their efforts to undermine them; their commentaries attacking these doctrines have also misrepresented Justice Black. It is thus worthwhile here briefly to discuss the doctrines of absolutism and literalism—at least for the purpose of establishing what he did not mean by them.

Absolutism and the Bill of Rights

In 1960, before an audience at New York University Law School, Justice Black delivered his James Madison Address, which stands as a major exposition of the premises and tenets of his constitutional jurisprudence. There he unfolded the doctrine of absolute rights contained in the Bill of Rights. All of the provisions of the Bill of Rights, not just the First Amendment, he said, contain absolute rights, and these liberties were not intended to be merely suggestions or admonitions to government but "were put there on purpose by men who knew what words meant, and meant their prohibitions to be 'absolutes.' " Speaking of the Sixth Amendment's guarantees of trial by an impartial jury, the right to confront witnesses, and the right to counsel, for instance, he asked: "Can it be that these are not absolute prohibitions?"[19] The Bill of Rights was not some misty congeries of uncertain liberties. In Justice Black's view the Bill of Rights (which he said included not only the first eight amendments but all constitutional provisions that limit governmental powers) represented an intentional effort to set limits to what government could do. The Bill of Rights was designed to preserve individual rights and liberties by barring official encroachment on these liberties, which were "marked by bound-

[19] Black, *The Bill of Rights*, 35 N.Y.U. L. REV. 865, 867, 872 (1960).

aries precisely defined." The task for the judiciary was quite clear: "[W]e have only to observe faithfully the boundaries already marked for us."[20]

Justice Black was insistent in his claim of precision and clarity emanating from the constitutional text: "Those principles [of freedom] are embodied for all who care to see in our Bill of Rights. . . . Their ineffectiveness . . . stems, not from any lack of precision in the statement of those principles, but from the refusal [of the Supreme Court] to apply those principles precisely stated."[21] But that the Bill of Rights does not precisely or clearly define all its particular guarantees is a fact too clear for argument. The First Amendment, for example, ensures "the free exercise of religion," but it does not explain what that right entails. The Fifth Amendment speaks of a right against double jeopardy, but it says nothing of what constitutes double jeopardy.

Answers to these unanswered questions are important if the rights contained in the Bill of Rights are to mean anything in practice. Aware of the obvious ambiguities and uncertainties in the Bill of Rights, Justice Black's critics have attacked his repeated assertions of its clarity and what appeared to be his simplistic view of constitutional adjudication. Wallace Mendelson, political scientist and former law clerk to Mr. Justice Felix Frankfurter, Justice Black's major jurisprudential antagonist on the Court, has characterized the justice's position as an "activist-idealist pretense that all answers to all problems are in (or above) the Constitution— and that the judicial process for extracting them is largely mechanical or automatic."[22] Former solicitor general and dean of the Harvard law school Erwin N. Griswold has described Justice Black's jurisprudence as the "fundamentalist theological" approach to law: "God said it. We believe it. That's all there is to it."[23]

The late Alexander M. Bickel of the Yale law school contended that Justice Black resorted to the notion of literally clear and precise absolutes in order "to disguise, as did his predecessors of a generation ago, the process of judgment."[24] Bickel equated the justice's statements with the

[20] Braden v. United States, 365 U.S. 431, 444–445 (1961) (Black, J., dissenting).

[21] Wilkinson v. United States, 365 U.S. 399, 422 (1961) (Black, J., dissenting).

[22] Mendelson, *The First Amendment and the Judicial Process: A Reply to Mr. Frantz*, 17 Vand. L. Rev. 479, 485 (1964).

[23] Griswold, *Absolute Is in the Dark*, 8 Utah L. Rev. 167, 172 (1963).

[24] A. Bickel, The Least Dangerous Branch 91 (1962).

disingenuous front for judge-made law announced by Mr. Justice Owen J. Roberts in 1936, when the Court was in the midst of piecemeal invalidation of the New Deal:

> The Constitution is the supreme law of the land ordained and established by the people. . . . When an act of Congress is appropriately challenged in the courts as not conforming to the constitutional mandate the judicial branch of the Government has only one duty,—to lay the article of the Constitution which is invoked beside the statute which is challenged and decide whether the latter squares with the former. . . . [A]nd having done that, [the Court's] duty ends.[25]

"Yet here is Justice Black," Bickel continued, "ignoring the lessons he had his share in teaching and reverting to the practice of laying articles of the Constitution beside federal and state statutes and finding, so to speak, a lack of squarage [*sic*]."[26] The only real difference between the judicial behavior of Justices Black and Roberts was a difference in policy. It was the "achievement" of Justice Black, Bickel wrote, "to adapt the old style [the Justice Roberts style] to a substance of his own."[27]

These are serious charges, not only because they are those of nationally recognized constitutional law experts, such as Bickel, but also because they offhandedly reduce Justice Black's jurisprudence to the activist contrivances invoked by the Court of the 1920s and 1930s in order to legitimate judicial efforts to repress the emerging welfare state, the very type of judicial philosophy against which Justice Black aimed his own. Yet his choice of language and his repeated assertions of precise and clear principles in the Bill of Rights invited such accusations from critics. Criticism comes, though more gently, even from Laurent B. Frantz, whose First Amendment posture is akin to Justice Black's but who has presented his position more cogently:

> Mr. Justice Black . . . has chosen to put his argument largely in the form that the first amendment "means what it says." But to treat this as a sufficient answer to questions of whether and how the first amendment applies in a particular case is to imply that its terms are self-defining, that prefabricated answers to all questions of this type can be found merely by consulting the text. . . . [H]is failure to spell out more clearly

---

[25] United States v. Butler, 297 U.S. 1, 62–63 (1936) (Roberts, J.).

[26] A. Bickel, *supra* note 24, at 91.

[27] A. Bickel, The Supreme Court and the Idea of Progress 19 (1970).

[what is meant by the First Amendment] has certainly contributed to the ability of his opponents to brush his arguments aside by putting this construction [of simplistic literalism] upon them.[28]

Justice Black's repeated exaggerations about the presumed precision and clarity in the language of the First Amendment, and the Bill of Rights in general, impelled his critics to the conclusion that his constitutional jurisprudence was naive, unrealistic, and fanciful. Bickel and Mendelson, both citing Thomas Reed Powell's criticism of the Court of the 1920s and 1930s, compared Justice Black's position to " 'these professions of nonparticipation in the judicial process.' "[29] Justice Black's constant rhetoric and exclamations about precise boundaries in the Bill of Rights served mostly to cloud the core of his absolutist argument. His ceaseless insistence on the validity of the truism that "no law" means no law contains the essence of an important legal concept which was mostly overlooked or ignored by his critics, who focused on the abundance of ambiguity in the Bill of Rights. Absolutism was Justice Black's response to the "balancing of interests" doctrine; it was a direct challenge to what has become the prevailing process of adjudication adopted by the Supreme Court in First Amendment cases, a process which he saw as subordinating to competing governmental interests "liberties *admittedly* covered by the Bill of Rights,"[30] the supreme law of the United States. Absolutism was a rejection of the judicial disposition represented by the following statement of the Court in upholding governmental incursions into First Amendment rights:

[W]e agree that compulsory disclosure of the names of an organization's members may in certain instances infringe constitutionally protected rights of association. . . . But to say this much is only to recognize one of the points of reference from which analysis must begin. To state that individual liberties may be affected is to establish the condition for, not to arrive at the conclusion of, constitutional decision. Against the impediments which particular governmental regulation causes to entire

[28] Frantz, *The First Amendment in the Balance*, 71 YALE L. J. 1424, 1432 (1962).

[29] Mendelson, *On the Meaning of the First Amendment: Absolutes in the Balance*, 50 CALIF. L. REV. 821, 825 (1962), *quoting from* T. POWELL, VAGARIES AND VARIETIES IN CONSTITUTIONAL INTERPRETATION 28 (1956). Bickel made the analogy between Justice Black's position and "judicial professions of automation.' " A. BICKEL, *supra* note 24, at 91, *quoting from* POWELL, *supra*, at 43.

[30] Black, *supra* note 19, at 867.

freedom of individual action, there must be weighed the value to the public of the ends which the regulation may achieve.[31]

Conceding that freedoms protected by the First Amendment might, indeed, be abridged by governmental action, the Court reasoned that such action is nonetheless constitutionally permissible if its purpose or effect is of sufficient value as to outweigh the importance of First Amendment freedoms.

Justice Black's reply to this reasoning was not the simpleminded literalism attributed to him by his detractors. It was a simple but trenchant argument which cannot easily be brushed aside: that the express purpose of the First Amendment was absolutely to remove governmental powers from this area, that the freedoms contained therein are absolute against all governmental attempts to abridge them, no matter how noble the government's intentions or how overwhelming, valuable, or compelling the countervailing public interest in abridging those freedoms.[32] As such, absolutism was an uncomplicated but quite important rebuttal to the balancing of interests approach to the resolution of conflicts involving incursions into individual rights protected by the Constitution.

Benjamin N. Cardozo, distinguished judge of the New York Court of Appeals, later a revered member of the United States Supreme Court, and a seminal figure in the development of American jurisprudence, explained the process of judging in his classic volume on this subject. Sometimes "[t]he rule that fits the case may be supplied by the constitution," he wrote. "If that is so, the judge looks no farther. The correspondence ascertained, his duty is to obey."[33] Similarly, Justice Black reasoned that balancing perverts the idea of constitutional guarantees in that balancing results in upholding as constitutional what otherwise is an admitted invasion of the First Amendment if the government can demonstrate that the interest in doing so is great enough. And this is often done in the name of "judicial self-restraint." But Justice Black retorted that his oath of office was to uphold and enforce the written Constitution, not "to 'balance' the

[31] Communist Party v. Subversive Activities Control Board, 367 U.S. 1, 90–91 (1961) (Frankfurter, J.).

[32] However, when governmental regulation is aimed at conduct as distinguished from speech, although indirectly infringing on First Amendment rights, Justice Black agreed that courts were required to balance interests. This aspect of his judicial philosophy is examined in chs. III and V, *infra*.

[33] B. CARDOZO, THE NATURE OF THE JUDICIAL PROCESS 14 (1921).

Bill of Rights out of existence."[34] "I took an obligation to support and defend the Constitution as I understand it," he said. "And being a rather backward country fellow, I understand it to mean what the words say. . . . [The First Amendment] says 'no law,' and that is what I believe it means."[35] To deny enforcement to a right recognized in the Constitution constituted a violation of the judicial duty to enforce the Constitution. Judges must restrain themselves by restricting themselves to enforcing what the law says. In this sense Justice Black was more restrained than the balancers on the Court who claimed adherence to the doctrine of judicial self-restraint.[36]

Justice Black's absolutism, then, was not a "device" which "induces a happy activism without afterthought and sometimes even without fore-thought,"[37] as Bickel sarcastically misunderstood it. Nor was it the naive and preposterous notion that all answers to all questions involving individual liberties emanate for all time, "absolutely," from the Bill of Rights. Absolutism for Justice Black was more narrowly focused; it was a standard for enforcing the rights contained in the Constitution, not a method for exacting the meaning, scope, or extent of those rights. The First Amendment was a command explicitly prohibiting government from infringing on certain freedoms—whatever their meaning or scope. In the keynote passage from his Madison lecture stating his view of absolutism, this is exactly what Justice Black said: "To my way of thinking, at least, the history and language of the Constitution and the Bill of Rights . . . make it plain that one of the primary purposes of the Constitution with its amendments was to withdraw from the Government all power to act in certain areas—whatever the scope of those areas may be. If I am right in this then there is, at least in those areas, no justification whatever for 'balancing' a particular right against some expressly granted power of Congress."[38]

The concept of absolutism was Justice Black's reaction to the prevailing doctrine and practice that even rights conceded to be protected by the Constitution—the supreme law—could be overridden by a claim of greater public interest; it was the antithesis of a judicial process which he re-

---

[34] Konigsberg v. State Bar of California, 366 U.S. 36, 61 (1961) (Black, J., dissenting).

[35] Cahn, *supra* note 7, at 553–54.

[36] *See* H. BLACK, *supra* note 11, at 20; Freund, *Mr. Justice Black and the Judicial Function*, 14 U.C.L.A. L. REV. 467, 469 (1967).

[37] A. BICKEL, *supra* note 24, at 97.

[38] Black, *supra* note 19, at 874–875.

pudiated as "that Constitution-ignoring-and-destroying technique"[39] because, in his view, it does not treat the Bill of Rights as binding law and arrogates to the judiciary the unauthorized power to choose when to disregard the terms of the Constitution. If judges could admit the existence of an infraction of constitutional rights, but then proceed nevertheless to subordinate such rights to competing interests, what would be the purpose of law? What would be the purpose of the Bill of Rights? In Laurent Frantz's words: "It is difficult to see why a process for amending the Constitution was thought necessary, unless it was conceived that there are some choices [or balances] that might not be made, *except by that process.*"[40] "When closely analyzed," Justice Black observed, "the idea that there can be no 'absolute' constitutional guarantees in the Bill of Rights is frightening to contemplate."[41] If, instead of the word "absolute" in this passage, one substitutes "legally binding," the meaning of Justice Black's absolutism appears unencumbered by his critics' commentaries: It was frightening to contemplate the idea that constitutional rights, enshrined in the highest law of the land, were not legally binding, that they could be balanced away when confronted with claims of superior interests, that—in effect—they were not guarantees at all.

Literalism and the Judicial Function

As Edmond Cahn once said: "To [Justice Black] the language of the Constitution is more than a source of law, it is the only authentic commission of his office."[42] In advocating a literal interpretation of the Constitution, Justice Black was not engaging in a hoax of mechanical jurisprudence or, in Mendelson's words, "pretending that decisions spring full-blown from the Constitution."[43] He seemed, however, to some critics to have propagated the idea that absolute rights are detectable merely by reading the written document, which, he said, contains principles "precisely stated." But it was the principles, not the practical reach of the rights, that he said were marked out clearly in the Bill of Rights. And Judge Cardozo

[39] Time, Inc. v. Hill, 385 U.S. 374, 399 (1967) (Black, J., concurring).

[40] Frantz, *Is the First Amendment Law?—A Reply to Professor Mendelson*, 51 Calif. L. Rev. 729, 741 (1963).

[41] Black, *supra* note 19, at 876.

[42] Cahn, *The Firstness of the First Amendment*, 65 Yale L. J. 464, 475 (1956).

[43] Mendelson, *supra* note 29, at 825.

had explained that "[p]rinciples are complex bundles."[44] That cruel and unusual punishments may not be inflicted is a clear, precise principle, but the definition of cruel and unusual punishments is not precisely stated anywhere in the Constitution.

Literalism involved a process of employing standards—the words of the Constitution—for determining constitutional rights. Absolutism and literalism, of course, were intimately intertwined, for the foundation of Justice Black's belief that the First Amendment is an absolute was primarily the literal command "Congress shall make no law." But, whereas absolutism was only a standard of enforcement, literalism—besides being a justification for absolutism—also involved the complex task of ascertaining the meaning of the rights and freedoms outlined in the Bill of Rights. The practice of literalism, Justice Black explained, comprises "the wholly different and complex problem of the marginal scope of each individual amendment as applied to the particular facts of particular cases." It involves a process of judgment which might result in "differences of construction."[45] But the standards of judgment are the words of the Constitution as written. Thus, if constitutional rights are to exist at all, they must be derivable from the specific provisions of the document. For example, unlike his brethren on the Court, Justice Black was unable to find in the Bill of Rights a general right to privacy—even the fundamental right of privacy of married couples in the bedroom—because such a right did not exist in the text of the document nor did it emanate from any one provision, or combination of various provisions, of the Bill of Rights.[46] He concluded also that prohibitions against wiretapping and electronic surveillance without authorized warrants were not within the proscriptions against unreasonable searches and seizures, because wiretapping and electronic eavesdropping do not involve physical searches or seizures of tangible items.[47] And he refused to rewrite the language of the Bill of Rights so as to create such rights, because, as he often repeated, his duty as judge was to enforce the Constitution as written.

Because, in his Madison lecture on the Bill of Rights, Justice Black did not elucidate the full (or "absolute") scope and extent of each guarantee in

[44] B. CARDOZO, *supra* note 33, at 64.
[45] Black, *supra* note 19, at 867.
[46] Griswold v. Connecticut, 381 U.S. 479, 507–27 (1965) (Black, J., dissenting).
[47] Katz v. United States, 389 U.S. 347, 364 (1967) (Black, J., dissenting).

[15]

the Bill of Rights—for the obvious reason that they cannot be completely comprehended in the abstract, but only, as he explained, in the context of actual cases—Bickel asserted that the justice was attempting to evade the problem, thereby confessing indirectly the futility of his literalism. The difficulty in determining the meaning of the vague and general terms of the Bill of Rights, Bickel remarked, "can be overcome by excluding it from consideration," "a debating tactic" to which one resorts in order to circumvent an impossible task. "So the Justice, having earlier excluded the 'problem' . . . proceeds to argue that, whatever difficulties might arise in some cases, surely 'admittedly excessive fines or cruel punishments' are absolutely outlawed and may not be allowed by any process of balancing reasonableness, proximity, and degree. But, after all, what is an 'admittedly cruel punishment'?"[48]

Like many of Justice Black's critics, Bickel demanded more from the doctrine of literalism than Justice Black himself ever did. The latter recognized the problem of discerning the practical scope of each provision of the Bill of Rights as "complex." Determining whether certain punishment inflicted in a particular case is "cruel and unusual," or whether a fine or bail is "excessive," is a matter necessarily involving individual judgment. Justice Black did not pretend that these obviously vague phrases are unambiguous or that their meanings are self-evident. "There may be differences of opinion," he said in the same lecture on which Bickel was commenting, "about whether a particular search or seizure is unreasonable and therefore forbidden by [the Fourth] Amendment."[49]

"And who," asked Bickel, "is to admit that it is admittedly [a 'cruel and unusual punishment']? The people of the United States? The people of the State of California? . . . The Supreme Court of the United States? Will a majority of judges do?"[50] Bickel sought to extract from Justice Black's literalism an exact, static, concrete meaning of "cruel and unusual punishments" apart from the contexts of specific cases. He interjected into the doctrine of literalism his confusion about absolutism and thus expected from literalism absolute definitions of each individual right to cover all cases for all time. He contrived a straw man readily destroyed by common sense.

As the Supreme Court said in *Robinson* v. *California*, in an opinion in

[48] A. Bickel, *supra* note 24, at 87.
[49] Black, *supra* note 19, at 873.
[50] A. Bickel, *supra* note 24, at 87.

which Justice Black joined, "the question [of what constitutes cruel and unusual punishment] cannot be considered in the abstract."[51] Even one day in jail, the Court pointed out, might equal cruel and unusual punishment under certain circumstances. On the other hand, in the context of another case, such as the Willy Francis Case, "death-plus" is not considered cruel and unusual punishment by the Court. In this case Justice Black joined in an opinion which held that cruel and unusual punishment did not result from the failure of the electric chair successfully to operate on the first try, despite both the acute pain inflicted upon the subject and the fact that he was to be subsequently executed. This technical accident, the Court majority agreed, did not violate the Constitution.[52] But it was regarded as cruel and certainly unusual—and therefore unconstitutional—by four dissenting justices.[53]

Thus, although there may be "much difference of opinion," Justice Black maintained that "courts are required to determine the meaning of such general terms as 'excessive' and 'unusual.' "[54] Given this statement, it is difficult to understand the contention that, in professing allegiance to the language of the Constitution in discharging his judicial duties, Justice Black pretended to abstract himself from the judicial process. To be sure, his position was replete with serious difficulties—especially in the realm of First Amendment freedoms—as Bickel and others have demonstrated, and as will be examined below. But how else except through the judicial process can courts "determine the meaning of [the] general terms" of the document?

Commenting on the meaning of the evasive "liberty . . . without due process of law" clause of the Fifth Amendment in his amendment-by-amendment rendition of the Bill of Rights, Justice Black said that its meaning was a matter of some controversy, that it was a clause not as unequivocal as some other provisions of the Fifth Amendment. "What-

[51] 370 U.S. 660, 667 (1962) (Stewart, J.)

[52] Louisiana ex rel. Francis v. Resweber, 329 U.S. 459 (1947).

[53] The dissenters were Justices Burton, Douglas, Murphy, and Rutledge. This case generated a great deal of sympathy for Willy Francis, who eventually chose to be executed rather than to continue protracted litigation of new claims to save his life. Given Justice Black's vote, it is somewhat difficult to comprehend the grounds for Wallace Mendelson's statement that the "cold, cerebral approach is not for Mr. Justice Black. His generous heart is ever responsive to those who excite sympathy." W. MENDELSON, CAPITALISM, DEMOCRACY, AND THE SUPREME COURT 104 (1960). *See also* Justice Black's vote in Sweeney v. Woodall, 344 U.S. 86 (1952).

[54] Black, *supra* note 19, at 871.

ever its meaning, however, there can be no doubt that it must be granted."[55] Citing this statement, Sidney Hook—one of the Justice's more vehement detractors—places the word "sic!" after "Whatever," presumably believing that he caught his target in a slip of the tongue.[56] Evidently Hook assumes, as did Bickel, that Justice Black said that from the most uncertain and amorphous phrases of the Bill of Rights emanate clear, automatic, absolute answers to the multitude of questions which their words provoke.

Hook and Bickel treated absolutism and literalism interchangeably. Bickel, for instance, argued that "Justice Black insists only on the force of the text of the Constitution, literally read. He insists that whatever else may be true, there is a core of absolute literal meaning in the text, which it is the duty of judges to render and apply literally."[57] As argued in the next section of this chapter, to a large extent this is true of Justice Black's view of the free speech guarantee of the First Amendment; and, no doubt, his repeated claims that his interpretation of the First Amendment was simply the result of "plain language, easily understood," can lead a critic to confuse absolutism with literalism. Still, whatever holes there were in Justice Black's First Amendment position and its defense, literalism, as his own remarks verify, was not simply a reliance on "the force of the text" in reaching constitutional decisions. Constitutional adjudication, "of course, involves interpretation," he said, "and since words can have many meanings, interpretation obviously may result in contraction or extension of the original purpose of a constitutional provision, thereby affecting policy."[58] Literalism did not pretend that the meanings of the various constitutional provisions are absolute or that words such as "unreasonable" and "cruel and unusual" have a single "force." As Justice Black explained: Some "constitutional provisions do require courts to choose between competing policies, such as the Fourth Amendment which, by its terms, necessitates a judicial decision as to what is an 'unreasonable' search or seizure."[59]

Justice Black was under no illusion that each provision of the Bill of Rights exhibited, through its words, "a core of absolute meaning." He

---

[55] *Id.* at 873.

[56] S. Hook, *supra* note 17, at 26.

[57] A. Bickel, *supra* note 24, at 88.

[58] Adamson v. California, 332 U.S. 46, 90–91 (1947) (Black, J., dissenting).

[59] Rochin v. California, 342 U.S. 165, 176 (1952) (Black, J., concurring).

believed, of course, that each such clause meant something, at least to those who had drafted the document and to those who had agreed to be bound by its terms. The obligation of courts was to decipher that meaning and enforce it absolutely against competing counterclaims. The meanings of the guarantees are not absolute in scope; they are not static, enclosed concepts which by themselves render the answers to all the questions which they might generate, thus obviating the need for judges and judgment. Assigned to judges is the task of interpreting the Constitution's words, the duty, as Justice Black said, "to explain and expound."[60] His critics' conclusions to the contrary, Justice Black did not delude himself into a belief that the process of judging was automatic or that literalism was abracadabra.

His message behind a literal construction of the Constitution was that, in discharging their duty to interpret the nation's highest law, judges are required to confine themselves to the words and phrases contained in the Constitution. A written document was crucial to his conception of the role judges should play in the American system of government. Judicial discretion and policymaking are unavoidable, but literalism confines such discretion to the elaboration of the words of the document. "The fact that the Constitution which he invokes is written," explains law professor Louis Henkin, "means that [the judge] must pay a substantial respect to the words in it, no matter how much he may feel that the society would be better if they had not been written, or if different words were in the Constitution. . . . Words limit the choices open to the Court. We can demand that Justices give words their due."[61] This is the essence of Justice Black's literalism.

Central to his constitutional jurisprudence were the beliefs that in a democracy lawmaking is the province of legislatures elected by the people and that the judiciary should be precluded from roaming at large in the field of social and economic policy—as the "old Court" of the 1920s and 1930s had done until such judicial legislation provoked the constitutional crisis and judicial revolution of 1937. During this period the Supreme Court often had invalidated hours and wages legislation on such tenuous grounds as that these laws were "unreasonable" or that they infringed on

---

[60] H. BLACK, *supra* note 11, at 20.

[61] Henkin, *Some Reflections on Current Constitutional Controversy*, 109 U. PA. L. REV. 637, 656 (1961).

the judicially created "freedom of contract."[62] Justice Black abhorred standards of judgment such as "shocks the conscience" of judges or "offends the sense of decency of the English-speaking world" or runs counter to "the universal sense of decency."[63] For such flexible and boundless standards invited this very sort of judicial policymaking and ultimate usurpation of the legislative function. Similarly, it was a patent distortion of the First Amendment to treat the words "Congress shall make no law . . . abridging the freedom of speech" as if they say that governmental infringements of expression are constitutional as long as they promote a loftier value or as long as such infringements are reasonably related to the furtherance of some valid governmental goal. Such treatment, Justice Black believed, rewrites the First Amendment and strips it of any legal force.[64]

Of course, such standards as "cruel and unusual," "excessive bail," "just compensation," or "unreasonable searches and seizures," for example, are no less vague and no less flexible than the variants of natural law, as he labeled standards such as "shocks the conscience." But the important difference for him was that the former are the words of the Constitution, not judge-made formulas superimposed on the Constitution. If, in carrying out their function of interpreting the supreme law, judges are inevitably to make policy, they must do so only within the margins of dispute that surround the words of the Constitution itself. Also, where it is conceded that governmental action abridges the freedom of speech, for instance, judges are obligated to enforce the unequivocal command "Congress shall make no law," despite earnest judicial prognoses that it would be far better to evaluate contending policies.

His insistence on a literal construction of the Constitution was Justice Black's attempt to bridle judge-made law that inheres in the judicial process; it was an effort to justify judicial action and simultaneously to prevent courts from invading the broad legislative function reserved to the people's representatives. To say that his purpose was to hide the process of

[62] *See, e.g.,* Morehead v. New York ex rel. Tipaldo, 298 U.S. 587 (1936); Adkins v. Children's Hospital, 261 U.S. 525 (1923).

[63] As quoted by Justice Black in Cahn, *supra* note 7, at 561, these were some tests and standards announced by Mr. Justice Frankfurter and others. *See* Rochin v. California, 342 U.S. 165 (1952) (Frankfurter, J.); Adamson v. California, 332 U.S. 46, 59-68 (1947) (Frankfurter, J., concurring).

[64] *See* Beauharnais v. Illinois, 343 U.S. 250, 267–75 (1952) (Black, J., dissenting).

judging or to foster a delusion about the judicial process is fundamentally to misrepresent Justice Black and his judicial philosophy.

Literalism and the First Amendment

His critics' accusations become more relevant, however, when one focuses on Justice Black's construction of the freedom of speech guarantee of the First Amendment. Charles L. Black, Jr., one of the justice's more sympathetic observers, commenting on the latter's Bill of Rights address, said: "Mr. Justice Black himself recognizes, as of course he must, that even 'absolute' rights have the limits that inhere in their own definitions; that the most absolutist view of free speech must begin by defining what 'free speech' consists in."[65] This would seem consistent with Justice Black's doctrine of literalism and absolutism; the judge must first define—"explain and expound"—the meaning of "the freedom of speech," a freedom not self-defined. Once defined, that freedom is to be absolutely protected against governmental abridgments, regardless of the weight of contending values. This was Justice Black's explanation of the process of judgment, at least with respect to "the less precise provisions" of the Bill of Rights.[66] Surely this same process should apply to the First Amendment because, in Mendelson's words, "perhaps it is not going too far to suggest that there is no more equivocal word in the English language than 'freedom.' "[67] As Harry M. Clor argues in his commentary on Justice Black's First Amendment position, the need for judicial definitions, which the justice saw as necessary in interpreting, for instance, the provisions against unreasonable searches and seizures and cruel and unusual punishments, does "not become less compelling as one enters the area of First Amendment freedoms." "But when he approaches the First Amendment, Justice Black does not appear to allow for even this degree of latitude for judgment. He does not seem to regard the terms of the First Amendment as problematic in the same way or to the same extent as are those of the Eighth and Fourth Amendments."[68]

[65] Black, *Mr. Justice Black, the Supreme Court, and the Bill of Rights*, 222 HARPER'S 63, 65 (February, 1961).
[66] Black, *supra* note 19, at 871.
[67] Mendelson, *supra* note 29, at 821.
[68] H. CLOR, OBSCENITY AND PUBLIC MORALITY 91, 93 (1969).

[2 1]

Justice Black, of course, recognized that the First Amendment's command "Congress shall make no law" does not answer all the questions arising under that amendment. For example, he marked out in punctilious detail what he believed to be embodied in the "establishment of religion" clause of the First Amendment.[69] And he stated that a balancing of interests is necessary when governmental regulations in question only indirectly encroach on freedom of expression.[70] Yet he argued resolutely that the "principles of the First Amendment are stated in precise and mandatory terms and unless they are applied in those terms, the freedoms of religion, speech, press, assembly and petition will have no effective protection."[71] In fact, he insisted that courts are forbidden to define the freedom of speech protected by the First Amendment: "The Founders of this Nation were not then willing to trust the definition of First Amendment freedoms to Congress or this Court, nor am I now."[72] Here Justice Black was, of course, attacking the balancing of interests doctrine. But, while these passages emphasize his redoubtable belief in absolutism, they also record his refusal to elaborate specific boundaries around the freedom of speech. He seemed, then, to propagate the idea that the First Amendment absolutely protects every utterance—an obviously absurd and impossible standard in a free and ordered society. Some of his colleagues on the Court ridiculed such a position, as Mr. Justice John M. Harlan did when he alluded to it as "an unlimited license to talk."[73]

Justice Black encouraged this sort of confusion and derision which accompanied his exclamations about the presumed precision of the Bill of Rights and his First Amendment posture in general. Drawing a line between speech and conduct, he left the impression that all speech is protected by the First Amendment. He seemed, in fact, to have said this when he offered his literalist justification for including libel and pornography within the purview of free expression: "Since the language of the Amendment contains no exceptions, I have continuously voted to strike down all laws dealing with so-called obscene materials since I believe such laws act to establish a system of censorship in violation of the First

[69] Everson v. Board of Education, 330 U.S. 1, 15–16 (1947) (Black, J.).

[70] This direct-indirect dichotomy is discussed extensively in ch. V, *infra*.

[71] Wilkinson v. United States, 365 U.S. 399, 422–23 (1961) (Black, J., dissenting).

[72] Braden v. United States, 365 U.S. 431, 445 (1961) (Black, J., dissenting).

[73] Konigsberg v. State Bar of California, 366 U.S. 36, 50 (1961).

Amendment. . . . Just as with obscenity laws, I believe the First Amendment compels the striking down of all libel laws."[74]

The late Alexander Meiklejohn, who also proclaimed his allegiance to an absolutist interpretation of the First Amendment, drew the necessary distinction between speech and free speech. The First Amendment, he said, "does not forbid the abridging of *speech*. But . . . it does forbid the abridging of the *freedom of speech*."[75] And Laurent Frantz, who advocates something of an absolutist position on the First Amendment, expresses the same idea when he says that there "are cases in which, though speech is involved, 'the freedom of speech' is not."[76] But Justice Black appeared to deny any need to delineate between speech per se and constitutionally protected expression. Thus, his position appeared as one immunizing every utterance.

On the other hand, however, he explicitly rejected this preposterous interpretation of the First Amendment: "Nobody has ever said that the First Amendment gives people a right to go anywhere they want to go or say anything in the world they want to say."[77] But, if some line is to be drawn between constitutionally protected and unprotected expression, who is authorized to draw such a line if everyone, according to Justice Black, is prohibited from defining the freedom of speech? In 1948 the Supreme Court held that calculated falsehoods in commercial advertising designed to defraud the public did not fall within the scope of free speech or press. Justice Black himself wrote the opinion for the Court, saying: "A contention cannot be seriously considered which assumes that freedom of the press includes a right to raise money to promote circulation by deception of the public." The First Amendment does not protect "swindling schemes."[78] Yet Justice Black would later insist that calculated falsehoods designed to ruin reputations are absolutely immune from criminal prosecution and civil damage suits. Both are fraudulent and deceptive expression, but only one merits constitutional protection; and the reason why, according to Justice Black, can be traced to "plain words, easily understood." As he said repeatedly, "all I am doing is following

---

[74] H. BLACK, *supra* note 11, at 46, 48.

[75] A. MEIKLEJOHN, *supra* note 1, at 21. *See also* H. CLOR, *supra* note 68, at 89.

[76] Frantz, *supra* note 40, at 736.

[77] Cahn, *supra* note 7, at 558.

[78] Donaldson v. Read Magazine, 333 U.S. 178, 191, 192 (1948).

what to me is the clear wording of the First Amendment that 'Congress shall make no law . . . abridging the freedom of speech, or of the press.' "

The statement "Congress shall make no law" contains an absolute command, and Justice Black was correct in insisting that words do mean what they say, otherwise language would have no purpose except confusion. But since Congress is empowered to make some laws, what kind of laws does the First Amendment forbid it to make? This is squarely the problem of freedom of expression. Invoking the words "Congress shall make no law" in the effort to confront this problem comes closer to a restatement of it rather than any solution to it. As one observer has put it well: "The weakness of [Justice Black's] doctrine lies in what he does not consider. . . . He looks at the plainest words with the plainest meaning, but . . . he ignores the words of the constitutional text whose meaning must be determined before the prohibition or the guarantee itself possesses any significance."[79] Justice Black stressed words that are not questionable—except to balancers who feel authorized to ignore them—and hence words that are not germane to the problem of designating the limits to free expression. In Justice Black's literal construction the major task is set aside—that of defining words and phrases over which there is considerable dispute, even among absolutists.

Is there anything self-executing or self-defining about the phrase "the freedom of speech, or of the press"? Do these words by themselves mark the scope of free expression? When is speech free? When is the press free? Does freedom of the press include the right not to be taxed as any other business enterprise ordinarily is taxed? If a person is considered hindered in the exercise of her or his religious freedom by the imposition of a tax or license, even when the freedom in question involves peddling religious pamphlets, why is the press not equally hindered in the exercise of its freedom when news media are taxed as business corporations?[80] Why

[79] J. Soles, Mr. Justice Black and the Defendant's Constitutional Rights 67, 68 (1968, Ph.D. dissertation in Department of Government and Foreign Affairs, University of Virginia, Charlottesville).

[80] *See* Murdock v. Pennsylvania, 319 U.S. 105 (1943). *See also* Follet v. McCormick, 321 U.S. 573 (1944) (complete immunity from such a tax or license bestowed by the Court upon a Jehovah's Witness whose entire income was derived from the sale of religious literature). Dissenting in *Follet*, Justice Roberts said: "If the First Amendment grants immunity from taxation to the exercise of religion, it must equally grant a similar exemption to those who speak and to the press . . . The Amendment's prohibitions are equally sweeping." 321 U.S. at 581–82.

should churches be exempt from the payment of property taxes while the broadcasting industry is not? Furthermore, is television or radio a form of "the press"? If so, are federal communications standards, which are imposed on the broadcasting industry, abridgements of the freedom of the press? And, assuming the existence of free speech and press, when is either abridged? Indeed, what would such an abridgment be? The answers to these and countless other questions cannot be made by restating the First Amendment or by emphasizing, even with italics or boldface type in the *United States Reports*, the fact that "no law" does literally mean no law.

It seems only to add fuel to the weak flames of Justice Black's argument to confront it as did former Solicitor General Erwin Griswold in pleading the case for the United States in the Pentagon Papers Case. During oral argument the solicitor general made this statement: "Now Mr. Justice [Black], your construction of . . . [the First Amendment] is well known, and I certainly respect it. You say that no law means no law, and that should be obvious. I can only say, Mr. Justice, that to me it is equally obvious that 'no law' does not mean 'no law,' and I would seek to persuade the Court that this is true. . . ."[81] Of course, Justice Black was not to be persuaded. In the last opinion he wrote as a member of the Supreme Court, he gave his predictable reply: "In other words, we are asked to hold that despite the First Amendment's emphatic command," no law does not mean no law.[82]

The solicitor general undoubtedly was aware of the ambiguity that encases the meaning of freedom of speech and press. But in his dialogue with Justice Black he focused on the only words that are not ambiguous, and instead of leading the justice directly into the problem of free expression—that is, determining whether the publication of the Pentagon Papers was, in fact, free expression—the solicitor general was diverting him away from it and onto a ground on which the justice's position is impossible literally to refute. Griswold apparently conceded that the publication of the excerpts from the Pentagon Papers was free expression which the First Amendment protects; yet he was urging that "the First Amendment was not intended to make it impossible for the Executive to function or to protect the security of the United States."[83] He was asking

---

[81] *As quoted by* Justice Black in New York Times Co. v. United States, 403 U.S. 713, 717–18 (1971) (Black, J., concurring).

[82] *Id.* at 718.

[83] *As quoted by* Justice Black, *id.*

Justice Black to "balance" away an "admitted" First Amendment right regardless of the clear command of that amendment, because in this case, "national security" outweighed freedom of the press. Not only had Justice Black during the previous two decades attacked and repudiated precisely this sort of balancing, but he had also earlier publicly equated national security with freedom of expression.[84] Moreover, since the government relied on no act of Congress to suppress further publication of the Pentagon Papers, it was asking the judiciary to issue an injunction to achieve that purpose. As Justice Black said, the government "makes the bold and dangerously far-reaching contention that the courts should take it upon themselves to 'make' a law abridging freedom of the press in the name of equity, presidential power and national security, even when the representatives of the people in Congress have adhered to the command of the First Amendment and refused to make such a law."[85] Thus, not only was Justice Black being asked to engage in balancing an admitted First Amendment right; he was also being asked to use the judicial power to create judge-made law—the very thing his judicial philosophy was intended to eliminate, or at least curtail.

Justice Black's literalist First Amendment position is unassailable if the expression in question is conceded to be embraced within the meaning of freedom of speech and press safeguarded by the amendment. Having disarmed himself by admitting that the publications here were within the margins of free expression, the solicitor general proceeded in the futile attempt to undermine the foundation on which Justice Black structured his absolutism. His argument not only was doomed to fail but served to invigorate Justice Black's interpretation of the amendment, to reinforce the assumption that the justice's position on the First Amendment was compelled by "plain language, easily understood."

Alexander Meiklejohn agreed with Justice Black that the statement "Congress shall make no law" is " 'composed of plain words, easily understood,' " but he acknowledged that there is much "ambiguity" in the "other phrases of the Amendment." "[I]t may . . . be taken for granted that the words 'abridging the freedom of speech, [or] of the press' . . . are not

---

[84] Cahn, *supra* note 7, at 555. There Justice Black said that government should preserve itself, but "I think it can be preserved only by leaving the people with the utmost freedom to think and to hope and to talk and to dream if they want to dream. I do not think this Government must look to force, stifling the minds and aspirations of the people."

[85] 403 U.S. at 718.

'plain words, easily understood.' " "The Framers of the Constitution," he said, "suffered from the same semantic difficulties as do its present-day interpreters."[86] But, in establishing his position in response to the Court's balancing of interests doctrine, Justice Black apparently saw no "semantic difficulties" with the meaning of the rights he thought should be absolutely protected. He seemed unmistakably to be saying that speech per se is thereby constitutionally shielded, and so critics such as Bickel, Hook, and Mendelson dismissed him as an eccentric judge and his doctrine of absolutism as something unrealistic and absurd.

Meiklejohn attempted to deflate and counter this criticism by restating what he believed to be Justice Black's true position. The justice meant to say that, as with the less clear provisions of the Bill of Rights, judges are required to determine the meaning of the freedom of speech. Meiklejohn's endeavor was provoked by more than common sense. Justice Black had said that courts are required to ascertain the meaning of the general terms of the Bill of Rights, and to most readers the words "the freedom of speech" are general enough to require determinations made by judges. Moreover, Justice Black had, after all, recognized that not every utterance is that kind of speech which the First Amendment protects. The people, he said, have no constitutional right to "say anything in the world they want to say." Finally, Edmond Cahn had written in 1956 that he knew that Justice Black regarded defamatory expression as outside the pale of the First Amendment's guarantees: "Certainly Justice Black has not contended that the sponsors of the First Amendment expected it to end civil actions for defamation. I understand he would freely grant the existence of this 'exception.' " According to Cahn, "[h]e would probably go on to respond that civil remedies for defamation are not only consistent with but were considered by the founding libertarians as virtually essential to the maintenance of free speech and press."[87]

But as Meiklejohn was seeking to clarify Justice Black's position, Justice Black was announcing his dissenting opinion in *Braden* v. *United States* (1961) in which he said that courts (and everyone) are forbidden to define the meaning of First Amendment freedoms. He concluded that libel, slander, and pornography are absolutely protected because the First Amendment's language admits of no exceptions. Presumably, he was advocating the idea that all speech is constitutionally protected, and

[86] Meiklejohn, *The First Amendment Is an Absolute*, 1961 Sup. Ct. Rev. 245, 246, 247.
[87] Cahn, *supra* note 42, at 476.

absolutely so—despite Meiklejohn's clarification, Cahn's understanding, Justice Black's own opinion for the Court that fraudulent speech is not free expression, and his recognition that no one has a First Amendment right to say anything in the world he wants to say. The Achilles' heel of Justice Black's position is that he made exceptions where he insisted none should be made, and he failed to explain why.

The broad sweep of his conception of the freedom of expression is not necessarily unjustifiable, or proscribed by or contrary to the words of the First Amendment. The discretionary element attending the effort to implement the "freedom" of expression safeguarded by that amendment conceivably would justify any, however comprehensive or narrow, definition of the reach of free expression, and any practical exceptions to such a definition. The case can be made that under certain circumstances even hard-core pornography and libel fall within the scope of free expression and thus within reach of the First Amendment's absolute prohibition. But such broad interpretations are not self-evident, nor are they products solely of a literal rendition of the language of the amendment.[88]

Justice Black was influenced by something other than the text of the Constitution, and he acknowledged that something other than language compelled him to reach his conclusions (although he insisted that the words of the First Amendment were compelling enough). What reinforced his literalist position, he explained, was the intent of those who wrote the Bill of Rights: "[I]t is language and history that are the crucial factors which influence me in interpreting the Constitution."[89] The historical evidence that he advanced in support of his First Amendment position is examined in the next chapter.

[88] *See, e.g.*, Paris Adult Theatre I v. Slaton, 413 U.S. 49, 73–114 (1973) (Brennan, J., dissenting); New York Times Co. v. Sullivan, 376 U.S. 254, 297–305 (1964) (Goldberg, J., concurring).

[89] H. BLACK, *supra* note 11, at 8.

CHAPTER II

Of Absolutism, History, and Freedom of Expression

Regardless of whether it might seem unsound or imprudent legal or social policy, Justice Black's narrowly focused absolutist position—to insist that admitted First Amendment rights are not to be balanced against competing interests—is difficult to refute by recourse to constitutional language. Not even a Harvard Law School dean could adduce support for the contention that the words "no law" do not mean what they say. But anyone can readily dispel the myth that, merely from a literal reading of the words of the First Amendment, the breadth of freedom of expression protected by the Constitution is self-evident and self-defined. And so it was easily and often derided as an illusion by Justice Black's critics.

Nonetheless, undaunted by his critics' attacks, Justice Black endeavored to offer further support for his view by recounting the historical background of the framing of the Constitution and by identifying the goals that had inspired those who compiled that document. He attempted to reinforce with historical evidence the claim that the First Amendment is to be absolutely enforced. He also sought to justify his interpretation of the boundaries of free speech and press by tracing his position to the intent of the framers of the First Amendment. In addition to the doctrines of absolutism and literalism, history—his own version—was the third, crucial underpinning of Justice Black's constitutional jurisprudence.[1] But before assessing the weight of his evidence and other evidence to the contrary, perhaps an important caveat on the whole enterprise of detecting the intent of the framers is in order.

Historic accounts purporting to reveal *wie es eigentlich gewesen*, and thus definitively to establish the original intent of the framers of the Constitution have become, in John P. Roche's apt words, "a big scholarly business . . . [wherein] . . . our greatest difficulty is that we know so much more about what the Framers *should have meant* than they themselves did."[2] Of these scholarly historical accounts, perhaps the most notorious is the effort of Charles A. Beard to convince the American people that their forefathers were in the main conspirators who sought to secure their own financial interests through the arm of a strong central government.[3] Beard's thesis, which temporarily generated enormous influence, has been effectively refuted.[4] It has been assigned a place in the history of political thought alongside other treatises inspired more by discontent with present times than by historical fact.[5]

The overwhelming obstacle confronting the historian in search of the intent of the framers is the inability to consult with the dead. Engaging in a historical appraisal of the Constitutional Convention himself, Roche concludes that it is perhaps a futile exercise to attempt to determine the intent of the framers, for "they may not have known what they meant, . . . there may not have been any semantic consensus." Roche continues:

> The delegates were in a hurry to get a new government established; when definitional arguments arose, they characteristically took refuge in ambiguity. If different men voted for the same proposition for varying reasons, that was politics (and still is); if later generations were unsettled by this lack of precision, that would be their problem.

---

[1] History (again, his own version) was also the major factor underlying his assertion that section 1 of the Fourteenth Amendment was designed to apply verbatim the provisions of the Bill of Rights against the states. This allowed him to bypass the most ambiguous and most litigated language of the Constitution.

[2] Roche, *The Founding Fathers: A Reform Caucus in Action*, 55 AM. POL. SCI. REV. 779, 814, 815 (1961).

[3] C. BEARD, AN ECONOMIC INTERPRETATION OF THE CONSTITUTION OF THE UNITED STATES (1913).

[4] *See, e.g.*, F. MCDONALD, WE THE PEOPLE: THE ECONOMIC ORIGINS OF THE CONSTITUTION (1958).

[5] *See* Hofstadter, *Beard and the Constitution: The History of an Idea*, 2 AM. Q. 195 (1950).

There was a good deal of definitional pluralism with respect to the problems the delegates did discuss, but when we move to the question of extrapolated intentions, we enter the realm of spiritualism. When men in our time, for instance, launch into elaborate talmudic exegesis to demonstrate that federal aid to parochial schools is (or is not) in accord with the intentions of the men who established the Republic and endorsed the Bill of Rights, they are engaging in historical Extra-Sensory Perception.[6]

The end product of the ongoing debate over what the framers actually did, and intended to do, has been (and most likely will continue to be) primarily further dispute and contention rather than final answers. But the difficulty involved in historical assessment is not sufficient grounds for abandoning the task of resorting to history to find approximate answers to complex constitutional questions.[7] Sometimes history must be brought in even to refute the plain words of some provisions of the Constitution, as with the Thirteenth Amendment, which states that "Neither slavery nor involuntary servitude, except as a punishment for a crime whereof the party shall have been duly convicted, shall exist with the United States, or any place subject to their jurisdiction." The language here is compelling enough to support the conclusion that compulsory military service is prohibited, yet it would be extraordinarily difficult to maintain that the Thirteenth Amendment was designed to prevent the United States from raising an army through national conscription,[8] or that the amendment was designed for any purpose other than the abolition of slavery as it had existed in the United States before the Civil War.

History, therefore, is relevant in constitutional adjudication; it is sometimes an essential aid in deciding cases. But it is extremely difficult, often impossible, to decipher the original intent of certain other provisions of the Constitution or to uncover the seeds of their creation. Even if discovered, the original meaning may be of little value in cases involving issues wholly unanticipated by the framers. Despite the difficulties involved in ascertaining the meaning of law through history, almost all judges explicate and bolster their reasoning with historical evidence. It is a valuable and sometimes indispensable vehicle for arriving at judicial decisions.

---

[6] Roche, *supra* note 2, at 815.

[7] *See* B. CARDOZO, THE NATURE OF THE JUDICIAL PROCESS 51f. (1921).

[8] *See* Arver v. United States, 245 U.S. 266 (1918).

ABSOLUTISM AND HISTORY

Although Justice Black built his argument of absolutism on the words of the Constitution itself, he also drew upon what he believed to be the purpose of the American Revolution and the framing of the American system of limited government. In his address on the Bill of Rights, he narrowed his argument to the current controversy over the degree to which the Bill of Rights is to be applied as a limitation upon governmental power. On the one side there are those, he said, "who regard the prohibitions of the Constitution, even its most unequivocal commands, as mere admonitions which Congress need not always observe." These included the advocates of the "clear and present danger test" and the "balancing of interests doctrine," or any other test designed to accommodate competing interests by curbing the reach of a constitutional right. This view approximates "the English doctrine of legislative omnipotence, qualified only by the possibility of a judicial veto if the Supreme Court finds that a congressional choice between 'competing' policies has no reasonable basis."[9]

Justice Black rejected this view, however, because he believed the Bill of Rights contained "absolute" rights in the sense that they were above any competing interests; they were marked off as areas of freedom within which government could not legislate. The Bill of Rights meant more than the first eight amendments to him. It included "all provisions of the original Constitution and Amendments that protect individual liberty by barring government from acting in a particular area or from acting except under certain prescribed procedures." It was a package of freedom absolutely removed from governmental intrusion:

> The whole history and background of the Constitution and Bill of Rights, as I understand it, belies the assumption or conclusion that our ultimate constitutional freedoms are no more than our English ancestors had when they came to this new land to get new freedoms. The historical and practical purposes of a Bill of Rights, the very use of a written constitution, indigenous to America, the language the Framers used, the kind of three-department government they took pains to set up, all point to the creation of a government which was denied all power to do some things under any and all circumstances, and all power to do other things except precisely in the manner prescribed.[10]

[9] Black, *The Bill of Rights*, 35 N.Y.U. L. REV. 865, 866–67 (1960).
[10] *Id.* at 865, 867. *See also* Bridges v. California, 314 U.S. 252 (1941) (Black, J.)

The establishment of the Bill of Rights was an epoch-making adventure, ushering in a revolution in civil liberty and a revolutionary relationship between government and the people. The American Constitution was unique in creating a "new kind of limited government."[11] It is "the unique American contribution to man's continuing search for a society in which individual liberty is secure against governmental oppression."[12] The contribution lies in the fact that "Parliament could change [the] English 'Constitution'; Congress cannot change ours. . . . It was one of the great achievements of our Constitution that it ended legislative omnipotence here and placed all departments and agencies of government under one supreme law."[13] The unique security of freedom obtained in the United States under the Constitution is that the provisions of the Bill of Rights—the bulwark of freedom, according to Justice Black—are themselves components of this supreme law. And, just as government cannot deny the supremacy of the Constitution, it cannot treat the Bill of Rights as anything but supreme law, alterable only by constitutional amendment.

The counterargument, which greatly, if not directly, influenced Justice Black's development of absolutism, was advanced by, among others, Mr. Justice Felix Frankfurter, who drew upon an opinion rendered by the Supreme Court in *Robertson* v. *Baldwin* (1897). There Mr. Justice Henry B. Brown had said:

> The law is perfectly well settled that the first ten amendments to the Constitution, commonly known as the Bill of Rights, were not intended to lay down any novel principles of government, but simply to embody guaranties and immunities which we had inherited from our English ancestors, and which had from time immemorial been subject to certain well-recognized exceptions arising from the necessities of the case. In incorporating these principles into the fundamental law there was no intent of disregarding the exceptions which continued to be recognized as if they had been formally expressed.[14]

Citing this passage in *Dennis* v. *United States* (1951), Justice Frankfurter agreed that "this represents the authentic view of the Bill of Rights and the spirit in which it must be construed" and that this view "has been recog-

---

[11] Black, *supra* note 9, at 870.
[12] H. BLACK, A CONSTITUTIONAL FAITH 3 (1968).
[13] Black, *supra* note 9, at 870.
[14] 165 U.S. at 281.

[3 3]

nized again and again in cases that have come here within the last fifty years."[15]

Under this "authentic view," the Bill of Rights was not the symbol and reality of a revolution in individual freedom and a novel concept of limited government, as Justice Black maintained that it was. In the latter's opinion, the American Revolution and the creation of the Constitution were the work of men who recognized "the ancient evils" that frequently surfaced in the British tradition of liberty. They were men who "knew firsthand the dangers of tyrannical governments" intrinsic to legislative supremacy. The inadequate protection of liberty under such a system of government was recognized and "forced [our] ancestors to flee to this new country and to form a government stripped of old powers used to oppress them."[16] "Although other traditions were important, there can no doubt," insisted Justice Black, "that knowledge of the English experience influenced our Founding Fathers most in adopting the Constitution."[17]

Although not directing his argument specifically against Justice Black, Daniel J. Boorstin implies that Justice Black may have been correct in holding that British experience was most influential in the framing of the Constitution, but for the wrong reasons. Boorstin contends that the American Revolution was not a radical break with British constitutionalism, but rather a "desire to remain true to the principles of British constitutionalism." "The Revolution," he claims, "was conceived as essentially affirming the British institutions."[18]

Justice Black felt that the British constitution was not a true or real constitution in the sense of being supreme law above and unalterable by mere legislation. In the United States the Constitution is supreme; in Britain it is Parliament which is supreme. He believed that the Revolution and the establishment of the written Constitution represented a departure from the essence of British constitutionalism, an abrupt break inspired by awareness of "ancient evils" and the potential tyranny inherent in the British system of parliamentary supremacy. The Bill of Rights in particular marked a birth of new liberty in that it set aside certain areas of freedom upon which governmental encroachment was absolutely forbidden.

[15] 341 U.S. 494, 524 (concurring opinion).
[16] Black, *supra* note 9, at 867.
[17] H. BLACK, *supra* note 12, at 4.
[18] D. BOORSTIN, THE GENIUS OF AMERICAN POLITICS 84, 95, 98 (1953). *See also* C. MCILWAIN, THE AMERICAN REVOLUTION: A CONSTITUTIONAL INTERPRETATION (1923).

Yet Boorstin and others view the Revolution and the Constitution as events along the continuous path of the British constitutional tradition. The rights protected by the American Constitution are attributable to "our inheritance from the British constitution." The American "readiness to think of these traditional rights of Englishmen as if they were indigenous to our continent" is characterized by Boorstin as "sometimes bizarre." The heroes of the American Revolution, after all, "were fighting not so much to establish new rights as to preserve old ones"—the rights of Englishmen.[19]

It is very difficult to assess the merits of these diametrically opposed positions. Is the "authentic view" of Justices Frankfurter and Brown valid? Is it true that the Bill of Rights established no "novel principles of government," but merely enshrined the rights inherited from our English ancestors? Furthermore, are these rights subject to exceptions that are adjudged to be merely "reasonable"? Are they not to be absolutely enforceable as supreme law above and beyond countervailing interests? These are not simply academic questions. As Justice Black observed: "How this difference is finally resolved will . . . have far-reaching consequences upon our liberties."[20] If rights elevated to the status of the supreme law are nonetheless susceptible to ad hoc exceptions that Congress should deem necessary, and which the courts sustain if they are "reasonable," then it is fair to conclude that such a system approaches the British concept of legislative omnipotence. When is legislation ever passed without reason? If the Bill of Rights stands as nothing more than a shield against legislation that has no reasonable basis, then it serves as a paper boundary around legislative supremacy.

Paralleling Justice Black, Alexander Meiklejohn attacked the "authentic view" as "a patent and disastrous absurdity—an absurdity in which our current suppressions of political freedom find their source." It is a view "which seems . . . to sap the very foundations of our American political freedom." In his efforts to refute the Frankfurter-Brown-Boorstin "authentic view," Meiklejohn asked: "Are we to believe that the American Revolution had no revolutionary *political* significance? Was the dictum, 'Congress shall make no law respecting an establishment of religion,' etc., 'inherited from our English ancestors'?" Certain provisions, of course,

[19] *Id.* at 98, 72.
[20] Black, *supra* note 9, at 866.

were products of English heritage—for example, the rights of habeas corpus, fair trial, and others. "But to say that the relation between the people and the legislature was now, in principle, as it had been before, is to miss the meaning, not only of the First Amendment, but of the Constitution as a whole."[21]

To support his view, Meiklejohn built upon the words of Alexander Hamilton, who argued against the attachment of a Bill of Rights to the original Constitution. Hamilton believed that there was no need for a Bill of Rights because the government was constructed on enumerated and limited powers. "For why declare that things shall not be done which there is no power to do? Why, for instance, should it be said that the liberty of the press shall not be restrained, when no power is given by which restrictions may be imposed?" In Hamilton's view, the original Constitution was itself a Bill of Rights: "Adverting therefore to the substantial meaning of a bill of rights, it is absurd to allege that it is not to be found in the work of the convention. It certainly must be immaterial what mode is observed as to the order of declaring the rights of citizens if they are to be found in any part of the instrument which establishes the government."[22] The government created by the Constitution was by its nature limited and could not act in certain areas regardless of the presence or absence of a Bill of Rights.

Meiklejohn continued his repudiation of the "authentic view" by citing the words of James Madison, who said:

[P]osterity will be indebted for the possession, and the world for the example, of the numerous innovations displayed on the American theater in favor of private rights and public happiness. Had no important steps been taken by the leaders of the Revolution for which a precedent could not be discovered, no government established of which an exact model did not present itself, the people of the United States might at this moment have been numbered among the melancholy victims of misguided councils, must at best have been laboring under the weight of some of those forms which have crushed the liberties of the rest of mankind. Happily for America, happily we trust for the whole human race, they pursued a new and more noble course. They

---

[21] A. MEIKLEJOHN, POLITICAL FREEDOM: THE CONSTITUTIONAL POWERS OF THE PEOPLE 101–2, 104 (1960).

[22] THE FEDERALIST NO. 84, *reprinted in* THE FEDERALIST PAPERS 513–14, 515 (C. Rossiter ed. 1961).

accomplished a revolution which has no parallel in the annals of human society. They reared the fabrics of governments which have no model on the face of the globe.[23]

According to Meiklejohn, therefore, the American Revolution and Constitution established an entirely new kind of limited government, one which secured political freedom by placing it beyond the reach of government.

Despite the fact that Madison and Hamilton in writing *The Federalist* were energetically trying to persuade their countrymen through popular approval to ratify the Constitution, which is itself an indication of the novelty of the American democracy, it can hardly be denied that both were sincere in their belief that the central government was to be one of limited powers, and not an American version of legislative supremacy. But how limited were federal powers to be? The "necessary and proper" clause of Article I of the Constitution, for example, as nearly two centuries of constitutional history demonstrate, contains the seeds for enormous growth and expansion of federal power as it gives Congress additional power to make all laws "necessary and proper" to carry out its already enumerated powers. Indeed, Edward S. Corwin argued that this provision grants Congress "broad" authority to restrict speech which it considers to be a threat to the national interest. And he concluded that "the cause of freedom of speech and press is largely in the custody of legislative majorities and of juries, which . . . is just where the framers of the Constitution intended it to be."[24]

But can it be said that the "necessary and proper" clause was meant to undo the limitations on governmental power built into the original constitution and through subsequent amendments? Writing in the same year that Corwin made his argument, Fred B. Hart, as if anticipating Corwin's thesis, maintained that all powers of Congress, including those implied by the "necessary and proper" clause, are limited and circumscribed by the Bill of Rights. "These prohibitions, adopted subsequently to the Constitution, limit and circumscribe every power in that instrument. The end may be lawful. The Constitution may approve it. But that end may not be accomplished and that thing must not be done by any means included in these amendments or forbidden by any provisions in the constitution."[25] Justice Black's answer was similar: "It seems obvious to me that Congress, in exercising its general powers, is expressly forbidden to use means prohibited by the Bill of Rights. Whatever else the phrase 'necessary and proper' may mean, it must be that Congress may only adopt such means to carry its powers as are 'proper,' that is, not specifically prohibited."[26]

The inclusion of the Bill of Rights was designed to limit the implications of the "necessary and proper" clause and to guard constitutional rights against the whims of legislative majorities. Justice Black agreed with his colleague, Mr. Justice Robert H. Jackson, whose eloquent prose has enshrined this theme in memorable words: "The very purpose of a Bill of Rights was to withdraw certain subjects from the vicissitudes of political controversy, to place them beyond the reach of majorities and officials and to establish them as legal principles to be applied by the courts. One's right to life, liberty, and property, to free speech, a free press, freedom of worship and assembly, and other fundamental rights may not be submitted to vote; they depend on the outcome of no elections."[27]

To support this view Justice Black could invoke the words of Madison, who, when introducing the first ten amendments to the First Congress, said: "[T]he great object in view is to limit and qualify the powers of Government, by excepting out of the grant of power those cases in which the government ought not to act, or to act only in a particular mode."[28] Justice Black accepted this as strong historical support for the seemingly radical contention that the guarantees contained in the Bill of Rights are "absolute" in that they cannot be balanced against competing governmental interests. Together with the explicit command "Congress shall make no law," they provide a foundation for his belief that the right of free speech cannot be weighed against, and subordinated to, conflicting congressional goals and interests. And, in support of his conception of judicial duty, he again quoted Madison, who said: "If they [the provisions of the Bill of Rights] are incorporated into the constitution, independent tribunals of justice will consider themselves in a peculiar manner the guard-

---

[25] Hart, *Power of Government Over Speech and Press*, 29 YALE L.J. 410, 422 (1920).

[26] Black, *supra* note 9, at 875.

[27] West Virginia Board of Education v. Barnette, 319 U.S. 624, 638 (1943).

[28] 1 ANNALS OF CONG. 437 (Gales & Seaton eds. 1789–91) *quoted in* H. BLACK, *supra* note 12, at 7.

ians of those rights; they will be an impenetrable bulwark against every assumption of power in the legislative or executive; they will be naturally led to resist every encroachment upon rights expressly stipulated for in the constitution by the declaration of rights."[29] Justice Black's duty as judge was thus clear and direct—to enforce absolutely the constitutional rights contained in the Bill of Rights.

In his relentless—and sometimes rapacious—effort to rebut this view, Wallace Mendelson, one of the justice's most prolific critics, asserts: "Of course, Madison introduced and fought for the Bill of Rights—and, in so doing, referred to judicial review in support of it, as libertarians emphasize ad infinitum. What they fail to mention is that this was Madison under pressure. If the 'father of the Constitution' had really wanted a bill of rights, why did he not introduce and fight for one in the constitutional convention?"[30]

Mendelson's answer to his own question is that Madison "foresaw a far more reliable, and far more sophisticated, shield for civil liberty [than] the Bill-of-Rights-Judicial-Review approach." For Madison, according to Mendelson, "the only reliable security against governmental inhumanity" was "majority rule." Madison regarded judicial protection of civil liberty through the enforcement of a bill of rights as "futile," because he understood a declaration of rights to be very "close to Learned Hand's thought that the Bill of Rights is not law." "Sooner or later," Mendelson concludes, we will all have to appreciate the fact that "[m]an after all is . . . not a legal animal."[31]

Mendelson creates his argument by drawing upon statements made in a letter from Madison to Thomas Jefferson. In it Madison explained why he was not enthusiastic about a bill of rights. Although he assailed others for reverting to "selective history" and "selective Jefferson" in developing their libertarian conclusions,[32] Mendelson, it seems, resorts to "selective Madison." In the same letter to Jefferson, for example, Madison forthrightly said: "My own opinion has always been in favor of a bill of rights; provided it be so framed as not to imply powers not meant to be included

[29] *Id.* at 439, *quoted in* Black, *supra* note 9, at 880.
[30] Mendelson, *On the Meaning of the First Amendment*, 50 CALIF. L. REV. 821, 826–27 (1962).
[31] *Id.* at 828.
[32] *Id.* at 822.

in the enumeration. . . . I have favored it because I supposed it might be of use, and if properly executed could not be of disservice."[33] Thus, if some rights were stipulated in a declaration of rights, Madison believed that this might lead to the conclusion that the national government had the implied power to invade the rights of the people not spelled out in the written document. This was also one of Hamilton's reasons for disclaiming the need or the desire for a bill of rights.[34]

Furthermore, Madison also agreed with Hamilton that a bill of rights would be superfluous. In his letter to Jefferson, Madison characterized a bill of rights as a surplusage by saying "the rights in question are reserved by the manner in which the federal powers are granted." Since he deemed such rights to have already been secured through the nature of the power delegated to the federal government, he "never thought the omission [of a bill of rights] a material defect," nor "viewed [it] in an important light."[35]

As stated above, Mendelson emphasizes that for Madison the only reliable check upon governmental interference with individual rights was "majority rule," and not " 'parchment barriers.' " Paper rules presumably are no match for political power. Acknowledging the potential fragility of paper rights, Madison explained that "[r]epeated violations of these parchment barriers have been committed by overbearing majorities in every State." He said further: "Wherever the real power in a Government lies, there is the danger of oppression. In our Government, the real power lies in the majority of the Community, and the invasion of private rights is *chiefly* to be apprehended, not from acts of Government contrary to the sense of its constituents, but from acts in which the Government is the mere instrument of the major number of the constituents."[36] But, if paper rules are to be violated repeatedly by determined majorities, how is liberty secured through "majority rule?" The enigmatic logic sustaining Mendelson's conclusion, which he says must be "sooner or later" faced by all, is difficult to comprehend: that for Madison "majority rule" is the surest mechanism for safeguarding individual rights, and that Madison believed that the violation of individual rights is chiefly the work of majorities.

---

[33] Letter from James Madison to Thomas Jefferson (Oct. 17, 1788), *printed in* 14 The Papers of Thomas Jefferson 18 (P. Boyd ed. 1958) [hereinafter cited as Papers].

[34] *See* The Federalist No. 84, *reprinted in* The Federalist Papers 510 (C. Rossiter ed. 1961).

[35] Letter from Madison to Jefferson, *printed in* 14 Papers 18.

[36] *Id.* at 19.

To be sure, Madison developed and believed in the validity of his theory of factions: that sociological diversification would automatically promote diverse factions which, in the interplay of a system of checks and balances and separation of powers, would inevitably impose moderation upon contending factions and ultimately upon policy. This is what Mendelson alludes to in claiming that majority rule was for Madison "the only reliable protection for basic substantive interests."[37] But this does not erase the fact, as stated in the above passage which Mendelson ignores, that Madison saw the threat to liberty in the tyranny of the majority.

Mendelson's scheme for ensuring individual rights is this:

> Faction would resist faction; ambition would weigh against ambition. The hopes and fears of each subgroup would check and balance those of all others. Government could act only after political compromise had found the common denominator of a host of mutually suspicious minorities. . . . No program that had survived the give and take necessary to attain support by a concurrent majority of our incredibly varied factional interests could depart substantially from the Nation's moral center of gravity.[38]

Presumably, in this world of political power, the only legal check on the public policies of the ruling majority would be the test of reasonableness: if a measure transgressed the bounds of reason or rationality, it would be invalid and hence unconstitutional.

There are countless millions of people who comprise numerous minorities without access to political power (and thus outside Mendelson's political system) who would react derisively, sardonically, or even with disgust, to such a system of preserving their liberty. Their impact on the great moral center is negligible at best; they are more often the victims rather than the beneficiaries of this system. If they are not legal animals, with rights legally binding against the majority, their freedom cannot be guaranteed by a political system which denies them real political power. As Laurent B. Frantz poignantly concludes, for Mendelson "justice is the interest of the stronger."[39] This was hardly the design of the Constitution, nor was it the intent of the framers. A system of power which excludes certain segments of society from access to that power, while simultane-

---

[37] Mendelson, *supra* note 30, at 826.
[38] *Id.* at 827–28.
[39] Frantz, *Is the First Amendment Law?*, 51 CALIF. L. REV. 729, 754 (1963).

ously professing to be guardian of their liberty, nourishes the germ of its own destruction.

Such a system, moreover, mistakes reasonable majority rule for just majority rule. Is liberty to be reliably ensured by a system which allows and sanctions a coalition of factions to tyrannize a dissentient, unorthodox faction? Are individual rights secure when a majority of "rational" congressmen enacts a "reasonable" security measure, such as the Smith Act, which nonetheless serves to persecute a hated minority faction in the name of national self-preservation? Is liberty guaranteed by majoritarian support of a military measure the purpose of which is surely reasonable—security in time of war—but which nevertheless indiscriminately confines thousands of Americans in relocation camps on the premise that the United States is at war with Japan, the nation to which these American citizens trace their national ancestry?[40]

The test of reasonableness or rationality can, and often does, support the notion of legislative supremacy. Certainly, there seems no other way to interpret the statement "We are to set aside the judgment of those whose duty is to legislate only if there is no reasonable basis for it."[41] Although the most articulate spokesman for this view of judicial self-restraint, Mr. Justice Frankfurter never meant that the legislatures were endowed with unlimited power to subordinate constitutional rights whenever a majority saw fit to do so.[42] But, in the hands of other judges—and sometimes in his own—the test of reasonableness and rationality can be used to obliterate constitutional limitations on legislative power.[43] Legislatures do not enact

[40] For a devastating critique of the Supreme Court's posture in the Japanese exclusion cases, see E. ROSTOW, THE SOVEREIGN PREROGATIVE: THE SUPREME COURT AND THE QUEST FOR LAW ch. 7 (1962). It is one of the ironies of his absolutism that it was Justice Black who wrote the Court's holding sustaining the military order. This will be discussed in ch. III, *infra.*.

[41] Dennis v. United States, 341 U.S. 494, 525 (1951) (Frankfurter, J., concurring). Justice Frankfurter made this statement in a case where he conceded that the Smith Act encroached upon free speech rights; yet, for him, the Court's only duty was to defer to the judgment of Congress unless it was without reason. Such a gingerly interpretation of the First Amendment obviously invites the charge of legislative supremacy.

[42] *See, e.g.*, his dissenting opinion in United States v. Kahriger, 345 U.S. 22 (1953). There have even been suggestions that Justice Frankfurter's adherence to judicial self-restraint was in fact a myth and a front for policymaking. *See* Spaeth, *The Judicial Restraint of Mr. Justice Frankfurter: Myth or Reality*, 8 MIDWEST J. OF POL. SCI. 22 (1964); *see also* Braden, *The Search for Objectivity in Constitutional Law*, 57 YALE L.J. 571 (1948).

[43] *See, e.g.*, Minersville School District v. Gobitis, 310 U.S. 586 (1940), *overruled in* West Virginia Board of Education v. Barnette, 319 U.S. 624 (1943). It is unclear why legislation

completely irrational laws; legislators are reasonable and rational. There is always some conceivably reasonable connection between legislative means and ends in even the most egregious infringement on constitutional rights. As Walter Berns argues, employing Frankfurter's criteria "[t]he Court will exercise its powers only when legislators are idiots."[44]

Some Americans, moreover, prefer to adhere to life-styles at odds with, albeit not detrimental to, "the Nation's moral center of gravity." Who or what is to protect them against the enormous force of majoritarian orthodoxy, especially when that orthodoxy is imposed upon a dissident faction without substantial political power? Where is protection to be found within a system of majority rule for factions outside the moral center—outside the mainstreams of public opinion? The only reliable assurance that majority rule provides for them is the real possibility of majoritarian oppression, not protection, of their rights.[45]

Even Mr. Justice Frankfurter, Mendelson's hero, believed that "[t]he treatment of its minorities, especially their legal position, is among the most searching tests of the level of civilization attained by a society."[46] The measure of a democratic polity's support for individual rights and liberties is not, as Mendelson assumes it to be, the frequency with which, or the extent to which, legislative output reflects the moral center. This is the test of the safety of a majority against the overlordship of a minority faction. But, as Madison said, "[w]here the power as with us is in the many not in the few the danger cannot be very great that the few will be thus favored. It is much more to be dreaded that the few will be unnecessarily sacrificed to the many."[47]

The ultimate measure of strength and security of civil liberties is

---

compelling children to salute the flag should be deemed reasonable by Justice Frankfurter, while legislation providing public funds to bus children to parochial schools or the practice of voluntary prayer in public schools is judged unreasonable. *See* the dissenting opinion of Mr. Justice Rutledge (in which Justice Frankfurter joined) in Everson v. Board of Education, 330 U.S. 1 (1947); *see also* the concurring opinion of Justice Frankfurter in McCollum v. Board of Education, 333 U.S. 203 (1948).

[44] W. BERNS, FREEDOM, VIRTUE, AND THE FIRST AMENDMENT 180 (1957). *See also* Alfange, *The Balancing of Interests in Free Speech Cases: In Defense of an Abused Doctrine*, 2 L. TRANSITION Q. 35 (1965).

[45] Martin Shapiro makes an excellent case for judicial protection of factions and interests unrepresented in Mendelson's majority. *See* M. SHAPIRO, FREEDOM OF SPEECH: THE SUPREME COURT AND JUDICIAL REVIEW (1966).

[46] Dennis v. United States, 341 U.S. 494, 548–49 (1951) (Frankfurter, J., concurring).

[47] Letter from Madison to Jefferson (17 October 1788), *printed in* 14 PAPERS 21.

something very different from that which Mendelson offers as a criterion: it is the degree to which the body politic permits its citizens to criticize and dissent from "the Nation's moral center of gravity." It is the extent to which diversity within unity is maintained. It registers the strength of law as an effective instrument of controlling political power. The raison d'être of a bill of rights is the establishment of a legal barrier by which individual freedom is safeguarded in that it is removed from the whims of politics.

In Mendelson's political world, however, we are not legal beings; and we merely delude ourselves in believing that our liberties can be protected by law. Of course, the power of law is limited. Individual rights, even those enshrined in our tradition and scrolled in gold, cannot withstand the profound political pressure of a majority overrun with fear and determined to crush dissent, no matter how innocuous such dissent might be. And a bill of rights may not be very efficacious in the hands of timid judges who might forget their independence or ignore their judicial duty. But Mendelson structures his analysis by exaggerating the weakness of law and constitutionalism; he focuses on Madison's articulation of the shortcomings of a declaration of rights which purports absolutely to guarantee individual rights. In times of dire necessity, Madison said, "no written prohibitions on earth would prevent the measure" sought by a majority to meet the emergency. "The restrictions however strongly marked on paper will never be regarded when opposed to the decided sense of the public."[48]

From all this Mendelson concludes that since a bill of rights cannot completely ensure individual liberties, it cannot protect them at all. Majorities will trammel over "parchment barriers' when they deem it necessary, wise, or reasonable. Yet it is nevertheless majority rule wherein he sees the most reliable protection of individual freedom. The synthesis of these two propositions is replete with confusion and contradiction: the greatest source of protection is also our greatest source of tyranny; our strongest shield is also our strongest foe. This is the realism Mendelson holds out to libertarians, something, he says, they must accept—sooner or later.

Even assuming the validity of the paradoxical assertion that majority rule is the best safeguard for minority rights, it is inconceivable that a

[48] *Id.* at 20, 21.

rational, coherent, and openly deliberative process of majoritarian democracy could take place without an already firmly established and protected freedom of expression. The political process of majoritarian decision-making requires, at the very least, knowledge and information, if responsible and rational decisions are to be made. Freedom of speech and press is thus an essential prerequisite to an effective and viable process of majority rule.[49] This is true, unless by majority rule Mendelson supposes a process which operates within a vacuum unresponsive to the demands of public sentiment. As a means—the only sure means, in Mendelson's words—of protecting individual freedom, majority rule can operate efficiently only if that very freedom is already protected at least by law. What the process of majority rule is theoretically designed to protect is thus the precondition for the successful operation of that process. This is another dilemma which Mendelson, intentionally or not, fails to recognize and resolve.

Madison was assuredly correct and justified in believing that in some instances "absolute restrictions" must be subordinated to overwhelming necessity, and that a declaration of rights constantly violated yields watered-down paper protection of individual liberties.[50] But, as Jefferson indicated in his reply to Madison, although a bill of rights cannot endure unimpaired against every unanticipated emergency, "it is of great potency always, and rarely inefficacious."[51] One cannot disagree with Judge Learned Hand, who said that law and courts cannot save a "society so riven that the spirit of moderation is gone," and "that a society where that spirit flourishes" is not in need of law and courts to save it.[52] The eloquence of these truisms does not add much to the debate; life in the United States takes place at neither extreme of Judge Hand's dichotomous analysis. Of course a bill of rights is meaningless in a society with a majority strong and tyrannical enough always to disregard it. But, as Paul A. Freund puts it, we are not "a people lost beyond redemption or healthy beyond the need of saving. In fact our situation falls between. The

[49] This point is developed most extensively by A. MEIKLEJOHN, FREE SPEECH AND ITS RELATION TO SELF-GOVERNMENT (1948). *See also* T. EMERSON, TOWARD A GENERAL THEORY OF THE FIRST AMENDMENT 9 (1966).

[50] Letter from Madison to Jefferson (17 October 1788), *printed in* 14 PAPERS 18.

[51] Letter from Thomas Jefferson to James Madison (Mar. 15, 1789), *printed in* 14 PAPERS 660.

[52] L HAND, THE SPIRIT OF LIBERTY 164 (2d ed. I. Dilliard ed. 1954).

question is not whether the courts can do everything but whether they can do something."[53]

Mendelson himself admits[54] that Madison explained his reservations about the effectiveness of a bill of rights without considering the role which the judiciary would play in the enforcement of individual rights. Without some force behind it, of course, a bill of rights would appear as mere admonitory words to a majority determined to implement its will. When Jefferson replied to Madison's objections, however, he mentioned that Madison had overlooked the crucial and important role of judicial review: "you omit [an argument] which has great weight with me, the legal check which [a bill of rights] puts into the hands of the judiciary."[55] In other words, the bill of rights would be more than a parchment barrier; it would be enforced by the judicial power of the United States.

Madison seems to have been persuaded by Jefferson's argument. Still convinced, however, that a bill of rights would be superfluous to a government already limited in its powers, he agreed with Jefferson that a declaration of rights would serve as an additional safeguard against tyrannical government. A bill of rights would no longer be mere paper; it would derive its strength from the legal and political power of the judiciary. The courts were to be incorporated politically into Madison's original system of checks and balances—the particular province of the courts being the protection of individual rights "against every assumption of power in the legislative or executive." The natural function of the courts would be "to resist every encroachment upon rights expressly stipulated for in the constitution by the declaration of rights."[56]

These are the words and arguments, not of Madison under pressure, but of "the now converted Madison," as Alpheus T. Mason has argued. "In piloting the proposed amendments [the Bill of Rights] through Congress," Mason explains, "Madison stressed the very point Jefferson had earlier called to his attention as a glaring omission"—the role of the courts and judicial review. If Madison was under pressure in presenting amendments to the First Congress, the pressure was directed from those who advocated not so much individual rights, but states' rights. He wanted to propose amendments that would preserve individual freedoms, but "[h]e

---

[53] P. Freund, The Supreme Court of the United States 88–89 (1949).

[54] Mendelson, *supra* note 30, at 827 & n. 35.

[55] Letter from Jefferson to Madison (15 March 1789), *printed in* 14 Papers 659.

[56] *See* note 29 *supra* and accompanying text.

firmly opposed any amendments which might sap the energy of the new government."[57]

After Madison had proposed his amendments protecting individual freedoms, the states' rights proponents of a bill of rights were less than satisfied; some of the most vociferous wanted amendments only to weaken the federal government vis-à-vis the states, not so much to protect individual rights.[58] Many felt that there was an overemphasis on personal liberty at the expense of states' rights claims. Pierce Butler, for instance, saw the proposed amendments as a "few milk-and-water amendments . . . such as liberty of conscience, a free press, and one or two general things already well secured." Richard Henry Lee acknowledged that they were valuable rights, but that they did not touch on the "great points"—namely, those powers of the national government which were previously under state control. Beyond the protection of a bill of individual rights, these avid states' rightists, according to Jefferson, were "moving heaven and earth to have a new Convention to make capital changes."[59] If pressure was upon Madison when he introduced the Bill of Rights, as Mendelson maintains, it was pressure from ardent Antifederalists who were concerned more with undoing the Philadelphia Convention than with worrying about the protection of civil liberties. There was indeed pressure generated from an argument which Madison in the end did not oppose, and to which he most likely subscribed. After making his proposals in the First Congress, he said: "I have proposed nothing that does not appear to me as proper in itself, or eligible as patronized by a respectable number of our fellow-citizens; and if we can make the constitution better in the opinion of those who are opposed to it, without weakening its frame, or abridging its usefulness, in the judgment of those who are attached to it, we act the part of wise and liberal men to make such alterations as shall produce that effect."[60] The result of all this has been summed up succinctly by Mason: "[A] significant gain had been made. Rights formerly natural became civil. Individuals could thereafter look to courts for their protection; courts . . . could look to the Constitution for standards."[61]

[57] A. MASON, FREE GOVERNMENT IN THE MAKING, 312–15, 316 (3d ed. 1965). *See also* A. MASON, THE STATES' RIGHTS DEBATE: ANTIFEDERALISM AND THE CONSTITUTION (1964).

[58] For a comprehensive development of this thesis, see R. RUTLAND, THE BIRTH OF THE BILL OF RIGHTS (1955).

[59] A. MASON, *supra* note 57, at 317–18.

[60] 1 ANNALS OF CONG. 459 (Gales & Seaton eds. 1789–91).

[61] A. MASON, *supra* note 57, at 318.

Rather than appearing, as Mendelson would have it, as the forerunner of Judge Hand's lonely view that the Bill of Rights is not law, the Madison who proposed the Bill of Rights seems to have endorsed, and adopted as his own, a view of law and judicial duty which comes very close to Justice Black's. Indeed, Madison went so far as to suggest that the rights of freedom of the press and trial by jury and other provisions of the Bill of Rights should be made applicable against the states as well as the central government.[62]

> I should therefore wish to extend this interdiction, and add, . . . that no State shall violate the equal right of conscience, freedom of the press, or trial by jury in criminal cases; because it is proper that every Government should be disarmed of powers which trench upon those particular rights. . . . [I]t must be admitted, on all hands, that the State Governments are as liable to attack these invaluable privileges as the General Government is, and therefore ought to be as cautiously guarded against.[63]

And, these "absolute restrictions" on governmental power, as he called them in his letter responding to Jefferson, were to have the full weight of judicial power behind them. Far from approximating the posture of Judge Hand, these statements reflect very much Justice Black's repeated insistence that the purpose of the Bill of Rights was to withdraw from governmental interference an area of civil freedom which was to be protected absolutely by the courts.

HISTORY AND THE MEANING OF FREEDOM OF EXPRESSION

Having reinforced with considerable historical support both his literalist defense of absolutism and the corresponding role of the judiciary, Justice Black, in seeking to demonstrate the validity of his far-reaching view of freedom of expression, still faced the task of explaining why that freedom is so broad in scope. Assuming the authenticity of the doctrine that the Bill of Rights was meant absolutely to insulate certain liberties from governmental suppression, it remains unclear what many of those freedoms

---

[62] Justice Black would later argue that the Fourteenth Amendment was designed to make all of the guarantees of the Bill of Rights applicable against the states. *See* ch. IV, *infra*.

[63] 1 ANNALS OF CONG. 459 (Gales & Seaton eds. 1789-91).

entail. This is true of the freedom of expression. Since its boundaries are not precisely defined—despite Justice Black's repeated claims that they are—the meaning of free speech and press cannot be elicited solely from the text of the Constitution. Therefore, if one cannot derive the definition of freedom of expression from the language of the First Amendment, and if public officials—including judges—are prohibited from defining those freedoms,[64] then, consistent with Justice Black's constitutional jurisprudence, one has no alternative but to look back into history in search of a constitutional definition of free speech and press.

Historical interpretation as verification for certain constitutional conclusions was not for Justice Black, as it was for Justice Holmes, an examination "in the light of our whole experience and not merely in that of what was said a hundred [or two hundred] years ago."[65] Historical analysis was not an exegesis on the organic growth of a constitutional provision over time, but rather a rendition of the original understanding of that provision at the time of its adoption. It was historical intent, not development through history, which mattered in constitutional interpretation. Justice Black's concern was confined to the intention of the framers—what they meant by the "freedom of speech and of the press."

But history reveals very little conclusive evidence on the original meaning of freedom of speech and press, as that freedom was understood by the Founding Fathers. Alexander Hamilton admitted the inherent difficulty of definition and the potential variety of interpretations that might spring from any formulation of freedom of the press.

> What signifies a declaration that "the liberty of the press shall be inviolably preserved"? What is the liberty of the press? Who can give it any definition which would not leave the utmost latitude for evasion? I hold it to be impracticable; and from this I infer that its security, whatever fine declarations may be inserted in any constitution respecting it, must altogether depend on public opinion, and on the general spirit of the people and of the government.[66]

---

[64] Justice Black had said flatly: "The Founders of this Nation were not then willing to trust the definition of First Amendment freedoms to Congress or this Court, nor am I now." Braden v. United States, 365 U.S. 431, 445 (1961) (Black, J., dissenting).

[65] Missouri v. Holland, 252 U.S. 416, 433 (1920) (Holmes, J.).

[66] THE FEDERALIST No. 84, *reprinted in* THE FEDERALIST PAPERS 514 (C. Rossiter ed. 1961).

Still, what history does unfold about the meaning of freedom of expression at the time of the adoption of the First Amendment is a conception of that freedom strikingly short of the meaning ascribed to it by Justice Black. Indeed, though exaggerating his point with colorful sarcasm, Sidney Hook is probably correct in saying that "fidelity to fact should compel us to recognize that, unfortunately, the way the Daughters of the American Revolution and kindred organizations today interpret the First Amendment is much closer to how the makers of the American Revolution actually understood it in *their* time than the way civil libertarians of most schools of thought do today, absolutist or not."[67]

Investigations into the original meaning of freedom of expression ought to begin with Zechariah Chafee's frank but appropriate acknowledgment: "The truth is . . . that the framers had no very clear idea as to what they meant by 'the freedom of speech or of the press.' " Nevertheless, one thing seems fairly certain. "It was the freedom which they believed they already had—what they had wanted before the Revolution and had acquired through independence."[68] The First Amendment "does not create the right of freedom of speech and of the press, but merely protects an existing right from abridgment or interference."[69] The question, therefore, becomes: what was the existing (or natural) right embodied in and secured by the First Amendment?

As an answer to this question, there are two prominent and competing theses which have emerged from the myriad probings into the conception of freedom of expression held by Americans of the late eighteenth century. The more liberal interpretation has generally been the more widely accepted. It holds that the First Amendment was established to ensure the abolition of prior restraint and the elimination of seditious libel from the common law. Chafee succinctly stated this version of the intent of the framers: "[T]he First Amendment was written by men to whom Wilkes and Junius were household words, who intended to wipe out the common law of sedition, and make further prosecutions for criticism of government, without any incitement to law-breaking, forever impossible in the United States of America. . . . [T]he fundamental policy of the First Amendment [is] the open discussion of public affairs."[70]

---

[67] S. Hook, The Paradoxes of Freedom 31 (1962).

[68] Chafee, Book Review, 62 Harv. L. Rev. 891, 898 (1949).

[69] Vance, *Freedom of Speech and of the Press*, 2 Minn. L. Rev. 239, 242 (1918).

[70] Z. Chafee, Jr., Free Speech in the United States 21, 28 (1941).

The second, more restrictive interpretation of what the framers accepted as freedom of expression had been the standard view until it was replaced by Chafee's. Advanced by, among others, Edward S. Corwin, it contended that freedom of speech and press incorporated nothing more than Blackstone's limited definition of freedom of the press. Of the First Amendment, Corwin thus wrote:

> This Amendment was written into the Constitution by students of Blackstone, in the pages of whose Commentaries the notion of the freedom of the press, from being a literary and political watchword, is first raised to the position of an accepted legal concept. But Blackstone's notion of freedom of the press, while it records the final result of an historical struggle, is a somewhat modest one. Briefly, Blackstone defined freedom of the press as on the one hand freedom from restraint previous to publication, and on the other hand, subjection to the law for abuse of this freedom. Of course, the law which he has in mind is the common law of his day and includes, therefore, the common law of seditious libel.[71]

Under this view, one could publish or say anything without prior censorship, but one could be subsequently punished if the utterance contravened the common law, which Corwin argued included the prohibition of seditious libel. In other words, a person could criticize government but could nevertheless be punished for seditious libel unless, in some jurisdictions, the truth of the accusations could be established. And, in some cases, even this meager defense was removed if malicious intent on the part of the speaker or publisher could be demonstrated. Serving as counsel for a defendant in a New York Criminal libel case in 1804, Alexander Hamilton offered what was then considered a liberal definition of freedom of the press, which Corwin cites to magnify and reinforce his position. Hamilton said: "The liberty of the press consists in the right to publish with impunity, truth, with good motives, for justifiable ends, though reflecting on government, magistracy, or individuals."[72]

"[T]his most widely prevalent definition of liberty of the press," as Corwin called it,[73] would hardly sustain even moderately libertarian notions of freedom of expression, which Justice Black denounced as too

---

[71] Corwin, *supra* note 24, at 49.
[72] *Quoted in id.* at 52, *quoting from* State v. Croswell, N. Y. Sup. Ct. 1804.
[73] *Id.* at 53.

niggardly in their scope.[74] Corwin's essay is a rebuttal to Mr. Justice Holmes's celebrated libertarian dissent in *Abrams* v. *United States*, where the latter announced his libertarian "clear and present danger" test. There Justice Holmes argues that expression of opinions can be legitimately suppressed only when they "so imminently threaten immediate interference with the lawful and pressing purposes of the law that an immediate check is required to save the country."[75] But this generous test was designed to protect seditious libel; Justice Holmes, as well as his critics, quite clearly presumed that the "clear and present danger" was to be applied only to political expression—the scope of the meaning of free expression.

The distance between Justice Black and Corwin in their interpretations of the First Amendment can be measured by the fact that Justice Black also rejected the Holmesian clear and present danger test and its confinement to seditious libel as a dangerously weak construction of the amendment. Thus, if Corwin had been correct in his interpretation of history, Justice Black's rendition of the original meaning and purpose appears as that of a fanciful judge not much in touch with reality; the justice's view is so far wide of the mark that it genuinely can be dismissed as an absurdity.[76]

Yet Chafee painstakingly sought to demonstrate that Corwin may have been wrong and to repudiate the assertion that the sole purpose of the First Amendment was merely to incorporate the narrow, Blackstonian definition of freedom of expression. The gist of his thesis is this:

> The men of 1791 went as far as Blackstone, and much farther. . . . All through the eighteenth century . . . there existed beside this definite legal meaning of liberty of the press, a definite popular meaning: the right of unrestricted discussion of public affairs. There can be no doubt that this was in a general way what freedom of speech meant to the framers of the Constitution.
>
> In short, the framers of the First Amendment sought to preserve the fruits of the old victory abolishing censorship, and to achieve a new victory abolishing sedition prosecutions.[77]

---

[74] *E.g.*, the "balancing" and "clear and present danger" tests which Justice Black rejected. *See* H. BLACK, *supra* note 12, at 49–52.

[75] 250 U.S. 616, 630 (1919) (Holmes, J., dissenting).

[76] This is Professor Hook's conclusion; *see* S. HOOK, *supra* note 67, ch. 1 *passim*.

[77] Z. CHAFEE, *supra* note 70, at 18, 19, 22.

Supporting this view, he argued a line similar to one of Justice Black's most important themes—the rejection of legislative supremacy and English constitutionalism generally. "It must not be forgotten," Chafee explained, "that the controversy over liberty of the press was a conflict between two views of government, that the law of sedition was a product of the view that the government was master, and that the American Revolution transformed into a working reality the second view that the government was servant, and therefore subjected to blame from its master, the people." The basis of the First Amendment, he concluded by quoting Madison, is " 'the essential difference between the British Government and the American constitution.' "[78] In England seditious libel was still a crime; in the United States it was no longer.

Whether more or less valid than Corwin's, Chafee's position seems to have prevailed until a significant challenge to his thesis emerged in the 1960s in the form of a revival of Corwin's conclusions. In his *Legacy of Suppression*, Leonard W. Levy concludes that, although the available evidence is somewhat ambiguous and fragmentary, "[i]f . . . a choice must be made between two propositions [that of Corwin and that of Chafee], the known evidence points strongly in support of the former proposition." Levy's investigation leads him to the conclusion "that libertarian theory from Milton to the ratification of the First Amendment substantially accepted the right of the state to suppress seditious libel." Of the people who adopted the First Amendment, "few among them, if any at all, clearly understood what they meant by the free speech and press clause, and it is perhaps doubtful that those few agreed except in a generalized way and equally doubtful that they represented a consensus."[79]

This is not the place to examine and assess the accuracy and validity of these contending accounts of history and the original meaning of freedom of speech and press.[80] It is enough merely to note that, assuming Justice Black's doctrine of absolutism—solely as a standard of enforcement—to be

[78] *Id.* at 22. *Id.* at 19, *quoting* Madison's Report on the Virginia Resolutions 1799. Chafee also quotes the conclusion of Professor Schofield, who said: "One of the objects of the Revolution was to get rid of the English common law on liberty of speech and of the press. . . . Liberty of the press as declared in the First Amendment, and the English common-law crime of sedition, cannot co-exist." *Id.* at 20.

[79] L. LEVY, LEGACY OF SUPPRESSION: FREEDOM OF SPEECH AND PRESS IN EARLY AMERICAN HISTORY, vii, 236, 247–248 (1960).

[80] For an interesting critique of Levy's book, see George Anastaplo, Book Review, 39 N.Y.U. L. REV. 735 (1964).

valid, the freedom of expression which is to be absolutely protected is either Corwin's limited or Chafee's more liberal definition, both of which Justice Black dismissed as being far short of the original understanding of freedom of speech and press.[81] Granting the benefit of doubt to Chafee— and, in the light of Levy's analysis, this is a generous concession—and accepting the doctrine of absolutism, what emerges is an absolute right to criticize government and discuss public affairs.

This understanding of freedom of expression, of course, comports with Alexander Meiklejohn's view, which Justice Black also rejected as too narrow. Chafee, himself, did not accept this conclusion, perhaps because he did not accept the standard of absolute enforcement, or perhaps because he believed freedom of expression had its own implied exceptions.[82] (He acknowledged implicit qualifications on the right to discuss public affairs. Speech that might provoke lawbreaking, for example, or antisocial conduct, was not part of the original freedom of expression that he uncovered. Moreover, private defamation and pornography are not even considered in his assessment of the original intent of the framers. They are presumed by common sense to be outside the realm of free speech.)

The important concern here deals not with the wisdom or validity or feasibility of the views of Corwin, Chafee, or Meiklejohn, but with the fact that Justice Black found even the broad view propounded by Meiklejohn to be a substantial distance from the original meaning of freedom of expression. Justice Black could find in the First Amendment constitutional protection for private libel and slander, all forms of hard-core pornography, and even incendiary harangues leading to violence.[83] He claimed to have arrived at this extreme position without recourse to judicial policymaking; for him, it was a matter of compelling judicial obligation. He accepted the premise that "the basic purpose" of the First

---

[81] This, of course, is assuming that one must be chained to a meaning of freedom of expression considered important in the eighteenth century.

[82] Professor Mendelson has made the argument that Corwin's view stands unrefuted, and that "even Chafee ultimately accepted it." Mendelson, *The First Amendment and the Judicial Process: A Reply to Mr. Frantz*, 17 VAN. L. REV. 479, 480 (1964). He refers to Chafee's review of Meiklejohn's book (*see* note 68 *supra*). But in that review there is little indication that Chafee retracted his earlier view that the original purpose of the First Amendment was the abolition of seditious libel. It is true that Chafee rejected absolutism, but he rejected it long before his review of Meiklejohn's book. His comments on Meiklejohn are consistent with his original thesis. See Z. CHAFEE, *supra* note 70, at 31–35, where Chafee had made the same argument which he made in his review of Meiklejohn's book.

[83] *See* H. BLACK, *supra* note 12, at 45–53.

Amendment was to protect political speech, "plus the fact that they [the framers] wanted to protect *religious* speech. Those were the two main things they had in mind."[84] Then, to extend the core of freedom of expression to include libel and obscenity, he employed the following reasoning:

> There is nothing in the language of the First Amendment to indicate that it protects only *political* speech. . . . Since the language of the Amendment contains no exceptions, I have continuously voted to strike down all laws dealing with so-called obscene materials since I believe such laws act to establish a system of censorship in violation of the First Amendment. . . .
>
> Just as with obscenity laws, I believe the First Amendment compels the striking down of all libel laws.[85]

The initial objection to this line of reasoning is that although the language of the First Amendment does not contain exceptions, it is because there are no definitions from which exception can be made. One might as well argue that since the First Amendment "free exercise" of religion clause also contains no exceptions, every law in the United States ought to be invalidated if it conflicts with someone's claim of a religious exercise. Yet Justice Black always recognized the need to set limits to what could be done in the name of free exercise of religion. It is true that the language contains no exceptions, but the reference is to the extent of enforcement—absolutism—and not the meaning of that which is to be enforced absolutely. Literally, there are no exceptions from absolute enforcement. But this is not the same thing as saying that all expression is free, and hence absolutely protected.

Justice Black again enlisted the words of the Founding Fathers to support his position, this time those of Jefferson, who said: "libels, falsehood and defamation, equally with heresy and false religion are withheld from the cognizance of federal tribunals."[86] From this, Justice Black elicited the libertarian conclusion that "I believe with Jefferson that it is time enough for government to step in to regulate people when they *do* something, not when they *say* something."[87]

---

[84] Cahn, *Justice Black and First Amendment "Absolutes": A Public Interview*, 37 N.Y.U. L. Rev. 549, 559 (1962).
[85] H. BLACK, *supra* note 12, at 46–47, 48.
[86] *Quoted in id.* at 48.
[87] *Id.*

However, although Jefferson was a believer in freedom of expression and perhaps an ardent libertarian, the words of Jefferson on which Justice Black built his libertarian conclusions seem more concerned with the proper jurisdictions between the federal and state governments than with libertarian principles. As Harry Clor writes, "Madison and Jefferson would deny to the federal government any power to restrain the licentiousness of the press, but they would not deny that power to the states."[88] Denouncing the Sedition Act of 1798, Madison said that "every libellous writing or expression can receive its punishment in the State Courts . . . whether it injured public officers or private citizens."[89] And, writing to Madison, Jefferson said in 1788: "A declaration, that the federal government will never restrain the presses from printing anything they please, will not take away the liability of the printers for false facts printed."[90]

In a letter to John Norvell, a resident of Virginia who had written to Jefferson about the possibility of starting a newspaper, President Jefferson had this to say about the press of his day:

It is a melancholy truth, that a suppression of the press could not more completely deprive the nation of its benefits, than is done by its abandoned prostitution to falsehood. Nothing can now be believed which is seen in a newspaper. Truth itself becomes suspicious by being put into that polluted vehicle. . . . [T]he man who never looks into a newspaper is better informed than he who reads them; inasmuch as he who knows nothing is nearer to truth than he whose mind is filled with falsehoods and errors.[91]

The following lengthy portion of President Jefferson's letter to Abigail Adams also should be read in the context of Justice Black's historical argument. Speaking of the Sedition Act of 1798, Jefferson wrote:

Nor does the opinion of the unconstitutionality and consequent nullity of that law remove all restraint from the overwhelming torrent of slander which is confounding all vice and virtue, all truth and falsehood in the United States. The power to do this is fully possessed by the several State Legislatures. It was reserved to them, and was denied to

---

[88] H. CLOR, OBSCENITY AND PUBLIC MORALITY: CENSORSHIP IN A LIBERAL SOCIETY 96–97 (1969).

[89] *Quoted in id.* at 97.

[90] Letter from Thomas Jefferson to James Madison (July 31, 1788) *printed in* THE LIFE AND SELECTED WRITINGS OF THOMAS JEFFERSON 451 (Koch & Peden eds. 1944).

[91] Letter from Thomas Jefferson to John Norvell (June 11, 1807) *printed in id.* at 581.

the general government, by the constitution according to our construction of it. While we deny that Congress have a right to control the freedom of the press, we have ever asserted the right of the states, and their exclusive right, to do so. They have accordingly, all of them, made provisions for punishing slander, which those who have time and inclination resort to for the vindication of their characters. In general the state laws appear to have made the presses responsible for slander as far as it is consistent with their useful freedom. In those states where they do not admit even the truth of allegations to protect the printer, they have gone too far.[92]

Although these passages from Madison and Jefferson seem to corroborate Justice Black's contention that the federal government was absolutely deprived of any power to regulate the law of libel, they provide very little material from which to build genuine libertarian doctrine. Implicit in these passages, indeed, is the recognition of the state power to punish even seditious libel. Only by ignoring these passages and many others of similar content could Justice Black say: "Our First Amendment was a bold effort . . . to establish a country with no legal restrictions of any kind upon the subjects people could investigate, discuss and deny. The Framers knew, better perhaps than we do today, the risks they were taking. They knew that free speech might be the friend of change and revolution. But they also knew that it is always the deadliest enemy of tyranny. . . . They were not afraid for men to be free. We should not be."[93]

Of course it is not true that there were no legal restraints on the subject matter which the people of the United States could discuss. In every state at that time there was substantial legislation narrowing such subject matter. Some of these statutes are still on the legal code of some states—especially obscenity regulations.[94] Perhaps also the framers were aware of the risks involved in depriving the central government of the power to punish libelous expression, and perhaps they were not afraid for men to be free, as Justice Black said. However, the "bold effort" of stripping the federal government involved very little risk: the states had ample, if not complete, power to regulate speech that transgressed the bounds of the

---

[92] Letter from Thomas Jefferson to Abigail Adams (Sept. 11, 1804) *printed in* 1 THE ADAMS-JEFFERSON LETTERS 279 (Cappon ed. 1959).

[93] Black, *supra* note 9, at 881.

[94] *See* Henkin, *Morals and the Constitution: The Sin of Obscenity*, 63 COLUM. L. REV. 391 (1963).

accepted definition of freedom of expression. Speech that might be dangerous could be quickly and legally suppressed by the states; in fact, there was nothing but their own constitutions to prevent the states from suppressing that freedom within their respective jurisdictions. According to Corwin, "prosecutions for seditious libel occurred even in the 19th century in States whose constitutions asserted 'liberty of the press' in the broadest terms."[95]

Jefferson's conception of freedom of expression is somewhat revealed in his letter to Abigail Adams. The states were going too far, he thought, if truth was not allowed as a defense in state criminal and civil libel cases. Given his distaste for "that polluted vehicle," Jefferson was apparently pleased that the states retained plenary power to regulate the press. To be sure, he denied that Congress had any power to abridge the freedom of the press, but it is evident that it was not only for libertarian purposes that he felt the federal government ought to be deprived of this power.

It appears that for Jefferson and perhaps Madison the First Amendment was as much a matter of delineating jurisdictional boundaries between state and federal governments as it was an isolated, heroic concern for freedom of expression. It is uncertain whether this jurisdictional preoccupation was meant to deprive the federal government of all power to regulate all speech and press or all power to quash only political criticism—that is, all power over seditious libel. The evidence is unclear, but it seems that here Madison and Jefferson were concerned primarily with removing from the federal government only the power to crush political dissent.[96]

In many moving dissenting opinions in free speech cases,[97] Justice Black developed sincere and strong libertarian arguments drawing upon the views of Madison and Jefferson to invigorate his position with the appearance that he was only following the intent of this nation's forefathers. But it is difficult to believe that the libertarian reasons and motives espoused by Justice Black prompted Madison and Jefferson to insist that the federal government be divested of all power to abridge free speech and press. Given their attitudes toward state power over the press,

---

[95] Corwin, *supra* note 24, at 49–50.

[96] *See* A. BICKEL, THE LEAST DANGEROUS BRANCH 100 (1962).

[97] *See*, e.g., Konigsberg v. State Bar of California, 366 U.S. 36, 56–80 (1961); *In re* Anastaplo, 366 U.S. 82, 97–116 (1961); Barenblatt v. United States, 360 U.S. 109, 134–62 (1959) (Black, J., dissenting).

it is doubtful that they shared Justice Black's cavalier conception of freedom of expression. Jefferson and Madison, of course, were surely libertarians: they objected to the idea of a central government moulding public opinion. But this is something very different from the views Justice Black would later trace to those he believed "were not afraid for men to be free."

CONCLUSION

The conclusions to which Justice Black was led from the events surrounding the creation of the Constitution, and the Bill of Rights in particular, are not entirely substantiated by the facts. There is real support for the doctrine of absolutism (purely as a standard of enforcement), and of course the language of the First Amendment supports absolutism. There is evidence that the Bill of Rights was to be strictly enforced and that the rights therein were not to be rebalanced and reweighed against contending governmental claims. But even Justice Black recognized (for a time, at least) that, in the course of the nation's history, compelling necessity might outweigh the people's constitutional rights.[98]

However, with regard to the First Amendment, it is very unclear just what it is that is to be absolutely protected. Justice Black seems to have assumed that the men of the eighteenth century were unanimous in their support for freedom of expression and that they accepted a uniform definition of that freedom. Legal scholars and historians, however, have demonstrated by their conflicting conclusions that no general consensus existed. The confusion is compounded further by the jurisdictional argument traceable to Jefferson and Madison. Justice Black's interpretation of the First Amendment is tenable only if the narrow, jurisdictional aspect can be deemed the fundamental purpose of that amendment, and then only if it can be shown that the amendment was meant to remove all matters of speech and press from federal control. Justice Black believed that the federal government was indeed deprived of all such power, and he

---

[98] In 1944 Justice Black said: "Compulsory exclusion of large groups of citizens from their homes, except under circumstances of direct emergency and peril, is inconsistent with our basic governmental institutions. But when under conditions of modern warfare our shores are threatened by hostile forces, the power to protect must be commensurate with the threatened danger." Korematsu v. United States, 323 U.S. 214, 219–20 (1944).

based this conclusion on the libertarian views of the framers. But the justification or rationale for the jurisdictional argument cannot be based on libertarian principles. The framers were well aware of, and encouraged, the power of the states to control expression considered dangerous or seditious. Jefferson himself was in the forefront of this recognition of, and desire for, state power over the press. An amendment the purpose of which was solely to deny one jurisdiction power to control the press, so as simultaneously to reserve that power to state legislatures, cannot be characterized as a libertarian instrument. Exclusively on a jurisdictional basis, the First and Tenth Amendments would serve absolutely to deny Congress power over speech and press. In such a context the concept of absolutism loses all its libertarian connotations.

Justice Black carried forward his position on the First Amendment by enforcing it against the states as well, exactly as he applied it to the federal government. He maintained that the Fourteenth Amendment (made part of the Constitution in 1868) incorporated the provisions of the Bill of Rights intact, and that they were therefore to be applied against the states as if they were being applied against the federal government.[99] Although the validity of his incorporation doctrine will be discussed in more detail in a later chapter, one important point is relevant here: If the purpose of the First Amendment was in fact jurisdictional, and thus aimed specifically at the federal government's authority over the matter of freedom of expression, how can it then be turned around to limit the states? As a restriction on federal power vis-à-vis the power of the states, how can the First Amendment apply to the states at all? Furthermore, if the reserved powers of the states over the press were suddenly to be abolished by the Fourteenth Amendment, suspicions must necessarily arise as to why this dramatic reduction in state power should take place arcanely and quietly in the vagaries of the Fourteenth Amendment. If the First Amendment is thus to be applied against the states in the first place, it must be the libertarian notions embodied in the amendment which thereby are incorporated into the Fourteenth Amendment against the states.

The First Amendment's freedom of expression has indeed been held by the Supreme Court to apply against the states. As the Court said in *Gitlow v. New York* (1925), "freedom of speech and press—which are

[99] His position on this matter is stated most fully in Adamson v. California, 332 U.S. 46, 68–123 (1947).

protected by the 1st Amendment from abridgment by Congress—are among the fundamental personal rights and 'liberties' protected by the due process clause of the 14th Amendment from impairment by the States."[100] Thus it was the notion of freedom of speech and press, not the First Amendment's absolutist standard, that the Court applied against the states in this case. Courts must therefore determine what this freedom involves. For Justice Black, however, judges were forbidden to redefine the meaning of freedom of expression as it was originally understood by the framers. But the most liberal definition that one can discern from history is that freedom of expression meant merely the right to criticize government—a right, moreover, which could be withdrawn if abused. Pornography, libel and slander, and inflammatory speech were not included in this freedom. It was a freedom of expression quite different from that which Justice Black drew from history and the intent of the framers. And, if the Corwin-Levy hypothesis is valid—if the freedom of speech was only freedom from prior restraint—then adherence to the original meaning would destroy the free press as we know it today.

One of Justice Black's admirers and former law clerks, A. E. Dick Howard, has said: "The question . . . is not whether Black is a good or bad, careful or slipshod historian, but rather what are we to make of the fact that Black thinks that to decide constitutional cases, he must be an historian."[101] Indeed, why should a judge deciding questions of profound importance to Americans of the twentieth century feel compelled to adhere to the conceptions of freedom and restraint considered important in the eighteenth century? To adhere to the original meaning of freedom of speech and press might place intolerable burdens on the freedom of the contemporary news media; it could impose undue restraints on the right of expression.

But an equally valid and fundamental question is: was Justice Black, in fact, "a good or bad, careful or slipshod historian"? If a judge on the highest court in the United States considers himself bound by the original definitions of ambiguous concepts of freedom, definitions derived to meet the conditions of another age, should he not be required to justify more

---

[100] 268 U.S. 652, 666 (Sanford, J.).

[101] Howard, *Mr. Justice Black: The Negro Protest Movement and the Rule of Law*, 53 VA. L. REV. 1030 (1967). Professor John Frank, another of the justice's former law clerks, says that "primarily [Justice Black] is a historian." J. FRANK, MR. JUSTICE BLACK: THE MAN AND HIS OPINIONS 47 (1949).

soundly his conclusions, especially when they are made so adamantly in the face of overwhelming evidence to the contrary? While there is historical evidence to support the concept of absolutism, there is almost none to validate Justice Black's notions of the freedom of expression to be protected and his claim that these views were nothing more or less than those which the framers sought to preserve and protect.

Answering his own question, Howard offers an explanation of why Justice Black felt bound by history: "The simple fact . . . is that for Justice Black the appeal to historical evidence, to the intent of the framers, and to the historical meaning of constitutional provisions is part and parcel of this philosophy of the role of the judge and the strict limits which traditions of the judicial process under a written constitution impose on him."[102]

It is true that Justice Black saw the role of the judge as limited, and that the creative lawmaking function of the judiciary was to be circumscribed by the written Constitution. Judges were not empowered to go outside the Constitution and into their own value schemes in reaching constitutional decisions. Where ambiguities appeared in the text of the Constitution, courts were required to clarify them; but in this capacity judges were obligated to ascertain the true meaning from the original intent of the framers—from history.

But in professing to be strictly limited in his policymaking role, Justice Black drew his extreme conclusions on the First Amendment from a version of history which, at many crucial points, is sharply and overwhelmingly contradicted by historical fact. What are the "strict limits" restraining a judge who professed allegiance to a doctrinaire and extreme interpretation of freedom of speech and who purported to have derived this interpretation from close adherence to the language and history of the First Amendment, when in fact the words of the amendment do not contain any definitions of freedom of expression, and when history yields at most a definition very removed from that proposed?

It is not impossible to employ history to develop a position which approximates Justice Black's posture on freedom of expression. The late Harry Kalven, Jr., for instance, a libertarian though not endorsing or subscribing to Justice Black's views, undertook such a process. First, he cited the "central meaning of the First Amendment,"[103] which follows

[102] Howard, *supra* note 101, at 1069–70.
[103] Kalven, *The New York Times Case: A Note on the "Central Meaning of the First Amendment,"* 1964 SUP. CT. REV. 191.

Chafee's conclusions—that is, the abolition of seditious libel. Around this central core, he then inferred the existence of an "ambit" which might extend constitutional protection eventually to expression—even obscenity[104]—not encompassed in the original meaning of free speech.[105] But Kalven's method of expanding the scope of free speech involved a process of conscious and deliberate policymaking not necessarily either commanded or forbidden by the First Amendment.

Justice Black advocated something more than Kalven's comprehensive definition of free speech; yet he denied that his position was based on any policy considerations of his own. He tried to justify his view by the "plain language" and clear history of the First Amendment. But there were factors and events other than history and language which influenced him in reaching his views, and they are perhaps best uncovered and explained by tracing through his long tenure on the Supreme Court Justice Black's constant search for "strict limits" through which to channel the judicial power.

[104] Kalven, *The Metaphysics of the Law of Obscenity*, 1960 SUP. CT. REV. 1.

[105] Kalven, *The Reasonable Man and the First Amendment: Hill, Butts, and Walker*, 1967 SUP. CT. REV. 267, 289.

CHAPTER III

Justice Black and the Balancing of Interests

In tracing the development of his absolutist interpretation of the First Amendment, Justice Black's long tenure on the Supreme Court can be divided into three different periods. The first, dating roughly from 1937 to 1949, begins with his appointment and ends with the deaths of Justices Frank Murphy and Wiley Rutledge, two vigilant and ardent libertarians who, together with Justices Black and Douglas, comprised the libertarian wing on the Court from 1943 to 1949. On First Amendment issues, these four justices almost always united and frequently attracted the votes of other justices, thereby creating a shifting majority upholding the free speech claim in most cases coming before the Court during this period. The shifting vote or votes were frequently cast by Chief Justice Harlan F. Stone, sometimes by Justices Stanley F. Reed or Roberts, and occasionally by Justice Jackson. Often the decision was unanimous, or nearly unanimous. Thus it was during this period that the First Amendment was elevated to a "preferred position," at times almost blindly to the exclusion of other societal interests.[1]

The second period, from 1949 to 1962, begins with the appointments

[1] *See, e.g.*, Terminiello v. Chicago, 337 U.S. 1 (1949); Martin v. Struthers, 319 U.S. 141 (1943).

of Justices Tom Clark and Sherman Minton (who replaced Justices Murphy and Rutledge) and ends with the retirement of Justice Frankfurter and the appointment of his replacement, Justice Arthur J. Goldberg. The deaths of Justices Murphy and Rutledge marked the end of the "preferred position" era of the First Amendment. The dominant issue of freedom of expression that came before the Court, in C. Herman Pritchett's characterization, shifted from "nonconformity" in the 1940s to "subversion" in the 1950s.[2] This factor, coupled with the important changes in the Court's membership, resulted in the plummeting of the previously vigorous judicial protection of freedom of expression to a point at which people at all sympathetic to the ideas of the Communist party could rely on little support from the Supreme Court. For a brief period between 1956 and 1957, the Court endeavored to reassert its power to enforce the guarantees of the First Amendment. But vituperative political pressure from Congress amidst continuing but exaggerated national concern over the issue of Communist subversion in the United States—a burning and consuming issue during the 1950s, an issue which had earlier been inflamed by the charges and accusations of Senator Joseph McCarthy—induced the Court, led by Justices Frankfurter and Harlan, to retreat into the background and all but abandon its role as protector of civil liberties when those liberties were asserted by suspected Communist subversives.[3]

It was during this second period, especially when the Court succumbed to congressional pressure, that Justice Black unfolded his doctrine of absolutism and announced his broad interpretation of the scope of free expression; his libertarian inclination merged with his search for objectivity into the far-reaching, absolutist construction of the First Amendment. Having lost the "preferred position" majority of the 1940s, he was forced to articulate his doctrine almost totally in dissenting opinions, some of which rank in the forefront of episodes of judicial fortitude and dedication to the principles of limited government and individual liberties,[4] even against what was for most of his colleagues on the Court overwhelming political pressure.

---

[2] C. PRITCHETT, CIVIL LIBERTIES AND THE VINSON COURT 4 (1954).

[3] For two excellent accounts of the political battle between the Court and Congress, see W. MURPHY, CONGRESS AND THE COURT (1962); C. PRITCHETT, CONGRESS VERSUS THE SUPREME COURT (1961).

[4] *See, e.g., In re* Anastaplo, 366 U.S. 82, 97–116 (1961) (Black, J., dissenting); Barenblatt v. United States, 360 U.S. 109, 134–62 (1959) (Black, J., dissenting).

The final period is from 1962 until his death in 1971. By the mid-1960s the government's crusade against communism had spent itself, and a new Court had revitalized freedom of expression and restored it to its proper place in a democratic society. It was during this period that a new activist and libertarian Court became involved for the first time in legislative reapportionment; revolutionized the constitutional law of libel and obscenity; found constitutional protection for the proliferation of novel modes of expression and communication characterized generally as "symbolic conduct"; and succeeded in fundamentally altering the administration of criminal justice. But it was also during this period, especially toward the end, that Justice Black disassociated himself from the libertarian wing of the Warren Court, whose activist majority continued to make advances into new fields of social policy. Several observers have maintained that from approximately 1964 until his death, Justice Black grew increasingly less libertarian and became more a voice of the conservative opposition and reaction to the Warren Court.[5] To be sure, his libertarian attitude began to wane amidst the turmoil of violent protest which he witnessed during the 1960s. But it was more than a change in attitude which prompted Justice Black to adapt and restructure his jurisprudence during the 1960s. Much of his judicial behavior then can be viewed as that of a judge struggling with the doctrine of absolutism—that of a judge attempting to control the effects of an absolutist construction of the First Amendment without destroying the concept of absolutism. His attempts will be discussed in Chapter V.

The thesis proposed in the present chapter is twofold. First, during the 1940s Justice Black was not an absolutist, nor did he comprehend the scope of free speech to be as broad as he would in the 1950s and 1960s. During the 1940s free speech to Justice Black meant merely free discussion of public affairs, primarily religious and political. Free speech also included artistic and literary expression, but it did not include libel and pornography; expanding the scope of free speech to include absolute protection of the latter two realms was undertaken only after he had embraced absolutism.

Moreover, since his interpretation of the freedom of speech was not the result merely of reading history and the language of the First Amendment, there were other reasons behind his sometimes dogmatic assertions concerning the sweep of that amendment. His position can be viewed as the

---

[5] G. Schubert, The Constitutional Polity 118–29 (1970); Snowiss, *The Legacy of Justice Black*, 1973 Sup. Ct. Rev. 187.

product of the interplay of libertarianism and his search for objectivity in constitutional adjudication. His construction of the First Amendment was an effort ideally to fuse together these two prominent values which permeate his opinions, an attempt culminating in the 1950s when the Court seemed almost always to subordinate First Amendment rights to the government's determination to purge the nation of all traces of communism. Absolutism was more than Justice Black's response to the decisions rendered by the Court during this period; it was as much—if, indeed, it was not more—a denunciation of the reasoning and process by which the Court reached those decisions. It was a rejection of judicial policymaking intrinsic to the Court's posture of balancing freedom of speech against competing governmental interests. Absolutism was the culmination of a libertarian's search for objectivity in constitutional adjudication as a means both to restrain the exercise of judicial power and to protect the right of expression. This will be examined in Chapter IV; the present chapter focuses on the Justice Black of the 1940s.

ABSOLUTISM AND THE 1940S: THE OTHER JUSTICE BLACK

If Justice Black's literal interpretation of the free speech and press guarantees of the First Amendment is obvious from plain language, it is clear that he was not persuaded by such alleged clarity during his initial encounters with governmental incursions into the domain of First Amendment freedoms. The doctrine of absolutism was alien to his jurisprudence during this first period on the Court, and he gave no indication that he contemplated his later, sweeping view of the scope of free speech. This is evident from several important opinions that he wrote or endorsed during the 1940s.

In 1940 the Supreme Court upheld the power of the school district of Minersville, Pennsylvania, to expel from school a student (a Jehovah's Witness) who refused, because of religious convictions, to salute the American flag. Justice Black aligned himself with a majority of justices whose decision in favor of the school authorities turned on a balancing of interests. Speaking for that majority, Mr. Justice Frankfurter said: "Our present task . . . , as so often the case with courts, is to reconcile two rights in order to prevent either from destroying the other." The Court's process of reconciling the conflicting interests was really no balance at all, since the Court deferred to the judgment of the school authorities. Arguing the curious and paradoxical position that the spirit of democracy is somehow advanced when "reasonable" majorities encroach on the rights of helpless minorities, and conceding that the governmental action under review itself infringed on such rights, Justice Frankfurter explained: "[T]o the legislature no less than to courts is committed the guardianship of deeply cherished liberties. . . . To fight out the wise use of legislative authority in the forum of public opinion and before legislative assemblies rather than to transfer such a contest to the judicial arena, serves to vindicate the self-confidence of a free people."[6] The net result of such deferential reasoning, of course, was the subordination of the right to refuse to salute the flag; for if the judicial test was whether the compulsory flag salute is reasonably related to the promotion of national unity (a legitimate governmental interest), it is difficult to see how the constitutional right could ever survive such a test.

Alone in dissent, Mr. Justice Stone—a libertarian, but surely no absolutist—pointed out the plain truth that the Court's reasoning and disposition was "no less than the surrender of the constitutional protection of the liberty of small minorities to the popular will."[7] He rejected, as Justice Black apparently then did not, the proposition that the state has the constitutional power to compel its citizens to pledge public affirmation to the United States despite their religious and political objections, and regardless of the First Amendment. National unity, however noble and valid as a governmental goal, could not be encouraged, according to Justice Stone, by suffocating the individual rights protected by the First Amendment.

Twenty years later Justice Black would categorically repudiate the very same test he helped apply in the *Gobitis* case. In his public rendition of the absolute nature of each guarantee contained in the Bill of Rights, he would say: "[I]t is sometimes said that the Bill of Rights guarantees must 'compete' for survival against general powers expressly granted to Congress [and government generally], and that the individual's right must, if outweighed by the public interest, be subordinated to the Government's competing interest in denying the right. . . . I cannot accept this approach to the Bill of Rights."[8]

Less than three years after the *Gobitis* ruling, Justice Black switched

[6] Minersville School District v. Gobitis, 310 U.S. 586, 594, 600 (1940).
[7] *Id.* at 606 (Stone, J., dissenting).
[8] Black, *The Bill of Rights*, 35 N.Y.U.L. Rev. 865, 866–67 (1960).

sides in the Second Flag Salute Case, apparently undergoing a change of mind and direction regarding the "plain meaning" of the First Amendment. But he explained his switch not on the basis of absolutism, but as a result of the application of still another "test" which he would also later denounce—the clear and present danger test. For himself and Justice Douglas, who also switched sides in the second case (as did Justice Murphy), Justice Black stated: "[W]e cannot say that a failure, because of religious scruples, to assume a particular physical position and to repeat the words of a patriotic formula creates a grave danger to the nation."[9] The Justice Black of the 1950s and 1960s would reject all such tests as judicial distortions of the simple and clear command of the First Amendment.

Further disavowals of absolutism appear in the majority opinion that he wrote for the Court in *Korematsu* v. *United States*. Over the dissent of three justices, Justice Black concluded that it was not beyond the constitutional power of Congress or the executive in time of war to exclude from the West Coast nearly 110,000 people of Japanese descent, most of whom were American citizens. Excluded from their homes and businesses on the West Coast, these people were forcibly relocated in detention camps in the Southwest United States. In reaching this result, he invoked a balancing of interests. "Nothing short of apprehension by the proper military authorities of the gravest imminent danger to the public safety," he explained "can constitutionally justify" this massive and cruel invasion of personal freedom and dignity. The hardships of war are real and affect everyone. "All citizens alike, both in and out of uniform, feel the impact of war in greater or lesser measure. Citizenship has its responsibilities as well as its privileges, and in time of war the burden is always heavier."[10]

Justice Black, of course, was aware, as were the dissenters, that "the impact of war" was here disproportionately far greater on those of Japanese ancestry, but unlike the dissenters he was unwilling to investigate the racial overtones of the exclusion order. Instead, he evaluated the order in terms of military necessity which could justify the measure, whereas "racial antagonism never can."[11] Yet racial antagonism was surely a weighty factor behind the issuance of the order. As Eugene

---

[9] West Virginia Board of Education v. Barnette, 319 U.S. 624, 644 (1943) (Black, J., concurring). Irving Dilliard saw Justice Black's change of view as "getting himself straightened out." Dilliard, *Hugo Black and the Importance of Freedom*, 10 AM. U. L. REV. 7, 14 (1961).

[10] 323 U.S. 214, 218, 219 (1944).

[11] *Id.* at 216.

Rostow later commented: "The dominant factor in the development of this policy was not a military estimate of a military problem, but familiar West Coast attitudes of race prejudice. The program of excluding all persons of Japanese ancestry from the coastal area was conceived and put through by the organized minority [The Native Sons and Daughters of the Golden West] whose business it has been for forty-five years to increase and exploit racial tensions on the West Coast."[12] Focusing the opinion of the Court exclusively on military necessity (as if the Court, as Justice Jackson said in dissent, could possibly have standards to adjudge military necessity), Justice Black thereby avoided the racial prejudice of the exclusion order by asserting that "the properly constituted military authorities feared an invasion of our West Coast and felt constrained to take proper security measures." He acknowledged that the exclusion order was "inconsistent with our basic governmental institutions. But when under conditions of modern warfare our shores are threatened by hostile forces, the power to protect must be commensurate with the threatened danger."[13]

Justice Black's holding in *Korematsu* evolved through judicial reasoning which could hardly be that of a judge preoccupied with the conviction that his official duty demands the absolute protection of basic civil rights. The Court's disposition rested squarely on the proposition that the power to wage war is the power to wage it successfully; the mother of invention was thus enlisted to legitimize broadside and degrading incursions into individual rights. It has been said that his opinion in *Korematsu* revealed Justice Black's "practical nature."[14] If "practical nature" means a rejection of absolute rights and a willingness to be persuaded by governmental claims of necessity, then *Korematsu* mirrored such a practical nature, for that ruling evinces a patent denial of the doctrine of absolute constitutional rights.

The Court's conclusion conferred constitutional approval upon an exclusion order which, in time of peace, Justice Black said, would not have been sustained. *Korematsu* might thus be viewed as a factor further impelling Justice Black's already entrenched determination to find concrete

---

[12] E. ROSTOW, THE SOVEREIGN PREROGATIVE 204 (1962). His analysis of this and other related cases was originally published as Rostow, *The Japanese American Cases—A Disaster*, 54 YALE L. J. 489 (1945).

[13] 323 U.S. at 223, 220.

[14] C. WILLIAMS, HUGO L. BLACK: A STUDY IN THE JUDICIAL PROCESS 171 (1950).

constitutional standards—such as absolutism—that would preclude another "major failure," as Rostow has characterized the holding in
Korematsu. [15] Though, as attorney general, and later governor, of California, Earl Warren had been an avid supporter of—and instrumental in
implementing—the Japanese exclusion order, [16] as chief justice of the
United States he criticized *Korematsu* and other lamentable wartime decisions involving Japanese Americans. Noting this, Carl Brent Swisher
added: "While Justice Black, a [judicial] participant in the wartime decisions as Chief Justice Warren was not, published no such criticism of the
Court's wartime handiwork, it may well be, in light of his growing
absolutism with respect to the Bill of Rights, that he has come to feel much
as does the Chief Justice."[17]

Justice Black never directly and specifically criticized his own opinion
in *Korematsu*. Yet he devoted much of the remainder of his judicial life to
condemning, as inconsistent with the idea of a written constitution, the
very reasoning employed to reach the result in *Korematsu*. Seeking to show
the inevitable danger to constitutional rights inherent in balancing and the
extent to which he opposed such balancing, he presented in his 1960 Bill of
Rights address "a practical demonstration of how [balancing] might
work."[18] Recounted by Justice Black, the facts of this hypothetical illustration were as follows.

While the United States was at war, in time of "great national
emergency, . . . a desperate condition," Congress enacted a statute
"authorizing seizure without compensation of lands required for the defense establishment." The plaintiff owned some 500 acres of "strategic
land for carrying out the defense program." Under the statute the military
expropriated his land without according him monetary compensation,
whereupon he brought suit in court challenging the constitutionality of
the statute, arguing that it violated the Fifth Amendment's provision that
private property shall not be taken for public use without just compensation. Was the act unconstitutional?

Employing the balancing of interests doctrine, "Judge X," as Justice

[15] Rostow, *Mr. Justice Black: Some Introductory Observations*, 65 YALE L. J. 451, 453 (1956).

[16] For an account of Warren's role in California, see L. KATCHER, EARL WARREN: A
POLITICAL BIOGRAPHY 137–51 (1967).

[17] Swisher, *History's Panamora and Justice Black's Career*, in HUGO BLACK AND THE SUPREME
COURT 17 (Strickland ed. 1967).

[18] Black, *supra* note 8, at 877. The excerpts depicting Justice Black's illustration of
balancing are taken from pp. 877–78.

Black called him, balanced in favor of the government, holding that the war power, together with the "necessary and proper" clause, gives the United States the power to wage war successfully. Judge X explained:

Driven by the absolute necessity to protect the nation from foreign aggression, the national debt has risen to billions of dollars. The Government's credit is such that interest rates have soared. Under these circumstances, Congress was rationally entitled to find that if it paid for all the lands it needs it might bankrupt the nation and render it helpless in its hour of greatest need. Weighing as I must the loss the individual will suffer because he has to surrender his land to the nation without compensation against the great public interest in conducting war, I hold the Act valid.

"Of course," said Justice Black, "I would not decide this case this way." Instead, he said he would have ruled against the government's claims of an urgent need because the Fifth Amendment's provision for just compensation is absolute, and, like all provisions of the Bill of Rights, it must be enforced "even in times of grave emergency." "The great danger of the judicial balancing process," he warned, "is that in times of emergency and stress it gives Government the power to do what it thinks necessary to protect itself, regardless of the rights of individuals. If the need is great, the right of the Government can always be said to outweigh the rights of the individual."[19]

In a lengthy biography of Justice Black which concentrates on his judicial career, Gerald T. Dunne briefly notes "this fictitious account of a nameless Judge X—no other, of course, than Felix Frankfurter—who 'balanced' the legislative findings of national necessity against uncompensated expropriation of private property notwithstanding the express command of the Fifth Amendment."[20] Justice Frankfurter was no doubt one of the most outspoken proponents and consistent practitioners of the method of adjudication invoked by Judge X, and it may well have been his chief jurisprudential antagonist to whom Justice Black alluded in the form of Judge X. But the factual context of military necessity that was persuasive to Judge X was equally persuasive to Justice Black in *Korematsu*. For Justice Black, as merciless critic of balancing, not even the gravest emergency was enough constitutionally to sustain otherwise invalid governmental actions; yet the assumed military necessity had been decisive

[19] *Id.* at 878.
[20] G. DUNNE, HUGO BLACK AND THE JUDICIAL REVOLUTION 358 (1977).

for him in *Korematsu*. Moreover, the facts that induced Judge X to reject the individual's monetary claim reveal "a desperate condition," an emergency far more compelling and severe than the disputed claims of urgency accepted by Justice Black in *Korematsu* to justify what the American Civil Liberties Union has called "the worst single wholesale violation of civil rights of American citizens in our history."[21] Indeed, the facts before Judge X render the doctrine of absolutism an absurdity if adherence to it in time of such dire conditions would result in prostrating the nation struggling to defend itself from foreign military attack. Yet Justice Black presented his "wholly fictitious" account of balancing in order to denounce balancing, not absolutism. "If 'balancing' is accepted as the test," he argued, "it would be hard for any conscientious judge [as it was for Justice Black in *Korematsu*] to hold [against the government] in times of dire need. And laws adopted in times of dire need are often very hasty and oppressive laws [as was the exclusion order in *Korematsu*]."[22]

Dunne's hasty presumption concerning the identity of Judge X should be considered in light of the behavior and jurisprudence of another Justice Black—justice of the Supreme Court who, in *Korematsu*, showed what can happen "if 'balancing' is accepted as the test." It might not be amiss to view Judge X as the author of *Korematsu* v. *United States*.

Beginning his fourth decade on the Supreme Court, Justice Black reviewed his past and said: "I can say categorically that I have not changed my basic constitutional philosophy—at least not in the last forty years. . . . And of course it is entirely too late in my life to say things I do not believe."[23] To be sure, he was never an avid or outspoken balancer, even during the 1940s.[24] More than any other member of the Supreme Court, he continuously and diligently sought to circumscribe judicial policy-making, pursuing an approach to constitutional adjudication which might yield an acceptable measure of consistency and objectivity. Aware of the inconsistency in his switch from *Gobitis* to *Barnette* (The Flag Salute

---

[21] *Quoted in* Preston, *The 1940s; The Way We Really Were*, 2 Civ. Lib. Rev. 4, 9 (1975).

[22] Black, *supra* note 8, at 878.

[23] H. Black, A Constitutional Faith, xvi–xvii (1968).

[24] Although he was undoubtedly a practitioner of the balancing of interests doctrine during this period, Justice Black often avoided the use of the word "balancing" in describing the process of judgment. Even in *Korematsu* he did not resort to that particular word in explaining the rationale whereby he arrived at the result. But in other cases he avowed his allegiance to balancing, forthrightly, and favorably using the word "balancing" in his opinions. *See, e.g.*, Marsh v. Alabama, 326 U.S. 501 (1946) (Black, J.)

Cases), he attempted in 1968 to explain his vote in the former case as an incorrect application of the sound principle that the Constitution should not be read as "a rigid bar against state regulation of conduct thought inimical to the public welfare." He insisted that "[t]his type of change is one thing and a change in basic constitutional philosophy is another,"[25] and then he maintained that he had never undergone a basic change in his constitutional jurisprudence while on the Court. But *Korematsu* stands to refute this claim of consistency.

Perhaps the glaring incongruity between that case and his later adherence to absolutism disappears on the assumption that, since only the uncertain "due process" clause of the Fifth Amendment was involved in *Korematsu*, no concrete, specific, or explicit constitutional right was violated when some seventy-five thousand American citizens were transplanted from their homes and confined to detention camps because they were of Japanese extraction. In 1965, for example, Justice Black refused to protect the right to marital privacy in the bedroom because he could not literally discern such a right even from a liberal reading of the specific provisions of the Bill of Rights.[26] He might have similarly defended his *Korematsu* decision as consistent with his later constitutional philosophy.[27]

But in his 1960 lecture attacking balancing he spoke of the absolute guarantees of the Bill of Rights. And when he reached the Fifth Amendment "due process" clause he said that, although its terms are not as clear as other guarantees, "[w]hatever its meaning, however, there can be no doubt that it must be granted."[28] The due process clause would hold out nothing at all if it contains no constitutional protection against, in the words of Mr. Justice Jackson, "an attempt to make an otherwise innocent act a crime merely because [one] is the son of parents as to whom he had no choice, and belongs to a race from which there is no way to resign."[29] Justice Black admitted as much in *Korematsu* when he conceded that in time of peace the military order would contradict our most basic freedoms.

Whether or not there exists some degree or dimension of jurispruden-

---

[25] H. BLACK, *supra* note 23, at xv–xvi.

[26] Griswold v. Connecticut, 381 U.S. 479, 507–27 (Black, J., dissenting).

[27] Justice Black never attempted such an explanation, at least not publicly (although, in a conversation with me, one of his former law clerks suggested—though he did not endorse —such an explanation of the nonabsolutist reasoning in *Korematsu*).

[28] Black, *supra* note 8, at 873.

[29] Korematsu v. United States, 323 U.S. 214, 243 (1944) (Jackson, J., dissenting).

tial consistency which one might discover between the constitutional approach and rationale in *Korematsu* and Justice Black's later condemnation of balancing, innumerable other cases decided in the 1940s reinforce the conclusion that absolutism was not then a part of his evolving constitutional jurisprudence.

One of his most deeply held libertarian beliefs was that the government has no legal power to divest a person of his or her American citizenship without the person's voluntary assent. In *Afroyim* v. *Rusk* (1967), Justice Black wrote for a Court which held that every citizen of the United States—including naturalized citizens—has "a constitutional right to remain a citizen . . . unless he voluntarily relinquishes that citizenship."[30] Four years later, a changed membership on a new Court upheld the power of the government to abolish the citizenship of an American citizen naturalized outside the United States, in Italy.[31] The Court there distinguished *Afroyim* by confining it only to citizens born or naturalized in the United States; the *Afroyim* holding, in other words, did not pertain to Bellei, who was naturalized in Italy.[32] (Afroyim had been naturalized inside the United States.)

Writing for the majority in *Bellei*, Mr. Justice Harry A. Blackmun had agreed that Congress was within its constitutional power in rescinding Bellei's citizenship. Citizenship itself, the Court held, is not absolute. Moreover, the condition imposed upon Bellei's citizenship was "not unreasonable, arbitrary, or unlawful." Finally, *Afroyim* did not apply in this case because Bellei "was not born in the United States. He was not naturalized in the United States. . . . He simply is not a Fourteenth-Amendment-first-sentence citizen. His posture contrasts with that of Mr. Afroyim, who was naturalized in the United States."[33]

In one of the last decisions of his life, Justice Black passionately dissented from the Court's holding and its Portia-like refusal to adhere to the dictates of *Afroyim*. He argued that Congress has the power to divest

[30] 387 U.S. 253, 268 (1967). In dissent, Justice Harlan convincingly argued that Justice Black distorted history in arriving at his conclusions.

[31] Rogers v. Bellei, 401 U.S. 815 (1971).

[32] Bellei was given conditional citizenship under federal law in that he was born outside the United States to parents only one of whom was an American citizen. At birth he was an American citizen subject to the condition that between the ages of 14 and 28 he reside in the United States for five consecutive years. He did not do this, and his citizenship was revoked. The constitutionality of this condition was the issue before the Court.

[33] 401 U.S. at 835, 831, 827.

no one of his or her citizenship, regardless of whether one is naturalized in or outside the territorial United States. He emphasized that the citizenship clause of the Fourteenth Amendment "did reach *all* citizens." Thundering with absolutist reverberations, his opinion concluded with his by then characteristic denunciation of the Court's "reasonableness" test:

> There was little need for the founders to draft a written constitution if this Court can say it is only binding when a majority finds it fair, reasonable, and right to make it so. That is the loosest construction that could be employed. . . . While I remain on the Court I shall continue to oppose the power of judges, appointed by changing administrations, to change the Constitution from time to time according to their notions of what is "fair" and "reasonable." I would decide this case not by my views of what is "arbitrary," or what is "fair," but rather by what the Constitution commands.[34]

Twenty-five years earlier, another Justice Black agreed that the citizenship clause is less than an absolute—that Congress could, under some circumstances at least, divest an American of his or her citizenship. During World War II, Congress authorized the denaturalization of Paul Knauer, a naturalized American citizen. He had obtained his citizenship fraudulently, working in the United States during the war as a spy for the Nazi government of Germany. Speaking through Justice Douglas (who later would join Justice Black's dissent in *Bellei*), the Supreme Court held that Congress was not "remediless to correct the wrong."[35] Justices Rutledge and Murphy dissented, arguing that the Court was treating Knauer as a second-class citizen. If a native-born citizen cannot be deprived of his or her citizenship, they asked, why can Congress deprive a naturalized citizen of his or her citizenship? With conspicuous reluctance, and in a separate opinion, Justice Black agreed with the Court's decision. Noting his reservations, he said: "I realize, as the dissent in this case emphasizes, the dangers inherent in denaturalizations. . . . I am unable to say that Congress is without constitutional power to authorize courts, after fair trials like this one, to cancel citizenship obtained by the methods and for the purposes shown by this record."[36]

To be sure, *Knauer* and *Bellei* are fundamentally different cases. Bellei's citizenship was revoked because he failed to fulfill the residence require-

---

[34] 401 U.S. at 842, 844–45 (Black, J., dissenting).

[35] Knauer v. United States, 328 U.S. 654, 674 (1946).

[36] 328 U.S. at 675–79 (Rutledge, J., dissenting), at 674–75 (Black, J., concurring).

ment, the condition for continuing his citizenship; Knauer was an enemy spy who had obtained his American citizenship fraudulently. The difference is substantial, and Justice Black's vote in *Knauer* is justifiable and not unpersuasive. But in *Bellei* his reasoning and denunciation of the majority opinion were based on absolutist language. He said that "the Fourteenth Amendment has put citizenship, once conferred, beyond the power of Congress to revoke."[37] He vehemently attacked the Court's unimpressive—somewhat ludicrous—attempt to distinguish *Afroyim*, reminding the majority of the holding in *Afroyim* that no citizen can constitutionally be divested of his or her citizenship, except through voluntary assent. No such view or absolutist language appears in Justice Black's concurrence in *Knauer*.[38] His willingness to make an exception, even though in the case of one who fraudulently acquires his citizenhip, stands to refute the view that he was an absolutist. An absolutist makes no exceptions, even in times of national peril.

There is an isolated example of absolutist rhetoric in his opinions prior to 1950. In *Feldman* v. *United States* (1944), the Supreme Court sustained, over the claim of self-incrimination, the use in a federal criminal prosecution of evidence compelled from a witness under a state immunity statute.[39] The Court narrowly defined the meaning of the right against compulsory self-incrimination by arguing that the right pertained only against the force of the federal government (since the Fifth Amendment at that time applied only to the national government). Since the federal agents had no part in eliciting the incriminating evidence against Feldman, the federal government was constitutionally empowered to use that evidence in a federal trial.

[37] 401 U.S. at 844 (Black, J., dissenting).

[38] Three years earlier in Schneiderman v. United States, 320 U.S. 118 (1943), a divided Court upheld Schneiderman's right to remain an American citizen. After he had become a naturalized citizen, the United States alleged that he was granted citizenship fraudulently in that he did not really support the Constitution since he was affiliated with the Communist party in 1927. Speaking through Justice Murphy, the Court (including Justice Black) concluded that the evidence failed to show that Schneiderman did not support the Constitution or that he did not have the requisite "attachment" to it. Moreover, the United States had failed to prove that the Communist party in 1927 was an organization which advocated violent action of a clear and present danger.

Although the question was not decided in *Schneiderman*, the Court appears to have conceded that Schneiderman could have lost his citizenship if the government could have proved its contentions and allegations of fraud. Justices Murphy and Rutledge rejected this view in *Knauer*; Justices Black and Douglas did not.

[39] 322 U.S. 487.

Justice Black vigorously dissented, asserting that compelled testimony is compelled testimony. "Testimony is no less compelled because a state rather than a federal officer compels it." The language of the Fifth Amendment contains "no exceptions based upon the persons who compel, their purpose in compelling, or their method of compelling." If evidence is compelled it makes no difference how it is compelled or who compels it because the Fifth Amendment contains an "unqualified prohibition against the extraction and use of compelled testimony."[40]

Justice Black was referring in *Feldman* to the scope or definition of the Fifth Amendment's right against compulsory self-incrimination. He was not criticizing the Court for balancing the importance or weight of the amendment against some other interest; rather, his dissent is based on his feeling that "there appears to be no justification for reducing its scope as the Court is now doing."[41] That he did not object to balancing individual rights against competing interests—and that he possibly would have considered some justifiable reason for reducing the scope of the Fifth Amendment in *Feldman*—is evidenced by his clearly nonabsolutist opinion for the Court in *Wade v. Hunter*,[42] five years after his *Feldman* dissent. As in *Korematsu*, military necessity in *Wade* appears once again to have been controlling for Justice Black.

During World War II, one Wade was being tried by a general court-martial of the Third Army, but before a decision could be reached the charges were withdrawn and the court-martial was directed to halt the proceedings. The commanding general of the Third Army then transferred the case to the Fifteenth Army, stating that the "tactical situation" of his command and the rapid advance of the army into Germany made it impossible to conduct the trial properly. Petitioner Wade claimed that he had been twice placed in jeopardy in violation of his Fifth Amendment rights. Rejecting the claim of double jeopardy, Justice Black explained:

[T]his record is sufficient to show that the tactical situation brought about by a rapidly advancing army was responsible for withdrawal of the charges from the first court-martial. This appears in the first order of transmittal of the charges. That order was made by the Commanding General of the 76th Division who was responsible for convening the court-martial and who was also responsible for the most effective

[40] 322 U.S. at 497, 500 (Black, J., dissenting).
[41] *Id.* at 499.
[42] 336 U.S. 684 (1949).

military employment of that Division in carrying out the plan for the invasion of Germany. There is no intimation in the record that the tactical situation did not require the transfer order. The court-martial was composed of officers of the invading Army Division. Momentous issues hung on the invasion and we cannot assume that these court-martial officers were not needed to perform their military functions.[43]

In 1960 Justice Black condemned his fictitious Judge X for balancing individual rights against real, even dire, military and wartime necessities. Yet in *Wade*, Justice Black had recognized "a pressing military tactical situation" and said: "[A] defendant's valued right to have his trial completed by a particular tribunal must in some instances be subordinated to the public's interest in fair trials designed to end in just judgments." "This case presents extraordinary reasons why the judgment of the Commanding General should be accepted by the courts."[44] But Justice Murphy, joined by Justices Douglas and Rutledge, dissented in an opinion which attacked the "exceptions" that he felt the Court was attaching to the provision against double jeopardy:

> The harassment to the defendant from being repeatedly tried is not less because the army is advancing. The guarantee of the Constitution against double jeopardy is not to be eroded away by a tide of plausible-appearing exceptions. The command of the Fifth Amendment does not allow temporizing with the basic rights it declares. Adaptations of military justice to the exigencies of tactical situations is the prerogative of the commander in the field, but the price of such expediency is compliance with the Constitution.[45]

Neither of the two volumes about Justice Black in print by the close of his first period on the Court—books that analyze his judicial philosophy—contains any reference to the concept of absolutism.[46] Charles Reich, a former law clerk for Justice Black, convincingly explains why: "Justice Black did not bring his philosophy with him to the Court. He came to the Court straight from politics, and nothing in his background suggested that he would make a contribution of a philosophical kind. His ideas grew strongly, and some of his most important views, including the 'absolute-

---

[43] *Id.* at 691–92.
[44] *Id.* at 685, 689, 692.
[45] 336 U.S. at 694 (Murphy, J., dissenting).
[46] *See* J. FRANK, MR. JUSTICE BLACK (1949); C. WILLIAMS, *supra* note 14.

ness' of the first amendment, appear very late in his writings."[47] Indeed, abundant evidence of this can be found in his participation in free speech cases in which the "self-defined" meaning of freedom of speech and press was more restrictive and less obvious for Justice Black in the 1940s than it would become in the 1950s and 1960s.

FREE SPEECH IN THE 1940S: "PREFERRED POSITION"

Wiley Rutledge's appointment to the Supreme Court in 1943 must be earmarked in the annals of constitutional history as a major contribution to the development of the First Amendment. Whereas previously the doctrine of "preferred position" had been used only sporadically and in dissent,[48] after 1943 it became temporarily the governing position impelling the Court into accepting a libertarian, even if sometimes dogmatic, policy on First Amendment issues. With the additions of Justices Rutledge and Jackson, together with the recantation by Justices Black, Douglas, and Murphy of their part in the *Gobitis* majority,[49] the libertarian wing of the Court proceeded to overrule the nonlibertarian decision in the *Gobitis* case.[50] Writing for a new majority, Mr. Justice Jackson rejected the Frankfurterian policy of subjecting the protection of First Amendment freedoms to the judgment and experimentation of legislatures and instead maintained that such freedoms "may not be submitted to vote; they depend on the outcome of no elections."[51] That same year the Court also overruled a previous decision upholding a municipal ordinance which imposed a flat licence tax on persons engaged in commercial ventures within the municipality, even those engaged in selling religious literature.[52] And, again in 1943, the Supreme Court struck down, as a violation

[47] Reich, *Mr. Justice Black and the Living Constitution*, 76 HARV. L. REV. 673, 673–74 (1963).

[48] The expression was first used by Chief Justice Stone in Jones v. Opelika, 316 U.S. 584, 608 (1942) (Stone, C. J., dissenting). For a brief evolution of that doctrine, *see* Kovacs v. Cooper, 336 U.S. 77, 90–94 (Frankfurter, J., concurring).

[49] *See* Jones v. Opelika, 316 U.S. 584, 623–24 (1942) (Black, Douglas and Murphy, dissenting).

[50] *Gobitis* was overruled in West Virginia Board of Education v. Barnette, 319 U.S. 624 (1943).

[51] *Id.* at 638.

[52] Jones v. Opelika, 316 U.S. 584 (1942), *overruled in* Murdock v. Pennsylvania, 319 U.S. 105 (1943).

of the First Amendment, a city ordinance prohibiting persons from ringing doorbells and knocking on doors for purposes of distributing pamphlets and handbills, despite the important counterclaim that many of the inhabitants of the city worked at night and slept during the day when such ringing of doorbells would disturb their quiet.[53]

The Court's treatment of First Amendment cases between 1943 and 1949, the era of "preferred position," elevated First Amendment freedoms to heights of importance above almost every other societal interest coming into conflict with them. At times the "preferred position" assigned to the First Amendment soared so high in the hands of the judiciary that Justice Frankfurter was prompted to comment that the majority was interpreting the amendment "as though it were a mathematical abstraction, an absolute having no relation to the lives of men."[54] He later characterized the Court's approach to free speech cases as "a doctrinaire attitude" which implies "that any law touching communication is infected with presumptive invalidity."[55]

One might be inclined to accept Justice Frankfurter's critique and conclude that Justice Black was indeed an absolutist in the 1940s but disguised his absolutism in "preferred position" rhetoric. This proposition ignores such cases as *Wade*, *Korematsu*, and *Knauer*, where the doctrine of absolutism (as he would later practice it) was forthrightly disowned. Yet even in the realm of freedom of expression, such a conclusion is misplaced. That Justice Black had been as libertarian on free speech issues in the 1940s as he was in the 1950s is certainly a valid argument, and in this sense the distinction between absolutism and "preferred position" is merely one of degree. But "preferred position" by its own words implies that some balancing of interests enters into the process of judgment—that some limits must be placed on freedom of expression, and that the process of judgment entails some judicial policymaking. The consistency from the 1940s through the 1950s in Justice Black's libertarian attitude in free speech cases reflects more on his devout libertarianism than on his constitutional jurisprudence. Absolutism involves a fundamentally different reasoning employed to reach those libertarian results. And, once committed to that doctrine, Justice Black was willing to protect constitutional rights even against the needs of a society struck by catastrophic

[53] Martin v. Struthers, 319 U.S. 141 (1943).

[54] *Id.* at 142 (Frankfurter, J., dissenting).

[55] Kovacs v. Cooper, 336 U.S. 77, 90 (1949) (Frankfurter, J., concurring).

emergency, as evidenced by his criticism of "Judge X." The transition from "preferred position" to absolutism involved not merely an intensification of Justice Black's libertarian attitude toward freedom of expression but also a basic change in the kind of judicial reasoning brought to the task of judicial decision-making. The transition to absolutism produced an uncompromising attitude toward the role of the judge and the judicial process.

In an interview in 1962, Edmond Cahn asked Justice Black whether he subscribed to the clear and present danger test; Justice Black said, "I do not."[56] Two years before, in his Bill of Rights address, he had demonstrated his unmatched ability to denounce the balancing of interests doctrine. Charles Reich has characterized Justice Black's approach to free speech cases during the 1940s as "basically an attempt to accommodate conflicting community interests, with a presumption in favor of speech and a strong dash of practicality."[57] In free speech cases the Justice Black of the 1940s applied the tests which the new Justice Black of the 1950s and 1960s would describe as judicial innovations designed to destroy the Constitution.

Clear and Present Danger and Balancing

In *Thornhill* v. *Alabama* (1940), Justice Black joined the Court's opinion invalidating a state statute which prohibited picketing in labor disputes. After concluding that picketing is a form of free expression, the Court through Justice Murphy applied the clear and present danger test to the case at hand: "Abridgment of the liberty of such discussions can be justified only where the clear danger of substantive evils arises under circumstances affording no opportunity to test the merits of ideas by competition for acceptance in the market of public opinion. We hold that the danger of injury to an industrial concern is neither so serious nor so imminent as to justify the sweeping proscription of freedom of discussion embodied in [the state statute]."[58]

That Justice Black did not always agree with everything announced in an opinion to which he would add his vote must, of course, be taken into

---

[56] Cahn, *Justice Black and First Amendment "Absolutes": A Public Interview*, 37 N.Y.U.L. REV. 549, 559 (1962).

[57] Reich, *supra* note 47, at 687.

[58] 310 U.S. 88, 104–5 (1940).

consideration in assessing his adherence to the clear and present danger test.[59] But it is doubtful, if not inconceivable, that he would join in the holding but not the premise or reasoning upon which the decision rests. Moreover, if the clear and present danger test was, in fact, a clear contradiction of the First Amendment, would not an absolutist be moved to point out in a concurring opinion the deficiencies in the Court's reasoning, as Justice Black frequently sought to do in later years,[60] especially when the Court's reasoning rejects absolutism?

Justice Black did not consider the clear and present danger test a violation of the First Amendment, and he demonstrated this repeatedly in the 1940s. Soon after *Thornhill* he dissented from the Court's refusal to extend the *Thornhill* ruling to an injunction enjoining picketing in a labor dispute. He rejected the Court's conclusions and examined the facts of the case for himself—a judicial task which he deemed imperative for arriving at satisfactory results: "A careful study of the entire record in this case convinces me that neither the findings nor the evidence, even viewed in the light most favorable to respondent, showed such imminent, clear and present danger as to justify an abridgment of the rights of freedom of speech and the press." After this statement, he cited in a footnote a series of cases where the Court had earlier applied the clear and present danger test and, in what appears to be a direct denial of the doctrine of absolutism, concluded in light of the facts that "the forfeiture of the right to free speech effected by the injunction is not warranted."[61]

Seven months later, Justice Black wrote the majority opinion in a landmark case which brought public criticism of a pending judicial proceeding within the reach of First Amendment freedoms. *Bridges* v. *California* involved the clash between freedom of speech and the public interest in courtroom decorum and fairness.[62] An editorial in the *Los Angeles Times* and a telegram sent by Harry Bridges, a prominent CIO official, both

---

[59] *See* Yarbrough, *Justice Black and His Critics on Speech-Plus and Symbolic Speech*, 52 Tex L. Rev. 257, 269n (1974).

[60] *See, e.g.*, New York Times Co. v. Sullivan, 376 U.S. 254, 293–97 (1964) (Black, J., concurring); Time, Inc. v. Hill, 385 U.S. 374, 398–401 (1967) (Black, J., concurring). Justice Black would later argue that picketing is not absolutely protected because it is conduct, not speech. H. Black, *supra* note 23, at 57. This attempt to seem consistent is discussed in ch. V, *infra*.

[61] Drivers Union v. Meadowmoor Co., 312 U.S. 287, 313, 316 (1941) (Black, J., dissenting).

[62] 314 U.S. 252 (1941).

[8 3]

commented on the outcome of pending litigation involving a labor dispute. The newspaper encouraged the court to render a decision against labor, while Bridges's telegram appears to have threatened a strike if the court's ruling were antilabor. Both Bridges and the *Los Angeles Times* were cited for contempt by the judge, and these citations were affirmed by the California Supreme Court.

Writing the opinion of a divided (5–4) Court reversing the decision of the state supreme court, Justice Black recognized that the First Amendment was framed in absolutist language: "[T]he unqualified prohibitions laid down by the framers were intended to give liberty of the press, as to the other liberties, the broadest scope that could be countenanced in an orderly society." But he disregarded absolutism by applying the clear and present danger test as a means of determining the limits of free speech required "in an orderly society." Indeed, he praised the test by stating that, although it is imperfect, it "has afforded practical guidelines in a great variety of cases in which the scope of constitutional protections of freedom of expression was in issue." The test provided "a working principle that the substantive evil must be extremely serious and the degree of imminence extremely high before utterances can be punished."[63]

He then explained the task before the Court: "We must turn to the particular utterances here in question and the circumstances of their publication to determine to what extent the substantive evil of unfair administration of justice was a likely consequence, and whether the degree of likelihood was sufficient to justify summary punishment."[64] These are the words and reasoning of a man deeply dedicated to freedom of expression, but aware that the right of free speech cannot be enforced absolutely. He found that there had been no clear and present danger involved and that the judicial citation for contempt had therefore contravened the First Amendment.

In his hands the clear and present danger test could almost always yield libertarian results. An extreme libertarianism short of absolutism is characteristic not only of Justice Black's posture during this period of "preferred position" but also of the views of Justices Douglas, Murphy, and Rutledge. The extent to which these four members of the Court elevated First Amendment freedoms without denying the existence of

---

[63] 314 U.S. at 265, 261–62, 263.
[64] *Id.* at 271.

some limits is illustrated by the following statement characteristic of "preferred position" policy:

The case confronts us again with the duty our system places on this Court to say where the individual's freedom ends and the State's power begins. Choice on that border, now as always delicate, is perhaps more so where the usual presumption supporting legislation is balanced by the preferred place given in our scheme to the great, the indispensable democratic freedoms secured by the First Amendment. . . . That priority gives these liberties a sanctity and a sanction not permitting dubious intrusions. And it is the character of the right, not of the limitation, which determines what standard governs the choice.

The line or balance that the Court recognized as acceptable was the clear and present danger test: "[A]ny attempt to restrict those liberties must be justified by clear public interest, threatened not doubtfully or remotely, but by clear and present danger."[65]

In *Pennekamp* v. *Florida* (1946), involving issues similar to those in *Bridges,* the Court upheld the claims of freedom of expression again by applying the clear and present danger test to two newspaper editorials and a cartoon criticizing some state court decisions as being too favorable to criminals. In an opinion by Mr. Justice Reed, in which Justice Black joined, the Court repeated the policy of "preferred position" and said: "We must, therefore, weigh the right of free speech which is claimed by the petitioners against the danger of coercion and intimidation of courts in the factual situation presented by this record. . . . [W]e must weigh the impact of words against the protection given by the principles of the First Amendment . . . to public comment on pending court cases." Examining the record for a clear and present danger, the Court, as in *Bridges,* found "that the danger under this record to fair judicial administration has not the clearness and immediacy necessary to close the door of permissible public comment."[66]

In *Craig* v. *Harney,* decided a year after *Pennekamp,* the Court was confronted with a third case involving criminal contempt citations for adverse comment on judicial proceedings. Here the publications involved inaccurate newspaper reports unfairly criticizing a lower Texas court's handling of a private lawsuit. Also at issue was an editorial which vehe-

[65]Thomas v. Collins, 323 U.S. 516, 529–30 (1945) (Rutledge, J.).
[66] 328 U.S. 331, 346, 349, 350 (1946).

mently criticized the judge. Justice Black again joined the Court's opinion, which again applied the clear and present danger test. Writing for the Court, Mr. Justice Douglas said: "The history of the power to punish for contempt . . . and the unequivocal command of the First Amendment serve as constant reminders that freedom of speech and of the press should not be impaired through the exercise of that power, unless there is no doubt that the utterances in question are a serious and imminent threat to the administration of justice." The test again was repeated. "The danger must not be remote or even probable; it must immediately imperil."[67] And once again the Court could find no such danger.

During the 1950s and early 1960s, the Supreme Court balanced interests in free speech cases, but if the claimants of constitutional protection were alleged subversives, the Court almost always struck the balance in favor of the government. In the 1940s, the Court had also balanced interests, but the balances had almost always been struck against governmental regulation. Since Justice Black would later denounce the Court for balancing interests in free speech cases, to be consistent with his own undisguised support of the balancing of interests doctrine in the 1940s, he would therefore be compelled to develop a rationale to reconcile his earlier behavior with his frequent denunciations of that doctrine in the 1950s and 1960s. His proposed rationale was the distinction between "direct" and "indirect" abridgments of freedom of expression. He explained the distinction on the basis of the language of the First Amendment—the free speech guarantee protects speech, not conduct. "In giving absolute protection to free speech . . . I have always been careful to draw a line between speech and conduct."[68]

> I do not agree that laws directly abridging First Amendment freedoms can be justified by a congressional or judicial balancing process. There are, of course, cases suggesting that a law which primarily regulates conduct but which might also indirectly affect speech can be upheld if the effect on speech is minor in relation to the need for control of the conduct. . . . But even such laws governing conduct . . . must be tested, though only by a balancing process, if they indirectly affect ideas.[69]

But let me make absolutely clear that this kind of balancing should be

---

[67] 331 U.S. 367, 373, 376 (1947).

[68] H. Black, *supra* note 23, at 53.

[69] Barenblatt v. United States, 360 U.S. 109, 141–42 (1959) (Black, J., dissenting).

used only where a law is aimed at conduct and indirectly affects speech.[70]

He repeatedly emphasized this distinction so as to deflate the inevitable charges that he was inconsistent with his earlier views.

In 1939, for instance, he joined Justice Roberts's opinion for the Court in *Schneider* v. *State*, which said that government "may enact regulations in the interest of the public safety, health, welfare or convenience, [but] these may not abridge the individual liberties secured by the Constitution to those who wish to speak, write, print or circulate information or opinion." But, since government can regulate in the interests of society, when do such regulations infringe on constitutional rights? The Court's answer was that "where [governmental] abridgment of the rights is asserted, the courts should be astute to examine the effect of the challenged legislation. . . . [T]he delicate and difficult task falls upon the courts to weigh the circumstances and to appraise the substantiality of the reasons advanced in support of the regulation of the free enjoyment of the rights."[71] This is the kind of balancing Justice Black would continue to endorse even after he had accepted absolutism, because the challenged regulation primarily regulates conduct and is constitutional, he said, "subject only to the condition that if such a law had the effect of indirectly impinging on freedom of speech, press, or religion, it would be unconstitutional if under the circumstances it appeared that the State's interest in suppressing the conduct was not sufficient to outweigh the individual's interest in engaging in conduct closely involving his First Amendment freedoms."[72]

It will be argued in Chapter V that Justice Black's speech-conduct distinction, designed not only as a bridge of consistency between his first and later periods on the Court but also to limit the consequences of absolutism, would insulate him from neither the charges of inconsistency nor the unwarranted consequences of his absolutism. Here, however, it is enough to argue that even conceding the viability and plausibility of such a distinction, it does not remove the fact that the Justice Black of the 1940s recognized the possibility—no matter how remote—that freedom of speech may be sacrificed to a greater public interest. Such a distinction does not

[70] H. BLACK, *supra* note 23, at 61.
[71] 308 U.S. 147, 160, 161 (1939).
[72] Cox v. Louisiana, 379 U.S. 536, 577 (1965) (Black, J., concurring).

make Justice Black an absolutist in the 1940s, because he was not; it does not narrow the cases in which he was engaged in balancing only to those involving legislation aimed at conduct apart from speech.

The clear and present danger test is a balancing test, except that the catchwords are different. Paul Freund aptly wrote: "No matter how rapidly we utter the phrase 'clear and present danger,' or how closely we hyphenate the words, they are not a substitute for the weighing of values. They tend to convey a delusion of certitude when what is most certain is the complexity of the strands in the web of freedoms which the judges must disentangle."[73] Kenneth Karst similarly equates the two: "The clear-and-present-danger test, even with its immediacy of threatened harm, was always a 'balancing' test."[74] Although some other observers have sought to distinguish the two,[75] the essence of both tests is a judicial weighing of the circumstances and competing interests involved in each case.[76] Both purport to support the greater interest in each instance, and both reject the idea that one of the interests in any case can be given an absolute value. Both tests recognize that the result in each case depends on the weight and importance which the Court attaches to each interest.

Attempting to explain or reconcile his participation in one type of balancing and not in another, Justice Black nonetheless never explained why he participated in the kind of balancing inherent in the clear and present danger test as used in cases such as *Bridges, Pennekamp*, and *Craig* where governmental punishment was imposed for utterances, not conduct. In all three cases the petitioners were cited for criminal contempt and punished for adverse commentaries on the judicial process; and in each case the Court weighed the merits of each side by applying the clear and present danger test. In *Pennekamp* the crucial test was stated rather pointedly by Justice Reed: "[W]e must weigh the impact of the words against the protection given by the principles of the First Amendment, as

[73] P. FREUND, THE SUPREME COURT OF THE UNITED STATES 44 (1949).

[74] Karst, *The First Amendment and Harry Kalven: An Appreciative Comment on the Advantages of Thinking Small*, 13 U.C.L.A. L. REV. 1, 10 (1965).

[75] *See, e.g.*, T. EMERSON, THE SYSTEM OF FREEDOM OF EXPRESSION (1970); M. SHAPIRO, FREEDOM OF SPEECH: THE SUPREME COURT AND JUDICIAL REVIEW (1966). Much of the reason for such distinctions derives from judicial misapplications of doctrines. *See* Alfange, *The Balancing of Interests in Free Speech Cases: In Defense of an Abused Doctrine*, 2 L. TRANSITION Q. 35 (1965).

[76] *See* Antieau, *Judicial Delimitation of the First Amendment Freedoms*, 34 MARQ. L. REV 57 (1950). The problem is inevitably one of drawing lines. *See* H. ABRAHAM, FREEDOM AND THE COURT 170–244. (3d ed. 1977).

adopted by the Fourteenth, to public comment on pending cases."[77] Balancing of interests, therefore, does not appear to have been confined in the 1940s only to cases involving merely governmental regulations of conduct. The contents of expression were also weighed against contending governmental claims of the need to curtail the right to speak and publish.

Moreover, in one of the earlier cases in which the balancing test was specifically announced, the Court seems to have indicated that judicial balancing must be made in all cases involving any alleged abridgment of First Amendment freedoms. Speaking for the Court in *Schneider* v. *State*, Justice Roberts said: "In every case . . . where legislative abridgment of the rights is asserted . . . the delicate and difficult task falls upon the courts to weigh the circumstances and to appraise the substantiality of the reasons advanced in support of the regulation of the free enjoyment of the rights."[78] Seven years later, quoting from *Schneider*, Justice Black said the same thing in *Marsh* v. *Alabama:* "As we have stated before, the right to exercise the liberties safeguarded by the First Amendment 'lies at the foundation of free government by free men' and we must in all cases 'weigh the circumstances and . . . appraise the . . . reasons . . . in support of the regulation . . . of the rights.' "[79] Perhaps both *Schneider* and *Marsh* involved what Justice Black described as "indirect" abridgments, governmental regulations aimed at conduct and only indirectly at freedom of speech. Nevertheless, the passages cited above explicitly state that a weighing of competing interests is necessary in all cases. Neither *Schneider* nor *Marsh*, nor any other case or opinion during this period, suggests that regulations aimed directly at speech, as opposed to conduct, are absolutely prohibited. *Bridges*, *Pennekamp*, and *Craig* present unambiguous examples of governmental action aimed specifically at the content of expression.

It is true that as early as 1942 Justice Black noted a distinction between indirect and direct abridgments and recognized that expression claimed greater constitutional weight when governmental abridgment is direct. In *Carpenters Union* v. *Ritter's Cafe* he said:

It is one thing for a state to regulate the use of its streets and highways so as to keep them open and available for movement of people and property . . . ; or to pass general regulations as to their use in the interest of

[77] 328 U.S. 331, 349 (1946).
[78] 308 U.S. 147, 161 (1939).
[79] 326 U.S. 501, 509 (1946).

public safety, peace, comfort, or convenience . . .; or to protect its citizens from violence and breaches of the peace by those who are upon them. . . . It is quite another thing, however, to "abridge the constitutional liberty of one rightfully upon the street to impart information through speech or the distribution of literature." . . . The Court below . . . barred the petitioners from using the streets to convey information to the public, because of the particular type of information they wished to convey. In so doing, it directly restricted the petitioners' rights to express themselves publicly concerning an issue . . . of public importance. It imposed the restriction for the reason that the public's response to such information would result in injury to a particular person's business, a reason which we said in the *Thornhill* case was insufficient to justify curtailment of free expression.[80]

But implicit in his dissent in *Carpenters Union* is Justice Black's weighing of the competing interests involved in the case. Despite the fact that, in his own words, the court injunction against the petitioners directly abridged their First Amendment rights, he did not argue that the injunction was thereby automatically and absolutely prohibited, as the later Justice Black would. Rather, as in *Thornhill* (where the Court applied the clear and present danger test to peaceful picketing—a form of expression the absolutist Justice Black would later eliminate from the scope of free speech), he posited that the asserted state interest was "insufficient to justify" the abridgment. He posed the question at issue:

Conveying this truthful information in the manner chosen by the union was calculated to, and did, injure the respondent's business. His business was injured because many of those whom the information reached were sympathetic with the union side of the controversy and declined to patronize the respondent's cafe or have any other business transactions with him. Does injury of this kind to the respondent's business justify the Texas courts in thus restricting freedom of expression?[81]

Justice Black balanced the conflicting claims and concluded that the injury to Ritter's Cafe was not enough to outweigh the interest in free expression—not a serious enough danger to justify an abridgment of the freedom of expression. Supporting his reasoning, he drew from and cited his own opinion in *Bridges* v. *California*. He viewed the First Amendment, he said quoting from *Bridges*, " 'as a command of the broadest scope that

[80] 315 U.S. 722, 731 (1942) (Black, J., dissenting).
[81] *Id.* at 729.

explicit language, read in the context of a liberty-loving society, will allow.' "[82]

This statement exhibits his profound commitment to as much free speech as possible; but, though it hovers very close to absolutism, this statement acknowledges that the First Amendment cannot be absolute, that it must have some limits—those that "a liberty-loving society" requires. How do courts determine such limits? In *Bridges*, where speech, not conduct, was punished, Justice Black found "a working principle" in the clear and present danger test. In *Carpenters Union*, although he did not mention the test by name, he applied the same "working principle" in a case which also involved a direct abridgment of the First Amendment.

In *Thomas* v. *Collins* the Court, joined by Justice Black, once more appears forthrightly to have ignored the standard he would later invoke to determine when courts should weigh the interest in free expression and, when courts should protect it absolutely. Speaking for the Court, Justice Rutledge said: "[W]hatever occasion would restrain orderly discussion and persuasion, at appropriate time and place, must have clear support in public danger, actual or impending."[83] Orderly speech made at appropriate time and place could be subordinated to the greater interest in preventing danger to the public welfare. Justice Black later rejected this view: "The First and Fourteenth Amendments take away from government, state and federal, all power to restrict freedom of speech, press, and peaceful assembly *where people have a right to be for such purposes.* That much is clear and to me indisputable."[84]

Justice Rutledge went on in *Thomas* to reject arguments that First Amendment protections are inapplicable to business or economic activity. Such conceptual distinctions do "not resolve where the line shall be drawn in a particular case . . . [They] are at once too simple, too general, and too inaccurate to be determinative." He then stated the Court's inclination toward balancing as a means of drawing the line "where the individual's freedom ends and the [government's] power begins."[85]

Where the line shall be placed in a particular application rests, not on such generalities, but on the concrete clash of particular interests and the community's relative evaluation both of them and of how the one

---

[82] *Id.* at 732, citing Bridges v. California, 314 U.S. 252, 263 (1941).

[83] 323 U.S. 516, 530 (1945).

[84] H. BLACK, *supra* note 23, at 53–54.

[85] 323 U.S. 516, 529, 531.

will be affected by the specific restriction, the other by its absence. That judgment in the first instance is for the legislative body. But in our system where the line can constitutionally be placed presents a question this Court cannot escape answering independently, whatever the legislative judgment, in the light of our constitutional tradition. . . . And the answer, under that tradition, can be affirmative, to support an intrusion upon this domain, only if grave and impending public danger requires this.[86]

These passages from *Thomas*, along with more from so many other speech cases of the 1940s, strongly indicate that the Court did not much adhere to absolutism or the distinction between indirect and direct abridgments. Instead, it appears that the Court would balance interests —in one way or another—in all free speech cases; it would weigh the merits advanced by both sides, regardless of whether the challenged governmental regulation directly or indirectly encroached on First Amendment freedoms. The weights were almost always set in favor of free speech during this period of "preferred position" of the First Amendment. But the absolutism and the speech-conduct dichotomy propounded by Justice Black in his later years found no advocates among his colleagues engaged in the free speech debate during this first period of Justice Black's judicial career.[87]

And Justice Black himself gave little attention to the distinction between "direct" and "indirect" infringements on freedom of speech. In a footnote to his application of the clear and present danger test in his dissenting opinion in *Meadowmoor Dairies*, he cited *Schenck*, *Abrams*, and *Gitlow* (all involving "direct" abridgments of the First Amendment) along with *Cantwell* (involving "indirect" abridgment) as examples of the Court's use of the clear and present danger test as an instrument for setting limits to freedom of expression.[88] In *Associated Press* v. *United States* (1945) he announced that the clear and present danger test applies to "utterances."[89]

---

[86] *Id.* at 531–32.

[87] This is not to say that the Court or Justice Black did not distinguish between speech and conduct. *See, e.g.,* Bakery and Pastry Drivers v. Wohl, 315 U.S. 769, 776 (1942) (Douglas, J., concurring), where Justice Douglas said that "[p]icketing . . . is more than free speech" and hence is subject to more restrictive regulation.

[88] *See* note 61 *supra*. In his footnote Justice Black also cited Schaefer v. United States, 251 U.S. 466 (1920), and the concurring opinion of Justices Holmes and Brandeis in Whitney v. California, 274 U.S. 357, 373 (1927). It would be difficult to conclude that Justice Black was distinguishing between direct and indirect abridgments when he wrote this footnote.

[89] 326 U.S. 1, 7 (Black, J.).

Only by insisting that the clear and present danger test is not a form of balancing could Justice Black later argue that the Court did not balance interests in *Bridges*, *Pennekamp*, and *Craig*. But, assuming that there is some significance in the semantic differential between balancing and the clear and present danger test as judicial efforts to circumscribe freedom of speech, the reasoning behind *Bridges*, *Pennekamp*, and *Craig* is not any less explicit in its renunciation of absolutism. In phrasing their rejection of absolutism in words other than "balancing," these cases are no less contradictions of Justice Black's later assertion that direct abridgments of freedom of speech are absolutely forbidden.

Another alternative response in defense of Justice Black's claim of consistency might be that almost all speech cases during this era of "preferred position" were, in fact, cases involving indirect violations of the First Amendment—insofar as very few governmental regulations openly disclose that their chief purpose is directly to stifle the enjoyment of individual liberties.[90] Indeed, an absolutist would have had little use of his doctrine if all abridgments were only indirect. Still, where governmental restraint was imposed on the contents of expression, as it was in *Bridges*, *Pennekamp*, and *Craig*,[91] Justice Black balanced interests by resorting to the clear and present danger test. The fact that he voted in favor of free speech in each instance does not obliterate, nor does it obscure, his frank acceptance of the premise of the clear and present danger test—that there are limits to freedom of expression even if only the seemingly theoretical or hypothetical limitations embodied in that test as applied by the Court during this period of "preferred position."

The Scope of Free Expression

After his interpretation of the First Amendment had become firmly established, in his own words Justice Black's position amounted to absolute protection for all speech and discussion short of conduct. The absolutist Justice Black would make no attempt to define the range of free

[90] This makes the practical application of Justice Black's dichotomy very difficult, because in almost every instance courts must second-guess the intent, purpose, and effect of the governmental regulation in question. *See* McBride, *Mr. Justice Black and His Qualified Absolutes*, 2 LOY. L.A.L. REV. 37, 51–53 (1969).

[91] *See* Fisher v. Pace, where Justice Douglas—joined by Justice Black—wanted to apply the clear and present danger test to contemptuous speech in the courtroom, 336 U.S. 155, 163–65 (1949) (Douglas, J., dissenting).

speech.[92] Speech is speech, including libel and pornography, and thus is absolutely protected. During the 1940s, however, his conception of the scope of free speech was much less expansive. Free speech during this period included political and religious speech; commercial advertisements, obscenity, and libel, as well as fraudulent speech, were not at all recognized forms of speech within the meaning of the First Amendment. Although the Court did not rule on the constitutionality of obscenity and libel laws until 1957 and 1964,[93] respectively, it was simply assumed by everyone, including Justice Black, that neither obscenity nor libel was protected by the First Amendment.

In one of the first speech cases in which Justice Black participated, the Supreme Court unanimously invalidated, as contrary to the First Amendment, a city ordinance which prohibited the distribution of pamphlets or leaflets within the city without prior written permission from the city manager. Chief Justice Charles Evans Hughes led the Court in holding that the ordinance constituted prior censorship; the regulation he said, was not confined to obscene and immoral literature or that which advocated unlawful conduct.[94] Implicit in the opinion is the recognition that if the ordinance were narrowly drawn to limit its effect to such expression, it would have met the requirements of the First Amendment.

Four years later, in *Chaplinsky* v. *New Hampshire*, a unanimous Court not only explicitly rejected absolutism but stated that libel and obscenity were not expression within the permissible scope of speech protected by the First Amendment. Speaking through Justice Murphy, the Court explained:

Allowing the broadest scope to the language and purpose of the Fourteenth Amendment [which incorporates the First], it is well understood that the right of free speech is not absolute at all times and under all circumstances. There are certain well-defined and narrowly limited classes of speech, the prevention and punishment of which have never been thought to raise any Constitutional problem. These include the lewd and the obscene, the profane, the libelous, and the insulting or

---

[92] Indeed, he believed that courts were forbidden to define the meaning of the First Amendment freedoms. Braden v. United States, 365 U.S. 431, 445 (1961) (Black, J., dissenting). *See* ch. I, *supra*.

[93] Roth v. United States, 354 U.S. 476 (1957); New York Times Co. v. Sullivan, 376 U.S. 254 (1964).

[94] Lovell v. Griffin, 303 U.S. 444, 451 (1938).

"fighting" words—those which by their very utterance inflict injury or tend to incite an immediate breach of the peace. It has been well observed that such utterances are no essential part of any exposition of ideas, and are of such slight social value as a step to truth that any benefit that may be derived from them is clearly outweighed by the social interest in order and morality.[95]

This frequently cited passage is crucial to the Court's holding in *Chaplinsky*. Justice Black's joining in this opinion suggests some answers to the questions of how obvious the First Amendment was to him, whether he balanced interests, and whether he considered all speech to be within the domain of free expression protected by the First Amendment.

Again, in 1946, the Court and Justice Black simply assumed that obscenity is not within the ambit of free speech. Construing section 14 of the Classification Act of 1879, Justice Douglas wrote for the Court:

We may assume that Congress has a broad power of classification and need not open second-class mail to publications of all types. The categories of publications entitled to that classification have indeed varied through the years. And the Court held in *Ex parte Jackson* . . . that Congress could constitutionally make it a crime to send fraudulent or obscene material through the mails. . . .

The validity of the obscenity laws is recognition that the mails may not be used to satisfy all tastes, no matter how perverted. But Congress has left the Postmaster General with no power to prescribe standards for literature or the art which a mailable [that is, not obscene] periodical disseminates.[96]

Two years later in *Winters v. New York* the Court struck down as overbroad a New York statute which forbade the distribution of magazines depicting scenes of bloodshed and lust that tend to incite violent or depraved crimes against the person. Justice Reed spoke for a Court including Justice Black and held that the standards embodied in the statute were too uncertain: "Men of common intelligence cannot be required to guess at the meaning of the enactment." Then, citing *Chaplinsky*, he said that states do have the power to punish if the publication in question is

[95] 315 U.S. 568, 571–72 (1942). Chaplinsky was a Jehovah's Witness who, on the streets of Rochester, N.H., said to the face of a potential convert:"You are a God damned racketeer" and "a damned Fascist and the whole government of Rochester are Fascists or agents of Fascists."

[96] Hannegan v. Esquire, Inc., 327 U.S. 146, 155–56, 158 (1946).

"lewd, indecent, obscene or profane." The constitutional defect in New York's law, however, was that it "does not limit punishment to the indecent and obscene, as formerly understood."[97] And when the Court in *Pennekamp* invoked the First Amendment to invalidate a judicial contempt citation, the Supreme Court, with Justice Black in agreement, offered the judge an alternative to punishing for contempt speech protected by the First Amendment. "[W]hen the statements amount to defamation," the Court explained, "a judge has such remedy in damages for civil libel as do other public servants."[98]

The absolutist Justice Black of the 1950s and 1960s hardly ever joined the Court's opinions in libel and obscenity cases; instead, he characteristically wrote a separate opinion in each case—even when he agreed with the Court's result—spelling out his interpretation of the First Amendment.[99] In the 1940s Justice Black is found agreeing—at least by silent consent—that libel and obscenity are not protected forms of expression. He could agree, moreover, that commercial publications do not enjoy the same degree of constitutional protection as do other kinds or forms of expression.[100] In 1948 he wrote the opinion for the Court holding that deliberately misrepresented, fraudulent publications are not free speech or press within the meaning of the First Amendment. "A contention cannot be seriously considered which assumes that freedom of the press includes a right to raise money," he said, "to promote circulation by deception of the public." The First Amendment does not protect "swindling schemes."[101]

The changed, absolutist Justice Black found no exceptions in the language of the First Amendment, and so he argued that another form of deliberate, fraudulent "swindling schemes" is safeguarded by the First Amendment. Deliberate libel and slander are deceptions on the public, "swindling schemes" calculated to misrepresent. But, even if designed to destroy the reputation of an innocent victim, deliberate lies must be protected absolutely, in Justice Black's words, "to save the press from

[97] 333 U.S. 507, 510, 515, 519 (1948).

[98] 328 U.S. 331, 348–49 (1946).

[99] *See, e.g.*, cases cited in note 60 *supra. See also* Smith v. California, 361 U.S. 147, 155–60 (1959) (Black, J., concurring); Associated Press v. Walker, 388 U.S. 130, 170–72 (Black, J., concurring).

[100] Valentine v. Chrestensen, 316 U.S. 52 (1942).

[101] Donaldson v. Read Magazine, 333 U.S. 178, 191, 192 (1948).

being destroyed by libel judgments."[102] Although in the 1950s and 1960s he could derive no exceptions from the language of the First Amendment, in the 1940s he could nonetheless draw distinctions between protected and unprotected speech. The only plausible explanation is that, despite his assertions to the contrary, Justice Black underwent a fundamental transformation in construing "plain words, easily understood," words that the absolutist would say "could never be misunderstood."

Conclusion

It would be an exaggeration to assume from this analysis that Justice Black made a sudden transition from the 1940s to the 1950s. He was very much concerned with enforcing the First Amendment to safeguard as much expression as possible, both in the 1940s and after. To have embraced absolutism at all, he surely had to be strongly inclined in that direction; indeed, he used the clear and present danger test to protect and broaden First Amendment freedoms, not to restrict them as other members of the Court had done and would soon do again. But he repeatedly admitted that the First Amendment cannot be given an absolute value in "an orderly society"; he clearly recognized, and practiced in cases like *Korematsu*, the view that individual rights cannot be enforced "without any ifs, buts, or whereases," as he later said,[103] against all dangers. In this first period Justice Black also recognized that the First Amendment did not and cannot protect all types of utterance; he excepted from the amendment's shelter certain forms of expression that surely were not contemplated in the intent or purpose of the amendment. He assumed then, as did everyone else, that obscenity, profanity, private libel, and fraudulent advertisements were speech which fell outside the pale of free expression.

The Justice Black of the 1940s followed a conception of the First Amendment akin to the libertarian views of Mr. Justice Holmes and Zechariah Chafee, Jr. He believed that the First Amendment was designed to ensure that the people would be allowed maximum freedom to discuss public affairs, but that in "an orderly society" there were implicit

[102] Curtis Publishing Co. v. Butts, 388 U.S. 130, 171 (1967) (Black, J., dissenting).
[103] H. BLACK, *supra* note 23, at 45. *See also* Beauharnais v. Illinois, 343 U.S. 250, 275 (1952) (Black, J., dissenting).

limits to that freedom,[104] and such limits were to be ascertained by applying the clear and present danger test.

But the events of the Cold War, McCarthyism, and congressional and public pressure soon would induce a different and timid Court majority to apply judicially created tests not to protect First Amendment freedoms, but to rationalize and encourage the government's determination to eradicate communism and punish its sympathizers. In turn, the Court's deliberate distortions of the clear and present danger test and the balancing of interests doctrine would induce Justice Black resolutely to denounce all such tests and renounce all limitations on freedom of speech, "even in times of grave emergency."[105] The transition to absolutism would come early in the 1950s, and it would not be the result merely of a stiffened libertarian posture. Nor would his subsequent inclusion of libel and obscenity within the meaning of free speech be the product of a closer, more careful reading of the language of the First Amendment. His reinterpretation would reflect his intensely held and increasingly strong conviction that judges must confine themselves to the words of the Constitution, the "rule of law," and that they should not be left at large to make policy on the basis of their own values and beliefs as to what is best for the people and their government. Absolutism would be the culmination of his search for objectivity in constitutional law: his disgust with the Court's willingness to balance away the constitutional rights of individuals, and his rejection of the idea of judges substituting their own notions of reasonableness and fairness for the words and commands of the Bill of Rights. The libertarian who once had been willing to set limits to freedom of speech would become an absolutist in theory and practice.

[104] Justice Holmes's view is well stated in his dissenting opinion in Abrams v. United States, 250 U.S. 616 (1919). For Chafee's view, see Z. Chafee, Free Speech in the United States 1–35 (1941). *See* the discussion of these views in ch. II, *supra*.

[105] Black, *supra* note 8, at 878.

CHAPTER IV

Justice Black and the Judicial Process:
The Road to Absolutism

THE END OF "PREFERRED POSITION"

Speaking for the Court in *Terminiello* v. *Chicago* (1949), Justice Douglas summed up the First Amendment policy of the 1940s:

> Speech is often provocative and challenging. It may strike at prejudices and preconceptions and have profound unsettling effects as it presses for acceptance of an idea. That is why freedom of speech, though not absolute . . ., is nevertheless protected against censorship or punishment, unless shown likely to produce a clear and present danger of a serious substantive evil that rises far above public inconvenience, annoyance, or unrest. . . . There is no room under our Constitution for a more restrictive view.[1]

Two months later, Justice Murphy died in Detroit; two months after this, Justice Rutledge died in York, Maine. Their sudden deaths mark the end of an era, the end of the "preferred position" of the First Amendment.

Whereas in the 1940s the doctrine of "preferred position" was the guiding policy of the Court in the disposition of free speech cases, in the

---

[1] 337 U.S. 1, 4 (1949).

1950s it commanded the allegiance only of Justices Black and Douglas, both of whom early in the decade would move beyond that doctrine; by 1960, both Justices Douglas and Black were vigorous absolutists. Whatever vitality remained of the "preferred position" of freedom of speech after the deaths of Justices Murphy and Rutledge was lost with the appointment of their replacements. President Truman in their places nominated Tom Clark and Sherman Minton, neither of whom shared or practiced the free speech policy of the "preferred position" doctrine. As it has happened so often, as it no doubt will happen again, the development of a doctrine was disrupted by the appointment process. The appointments of Justices Clark and Minton served in part to destroy the doctrine of "preferred position."[2]

Although this was crucial, other factors were instrumental in destroying the doctrine. The political environment and the social context, within which the First Amendment, as any law, must function, shifted enormously from the 1940s to the 1950s. Issues and the direction and strength of public opinion in the later decade were shaped and determined by forces unlike those of the 1940s. In the early and middle forties, Russians and the Soviet Union were depicted by Americans and the United States as allies and comrades ready to cooperate in peace efforts to prevent the recurrence of war. Even Mrs. Tryphosa Duncan Bates Batchellor, a prominent member of the Daughters of the American Revolution, praised Joseph Stalin as "a man who, when he sees a great mistake, admits it and corrects it."[3] In the air was the pervading optimism flowing from the anticipation of total defeat of Nazi aggression: the Soviets were America's allies; communism was tolerated as another political doctrine, although one commanding the allegiance of very few Americans.

Within a few years, however, old antagonisms were renewed with a vengeance: the Soviet Union became America's rival and enemy; communism became the enemy of democracy and freedom, a creeping plague to be rooted out of the political and social fabric of the United States. The process of eradication at home took the form of an official, comprehensive regulation of the Communist party and anyone suspected of having sympathized with that organization. Regulation eventually evolved into per-

---

[2] For an analysis of the appointment process and its effects on the law, see H. Abraham, Justices and Presidents (1974); H. Chase, Federal Judges: The Appointing Process (1972).

[3] I. Howe and L. Coser, The American Communist Party 413 (1962).

secution, especially as the government employed the effective weapon of public opinion. Suspected Communists and sympathizers, once their names were exposed, were subjected to the passions and powers of public wrath against communism.

It was only a matter of time before the Court would be confronted with the task of ruling on the constitutionality of the domestic war against communism. By the time the obvious questions involving the rights of freedom of belief and association were before the Court for review, cold war and national hysteria had struck the United States and, via the Court, the First Amendment in such a way as almost to deprive a society of its senses. It has been said that "[t]he anti-Communist movement . . . was compounded of a modest element of intelligent concern for public security in an age of international conspiracy and espionage and a very large component of emotionalism, irrationalism, and downright hysteria."[4] In the face of the consuming and panicky nature of the issue, the Court seemed simply to step aside. For more than a decade, with a brief hiatus between 1956 and 1957, the Supreme Court more or less abdicated its function of protecting individual rights whenever those rights were asserted by suspected "subversives." Its decision and opinion in *American Communications Association* v. *Douds* in 1950, the Court's first encounter with the issue, depicted the inclination the Court would assume in the ensuing decade throughout the government's war against communism. Only during the brief interlude between 1956 and 1957 did the Court itself enter the battle to attempt to undo what it had allowed to be done—only quickly to retreat.[5]

In *Douds* the Supreme Court demonstrated that it was prepared to refuse enforcement of the First Amendment by sustaining as a valid regulation of interstate commerce the loyalty-oath provision of the Taft-Hartley Act. Under this provision individual labor unions were denied the right to solicit intervention by the National Labor Relations Board in questions of commerce raised by the labor unions

> unless there is on file with the Board an affidavit executed contemporaneously or within the preceding twelve-month period by each officer of such labor organization and the officers of any national or international organization of which it is an affiliate or constituent unit

[4] A. KELLY AND W. HARBISON, THE AMERICAN CONSTITUTION 887–88 (4th ed. 1970).
[5] *See* W. MURPHY, CONGRESS AND THE COURT (1962); C. PRITCHETT, CONGRESS VERSUS THE SUPREME COURT (1961).

that he is not a member of the Communist Party or affiliated with such a party, and that he does not believe in, and is not a member of or supports any organization that believes in or teaches, the overthrow of the United States Government by force or by any illegal means.[6]

This provision was challenged by the American Communications Association as a violation of the First Amendment's guarantee of free speech and association. The United States government defended the regulation as a valid exercise of Congress's power to remove obstructions from interstate commerce. Political strikes were the alleged obstructions, and they presumably were the work of the Communist party. Under its plenary power to remove undue burdens from the free flow of interstate commerce, Congress thus claimed authority to coerce labor union leaders to renounce the Communist party or forgo the benefits of the National Labor Relations Board.

With three justices (Douglas, Clark, and Minton) not participating, Chief Justice Fred M. Vinson spoke for the Court and accepted the government's argument, though he acknowledged that "Congress has undeniably discouraged the lawful exercise of political freedoms." But, unsuccessfully, the Court sought to avert an obvious confrontation with the First Amendment by insisting that the loyalty oath was aimed at conduct, not speech, belief, or association. The chief justice contended that the loyalty oath "is designed to protect the public not against what Communists and others identified therein advocate or believe, but against what Congress has concluded they have done and are likely to do again." The regulation is aimed at "harmful conduct which Congress has determined is carried on by persons who may be identified by their political affiliations and beliefs."[7] In short, the Court upheld the loyalty-oath provision by concluding that Congress was attempting—via its power over interstate commerce—to regulate conduct, not beliefs, while nonetheless conceding that in order to regulate such conduct, Congress must regulate beliefs by singling out those who hold such beliefs. Despite reassurances that "[b]eliefs are inviolate" and that the First Amendment still retained its "high place,"[8] the chief justice's reasoning discloses a marked inability to disguise an unwillingness to enforce the First Amendment against official

[6] 339 U.S. 382, 385–86 (1950).
[7] *Id.* at 393, 396.
[8] *Id.* at 393, 399.

attempts to throttle the freedoms of association and belief when aimed at members of the Communist party or its sympathizers.

Justice Black dissented on the basis of the constitutional principle—to which the Court proclaimed allegiance—that freedom to think and believe is inviolable. He dissented because he was willing to enforce that principle, whereas the Court was not. Like the Court, he was aware of the public paranoia over the issue of communism: "At such times the fog of public excitement obscures the ancient landmarks set up in our Bill of Rights. Yet then, of all times, should this Court adhere most closely to the course they mark." The issue in *Douds* for him was not one of regulating conduct, but "the right to think," which, in his view, was absolute. No illegal conduct had taken place; yet the Court was allowing the government to "tamper in the realm of thought and penalize 'belief' on the ground that it might lead to illegal conduct."[9] He also attacked the government's premise, and the Court's acceptance of it, that the loyalty oath was a valid means of regulating interstate commerce. The Court had phrased the issue before it as one of balancing the right of Congress to regulate interstate commerce against the impact of the regulation on the freedom of association and belief.[10] But, to Justice Black, "the First Amendment was added after the adoption of the Constitution for the express purpose of barring Congress from using previously granted powers to abridge belief or expression."[11]

"[B]eginning perhaps with the *Douds* case in 1950," writes Wallace Mendelson, "the First Amendment seems to have acquired a fresh clarity for Mr. Justice Black."[12] It is doubtful that his dissenting opinion in *Douds* marks a sudden change in Justice Black's interpretation of the First Amendment or his judicial philosophy generally. The issue for him there was freedom of belief, a freedom which at least as early as 1942 he had recognized as absolute insofar as government had no power to penalize mere belief short of any action. The first sentence of his dissenting opinion quoted from Justice Murphy's earlier dissent in *Jones* v. *Opelika* (1942), an opinion then joined by Justice Black. There Justice Murphy had said:

Freedom of speech, freedom of the press, and freedom of religion all have a double aspect—freedom of thought and freedom of action.

---

[9] *Id.* at 453, 446 (Black, J., dissenting).

[10] *Id.* at 400.

[11] *Id.* at 446 (Black, J., dissenting).

[12] THE SUPREME COURT: LAW AND DISCRETION 29 (Mendelson, ed. 1967).

Freedom to think is absolute of its own nature; the most tyrannical government is powerless to control inward workings of the mind. But even an aggressive mind is of no missionary value unless there is freedom of action, freedom to communicate its message to others by speech and writing. Since in any form of action there is a possibility of collision with the rights of others, there can be no doubt that this freedom to act is not absolute but qualified, being subject to regulation in the public interest which does not unduly infringe the right.[13]

For Justice Black, the question raised in *Douds* was no more than whether government had the power to penalize political belief. He did not argue that freedom of speech was absolute. His opinion holds the thoughts of a judge astonished that the Court could actually have sustained the loyalty-oath provision and accept the government's makeshift justification for violating the First Amendment. His dissent was unlike his later, thundering dissents in free speech cases involving suspected subversives; there his dissents would be almost automatic, characteristic reactions to the Court's decisions and reasoning. There he would be too well aware of what the Court was doing—refusing to enforce the First Amendment. But in *Douds* his dissent reads as if he were genuinely amazed that the Court could even contemplate the constitutionality of a regulation aimed at belief. "Never before," he lamented, "has this Court held that the Government could for any reason attaint persons for their political beliefs or affiliations. It does so today."[14]

Having the benefit of hindsight, one can say that Justice Black, or even the Court itself, was unaware that the Court's opinion in *Douds* would be characteristic of a decade-long policy of abandoning the principles of the First Amendment in order to sustain governmental attempts to exterminate the Communist party and punish anyone who sympathized with any of its political goals.[15] But, soon thereafter, Justice Black recognized that a reconstituted Court had abandoned the doctrine of "preferred position," not only in cases involving alleged subversives but as the governing policy

[13] 316 U.S. 584, 618 (1942) (Murphy, J., dissenting). Of course, his agreement with this passage is further evidence contradicting his later statement that he had always believed that the freedom of speech is absolute and undermining his later distinction between speech and conduct.

[14] 339 U.S. 382, 449 (Black, J., dissenting).

[15] *See, e.g.*, Carlson v. Landon, 342 U.S. 524 (1952).

of the Court in free speech cases generally.[16] On June 4, 1951, he dissented from the Court's judgment in *Dennis* v. *United States* and from the several opinions rendered to reach that judgment. The *Dennis* case was of major significance in demonstrating the Court's forthright and undisguised willingness to remove the First Amendment, as a constitutional obstacle, from the path of the United States government in its frenetic crusade to expunge communism. Justice Black dissented in a very brief opinion, saying: "[M]y basic disagreement with the Court . . . springs from a fundamental difference in constitutional approach. Consequently, it would serve no useful purpose to state my position at length."[17] By this time, he was on the road to absolutism, convinced that the Court's previous First Amendment policy of "preferred position" had passed into history.

Dennis v. United States

Dennis involved the constitutionality of certain provisions of the Smith Act that made it a crime for any person "willfully" or "knowingly" to teach or advocate the violent overthrow of the United States government, to be a member of a group which teaches or advocates such doctrine, to organize or help organize any group which does so, or to conspire to do so. The Smith Act, or the Alien Registration Act as it was also called, was passed in 1940 as a wartime sedition measure; and, as such, it was not specifically intended as a weapon in the government's arsenal in the postwar frenzy over communism. When the above provisions of the act reached the Court for review in 1951, Justice Black viewed the provisions as patently unconstitutional—"a virulent form of prior censorship of speech and press, which I believe the First Amendment forbids."[18] In 1943, however, when the issue of the constitutionality of this act came before the Court in a case for the first time, Justice Black was among the majority who denied certiorari (precluding the Court from hearing the case at all) and thereby

---

[16] In a free speech case upholding an Illinois law and the conviction under it, the Court did not even mention the First Amendment, let alone the doctrine of "preferred position." Beauharnais v. Illinois, 343 U.S. 250 (1952).

[17] 341 U.S. 494, 579 (1951) (Black, J., dissenting).

[18] *Id.*

upheld the provisions of the Smith Act.[19] This was the Justice Black of the 1940s, in wartime—the nonabsolutist author of *Korematsu*. By 1951, he not only chided the Court for upholding this obvious infringement on First Amendment freedoms but also criticized the Court's "severely limited grant of certiorari."[20] The Court agreed to review the constitutionality of the legislation but refused to consider the facts of the case.

In its endeavor to uphold the Smith Act, the majority of the Court could not agree on a governing rationale: Chief Justice Vinson announced the judgment of the Court in an opinion joined by Justices Reed, Burton, and Minton; Justices Frankfurter and Jackson both concurred in separate opinions. Justices Black and Douglas dissented separately. Justice Clark, who was attorney general when the indictment was brought, did not participate. The chief justice's opinion, like his opinion in *Douds*, unveiled his ability to limit the First Amendment whenever it collided with governmental efforts to extinguish communism in the United States. Here the interest was the prosecution of the Communist party and its sympathizers in the name of national security. The chief justice applied the clear and present danger test, as reformulated into no test at all by Judge Learned Hand (who had written the opinion for the Court of Appeals affirming the conviction of Dennis and his associates). As Chief Justice Vinson quoted that reformulation: "In each case [courts] must ask whether the gravity of the 'evil,' discounted by its improbability, justifies such invasion of free speech as is necessary to avoid the danger." We adopt this statement of the rule," the chief justice said. "It takes into consideration those factors which we deem relevant, and relates their significance. More we cannot expect from words."[21]

As a test specifically designed to uphold this unmistakable invasion of the First Amendment, no more could be expected from words. Under this test the Smith Act was constitutional as a matter of course. Since the gravity of the evil—the overthrow of the United States government—is infinite, it does not matter whether the actuality of the event is probable or not; in fact, that factor is not even relevant. Chief Justice Vinson could thereby dispose of the case by saying: "Overthrow of the Government by

---

[19] Dunne v. United States, 138 F. 2d 137 (8th Cir. 1943), *cert. denied*, 320 U.S. 790 (1943). Here the government prosecuted a group of Minneapolis Trotskyites who allegedly advocated insubordination in the armed forces.

[20] 341 U.S. 494, 581 (Black, J., dissenting).

[21] *Id.* at 510.

force and violence is certainly a substantial enough interest for the government to limit speech. Indeed, this is the ultimate value of any society, for if society cannot protect its very structure from armed internal attack, it must follow that no subordinate value can be protected."[22]

Even Justice Jackson, a literary stylist usually at pains to make sense, sustained the government's attempt to destroy the American Communist party in the name of national security. He rejected the clear and present danger test because it would require the Court to "appraise imponderables, including international and national phenomena which baffle the best informed foreign offices and our most experienced politicians." (Of course, as applied by the plurality through Judge Hand's reformulation, the test precludes thinking; confronting "imponderables" is obviated if "national self-preservation" is inserted into the test as the "ultimate value.") The issue for Justice Jackson was "a conviction of conspiracy, after a trial for conspiracy, on an indictment charging conspiracy, brought under a statute outlawing conspiracy."[23] Even though the conviction was based on a conspiracy of thoughts rather than a conspiracy of overt acts, in his view "the end being punishable"—attempting to overthrow the government—"the power to punish conspiracy for the purpose" is obvious.[24] This syllogism succeeds only in avoiding the question: Is advocacy or teaching the doctrine of communism or membership in an organization which adheres to that doctrine a crime compatible with the principles of the First Amendment? Justice Jackson premised the issue in such a way as if the First Amendment were entirely inapplicable to a resolution of the problem. Following this reasoning, since Congress can punish civil disobedience, Congress can therefore punish or outlaw an organization which conspires to advocate the desirability or utility of civil disobedience. Believers in natural law who organize to teach and advocate the virtue and higher duty of disobeying "unjust" positive law may constitutionally be jailed under the analysis offered by Justice Jackson to sustain the Smith Act.[25]

[22] *Id.* at 509.

[23] 341 U.S. 494, 570, 572 (Jackson, J., concurring). Of Justice Jackson's opinion it has been said: "Eleven times in two paragraphs in his opinion he used the noun 'conspiracy,' commenting that the 'Constitution does not make conspiracy a civil right.' " H. ABRAHAM, FREEDOM AND THE COURT 202 (3d ed. 1977).

[24] 341 U.S. 494, 575.

[25] Given the frailty of Justice Jackson's position, it has been suggested that he was "probably . . . saying . . . that the defendants were really being charged with a conspiracy to

Also concurring in the Court's judgment, Justice Frankfurter posed the issue squarely as one of balancing conflicting interests, neither of which can be assigned an absolute value. Government has the right to protect itself, "[but] even the all-embracing power and duty of self-preservation are not absolute. . . . [They are] subject to applicable constitutional limitations. . . . The First Amendment is such a restriction." But neither is the First Amendment absolute. "Free speech is subject to prohibition of those abuses of expression which a civilized society may forbid." For him a resolution of the problem involved in *Dennis* could result only after "candid and informed weighing of competing interests."[26]

Having said all this, Justice Frankfurter refused to do any balancing. It was not his or the Court's duty to weigh the merits of these interests, he explained, because the process inextricably involves making social policy. For the Court to make such policy is to usurp the legislative power that is reserved to the people through their representatives.

> Free speech cases are not an exception to the principle that we are not legislators, that direct policy-making is not our province. How best to reconcile competing interests is the business of legislators, and the balance they strike is a judgment not to be displaced by ours, but to be respected unless outside the pale of fair judgment.[27]
>
> We are to set aside the judgment of those whose duty is to legislate only if there is no reasonable basis for it.[28]

Like Chief Justice Vinson's distortion of the clear and present danger test, Justice Frankfurter's policy of deferring to legislative judgment deflates the impact of the First Amendment against official attempts to suppress expression. Like the chief justice's "test," Justice Frankfurter's test of reasonableness almost completely removes the First Amendment's prohibitions from the path of legislators. Of course, the First Amendment retains its full force when it stands in the way of legislation that has no

---

overthrow the government, not merely to advocate, and that evidence of advocacy could be used to prove such a conspiracy." T. EMERSON, THE SYSTEM OF FREEDOM OF EXPRESSION 119 (1970).

[26] 341 U.S. 494, 520, 523, 525 (Frankfurter, J., concurring).

[27] *Id.* at 539–40.

[28] *Id.* at 525.

basis in reason; the First Amendment stands as a legal barrier against laws made by idiots.[29] When do legislatures ever make laws that are not based in reason? Mere legislative debate may make a legislative proposal reasonable, although the legislative product may not be constitutional. If one applies Justice Frankfurter's policy faithfully and consistently, any law stifling freedom of expression is constitutional as long as there exists a reason for such a law.

Justice Frankfurter's answer to those who challenged the Smith Act on grounds that it violated the First Amendment was: "The Smith Act and this conviction under it no doubt restrict the exercise of free speech and assembly." But Congress itself decides whether Congress is justified in violating the First Amendment, despite its statement that "Congress shall make no law . . . abridging the freedom of speech . . . or the right of the people peaceably to assemble." The Supreme Court must practice the virtue of "perceptive humility" and thus defer judgment to the people's representatives unless they cannot make a reasonable judgment.[30] If Congress has reason to pass a law abridging freedom of speech, that law must be sustained as constitutional because Congress has reason to pass a law abridging the freedom of speech. Apparently judicial humility requires the Court to ignore the command of the First Amendment.[31]

[29] In Walter Berns's words: "The Court will exercise its powers only when legislators are idiots." W. BERNS, FREEDOM, VIRTUE AND THE FIRST AMENDMENT 180 (1957).

[30] 341 U.S. 494, 521, 552 (Frankfurter, J., concurring). Justice Frankfurter's "perceptive humility" has been aptly characterized as the "ultimate surrender." M. SHAPIRO, FREEDOM OF SPEECH: THE SUPREME COURT AND JUDICIAL REVIEW 88 (1966).

[31] It has never been adequately explained why Justice Frankfurter was willing to ignore the commands of the First Amendment and defer to Congress (and the states) in cases involving free speech and association, yet determined to enforce the principle of the separation of church and state. Of the latter he said: "It is the Court's duty to enforce this principle in its full integrity." McCollum v. Board of Education, 333 U.S. 203, 231 (1948) (Frankfurter, J., concurring). Why were legislatures which subvented aid to parochial schools not the beneficiaries of Justice Frankfurter's virtues?

Wallace Mendelson, Justice Frankfurter's devoted admirer and Justice Black's constant critic, unblushingly attempts to explain the difference "in terms of crystal clarity in the Constitution." W. MENDELSON, JUSTICES BLACK AND FRANKFURTER 63 (2d ed. 1966). Presumably, then, the meaning of "Congress shall make no law respecting an establishment of religion" came across to Justice Frankfurter with "crystal clarity," while the hopelessly vague words "Congress shall make no law . . . abridging the freedom of speech" reduced him to humility. The "crystal clarity" of the establishment clause compelled Justice Frankfurter to strike down all state laws purporting to aid parochial schools and to invalidate the practice of prayer in the public schools. Aside from the fact that the phrase "respecting an establish-

Applying the clear and present danger test as it was used by Justices Holmes and Louis D. Brandeis,[32] or as applied by the Court during the "preferred position" era of the 1940s, one would have difficulty in not invalidating the Smith Act convictions under review in *Dennis*. Dissenting, Justice Douglas did apply the clear and present danger test and concluded that the convictions should have been reversed by the Court:

[T]he primary consideration is the strength and tactical position of the petitioners and their converts in this country. On that there is no evidence in the record. If we are to take judicial notice of the threat of Communism within this nation, it should not be difficult to conclude that *as a political party* they are of little consequence. Communists in this country have never made a respectable or serious showing in any election. I would doubt that there is a village, let alone a city or county or state, which the Communists could carry.

How it can be said that there is a clear and present danger that this advocacy will succeed is, therefore, a mystery. . . . The fact that their ideas are abhorrent does not make them powerful.[33]

The government, of course, had cause to worry about espionage in the United States; the Cold War being waged was unique, as were the stakes involved. But the American Communist party was impotent as a force capable of overthrowing the United States. The idea that it could, it has been bluntly but aptly said, "was an idea which could be entertained seriously only by the profoundly naive, the politically unsophisticated, and those with deeply disturbed and confused minds."[34] "We might as

---

ment of religion" is as vague, if not more vague, than the phrase "freedom of speech," for Justice Frankfurter the First Amendment did not even apply to the states; for him, the governing principle was the "due process" clause of the Fourteenth Amendment, and there is not much of "crystal clarity" to be found in the vague contours of that clause.

Moreover, in his dissenting opinion in Board of Education v. Barnette, 319 U.S. 624, 659 (1943), Justice Frankfurter implied that the Court has no power to deny "states the right to entertain such convictions in regard to their school systems." One such conviction which he mentioned was compulsory Bible-reading, a conviction which he later struck down as unconstitutional—not "unreasonable"—in *McCollum*.

[32] Justice Holmes held that expression of opinions can be suppressed only when they "so imminently threaten immediate interference with the lawful and pressing purposes of the law that an immediate check is required to save the country." Abrams v. United States, 250 U.S. 616, 630 (1919) (Holmes, J., dissenting).

[33] 341 U.S. 494, 588 (Douglas, J., dissenting).

[34] A. KELLY AND W. HARBISON, *supra* note 4, at 887.

well say," said an exasperated Justice Douglas, "that the speech of petitioners is outlawed because Soviet Russia and her Red Army are a threat to world peace."[35] He was not far from the truth, for his frustration reflected the "threat" as seen by myopic crusaders who were leading the fight against communism at home.

Justice Black was the other dissenter in *Dennis;* by this time he understood full well the distressed state in which the Court since *Douds* had left the First Amendment. In his opinion of less than three pages, he explained that it was unnecessary for him fully to elaborate his views because his disagreement with the majority derived "from a fundamental difference in constitutional approach." What exactly did he mean by this? The words of his opinion reveal the lament he felt over the passing of the "preferred position" of the First Amendment; he could see that those who voted to sustain the convictions in *Dennis* had done so by debasing the First Amendment:

> I cannot agree that the First Amendment permits us to sustain laws suppressing freedom of speech and press on the basis of Congress' or our own notions of mere "reasonableness." Such a doctrine waters down the First Amendment so that it amounts to little more than an admonition to Congress.
>
> Public opinion being what it now is, few will protest the conviction of these Communist petitioners. There is hope, however, that in calmer times, when present pressures, passions and fears subside, this or some later Court will restore the First Amendment liberties to the high preferred place where they belong in a free society.[36]

On the surface of his opinion, it appears that the "fundamental difference" is merely that Justice Black would have had the Court return to the policy of "preferred position." But beneath the surface was a realization of his fear that freedom of expression could not be guaranteed by fluctuating Court majorities and changing political climates; he became hardened with the conviction that freedom of expression was to be protected, not merely because it was to be "preferred" over other values which might collide with it, but because the First Amendment to the Constitution protected it absolutely—against all conflicting interests.

[35] 341 U.S. 494, 587–88 (Douglas, J., dissenting).
[36] *Id.* at 579, 580, 581 (Black, J., dissenting).

THE TRANSITION TO ABSOLUTISM

The "preferred position" doctrine was implicitly a balancing test—although, in the scales, First Amendment freedoms were heavily favored. Speech could have been prohibited if the requirements of the clear and present danger test, a concomitant of the "preferred position" doctrine in the 1940s, were met. In his dissent in *Dennis*, Justice Black professed allegiance to the "preferred position" doctrine, but he did not apply the clear and present danger test. On the same day in another First Amendment case, he again said: "I adhere to that preferred position philosophy." Here too he stated the doctrine but did not bother to assess the possibility of a clear and present danger. Instead he echoed the theme of absolutism. "It is my belief that the freedom of the people of this Nation cannot survive even a little governmental hobbling of religious or political ideas." And, as in *Dennis*, he reiterated that his constitutional approach to free speech cases was the primary reason for his disagreement with the Court:"[I]t should be plain that my disagreement with the majority of the Court as now constituted stems basically from a different concept of the reach of the constitutional liberty of the press [and speech] rather than from any difference of opinion as to what former cases have held."[37]

The fall of "preferred position," as Justice Black correctly implied, was the product of a reconstituted Court. *Douds* and *Dennis* were indicative of the Court's new posture in matters raising issues under the First Amendment involving the government's and the public's frantic concern with communism. "As the era of tensions continued," wrote Irving Dilliard, "Justice Black found it necessary to strike his blows for freedom harder and harder." Similar sentiments were expressed by Charles Reich, who observed that "the Court's decisions pressed Black further and further."[38] Justice Black indeed stiffened his attitude in response to the Court's results, but his approach was primarily a response to the Court's method of reaching those results. He announced his adherence to the previous policy of "preferred position," but by the time of the *Dennis* decision he was no longer willing to include in that position the application of the clear and present danger test, or any test. Freedom of speech was to be absolutely protected.

---

[37] Breard v. Alexandria, 341 U.S. 622, 650 (1951) (Black, J., dissenting).

[38] Dilliard, *Hugo Black and the Importance of Freedom*, 10 AM. U. L. REV. 7, 23 (1961); Reich, *Mr. Justice Black and the Living Constitution*, 76 HARV. L. REV. 673, 696 (1963).

The transition from "preferred position" to absolutism seems to have been made sometime between *Douds* and *Dennis*. The first appearances of his attempt to disassociate himself from the Court's approach to free speech cases can be detected five months before *Dennis*, on January 15, 1951, when the Court handed down three decisions involving freedom of speech. In two of them, *Niemotko* v. *Maryland* and *Kunz* v. *New York*,[39] the Court invalidated two regulatory provisions, each as a prior restraint in violation of the First Amendment. When the Court had struck down similar state or municipal measures for similar reasons in the 1940s, Justice Black without reservation had agreed with the Court's reasoning and results.[40] In *Kunz* and *Niemotko*, however, he concurred in the judgments, but wrote no opinion explaining his votes or why he did not join the Court's opinion.

In another case decided on that same day in 1951, the Court upheld the conviction of Irving Feiner, who was accused of making an inflammatory speech to an allegedly hostile and restless crowd. Applying the clear and present danger test, and finding no evidence of such a danger, Justice Douglas, joined by Justice Minton, dissented. Justice Black also dissented, but by himself; he did not join the opinions of Justice Douglas, nor did the latter join that of Justice Black, who blasted the Court for sustaining the conviction and who rejected the Court's conclusions that disorder was about to erupt as a result of Feiner's speech. Both Justices Douglas and Black concluded that no such disorder or danger was discernible from the facts of the case. But a crucial difference between the two dissenters was registered in that Justice Douglas conceded that Feiner could have been constitutionally prevented from speaking if there were a real possibility of danger. Citing *Chaplinsky* v. *New Hampshire*, he said: "A speaker may not, of course, incite a breach of the peace by using 'fighting words.' "[41] In contrast, however, Justice Black said: "Even accepting every 'finding of fact' below, I think this conviction makes a mockery of the free speech guarantees of the First and Fourteenth Amendments."[42]

Dissenting in the *Kunz* case, Justice Jackson intimated that Justice Black was on the verge of absolutism, although the latter did not specifi-

[39] 340 U.S. 268 (1951); 340 U.S. 290 (1951).
[40] *See, e.g.*, Saia v. New York, 334 U.S. 558 (1948); Murdock v. Pennsylvania, 319 U.S. 105 (1943); Cantwell v. Connecticut, 310 U.S. 296 (1940).
[41] Feiner v. New York, 340 U.S. 315, 331 (1951) (Douglas, J., dissenting).
[42] *Id.* at 323 (Black, J., dissenting).

cally mention the notion of absolutism in his *Feiner* dissent. As Justice Jackson put it:

> I understand, though disagree with, the minority in the Feiner case, who, so far as I can see, would require no standards since they recognize no limits at all, considering that some rioting is the price of free speech and that the city must allow all speech and pay the price. But every juristic or philosophic authority recognized in this field admits that there are some speeches one is not free to make. The problem, on which they disagree, is how and where to draw the line.[43]

Presumably Justice Jackson included Justices Douglas and Minton, as well as Justice Black, in the "minority" of which he spoke. But both Justices Douglas and Minton applied the clear and present danger test, stating that speech could be limited if the record evinced evidence of a clear and present danger resulting from the speech. Moreover, surely Justice Jackson was not unleashing his impatience at Justice Minton, who had joined Justice Douglas; surely Justice Jackson could not have regarded the meek and ineffectual Justice Minton as an absolutist. It seems, then, that the target of his criticism was Justice Black, whose *Feiner* dissent appears to have rejected even the clear and present danger test as a limitation on expression. Justice Black did not use the word "absolute" in his dissent but might have done so in conference or perhaps in an earlier draft of his opinion.

Perhaps in *Dennis* Justice Black again raised the idea of absolutism, either in conference or in an earlier draft of his opinion. Perhaps this is what he meant by a "fundamental difference in constitutional approach." Chief Justice Vinson may have been referring to Justice Black in his plurality opinion in *Dennis* when he said: "Nothing is more certain in modern society than the principle that there are no absolutes, that a name, a phrase, a standard has meaning only when associated with the considerations which gave birth to the nomenclature. . . . To those who would paralyze our government in the face of impending threat by encasing it in a semantic straightjacket we must reply that all concepts are relative."[44] Whether or not Justice Black did pose the alternative of absolutism to the Court in *Feiner* or *Dennis*, a transition in his approach to free speech cases was undoubtedly taking place. Underway was his attempt to disassociate

[43] Kunz v. New York, 330 U.S. 290, 300 (1951) (Jackson, J., dissenting).
[44] 341 U.S. 494, 508.

himself from the Court majority and even from Justice Douglas, who at this time still professed allegiance to the clear and present danger test.

In *Dennis* Justice Black claimed adherence to the "preferred position" doctrine; yet he obviously meant something other than that doctrine as it was explained and practiced in the 1940s. In his dissent Justice Douglas in *Dennis* applied that doctrine, together with its concomitant clear and present danger test, as he and its other advocates (including Justice Black) had applied it in the 1940s. His dissent reads much like the "preferred position" philosophy of the previous era. If in *Dennis* Justice Black was faithful to that doctrine, or if he was concerned solely with a result favorable to free speech, why did he not join Justice Douglas's opinion, as he had customarily done in many cases during the 1940s, and as he would do later in free speech cases? As in *Feiner*, both Justices Douglas and Black wrote separate opinions in *Dennis*, and neither signed his name to the other's—an unusual occurrence in free speech cases.

In *Murdock* v. *Pennsylvania* (1943), Justice Douglas wrote for the Court and Justice Black in "preferred position" style, stating that "the rights with which we are dealing [freedom of speech and religion] are not absolutes."[45] And in *Terminiello* v. *Chicago* (1949), he wrote again for the Court and Justice Black, observing that "freedom of speech . . . [is] not absolute."[46] The Justice Black of the 1940s could join these opinions. But, by 1951, the new, absolutist Justice Black could not continue to do so if Justice Douglas, or any other member of the Court, persisted in rejecting absolutism. In *Dennis* Justice Douglas said:

> The freedom to speak is not absolute; the teaching of methods of terror and other seditious conduct should be beyond the pale along with obscenity and immorality.
>
> There comes a time when even speech loses its constitutional immunity. Speech innocuous one year may at another time fan such destructive flames that it must be halted in the interests of the safety of the Republic. That is the meaning of the clear and present danger test.[47]

If that was the meaning of the clear and present danger test, the reason why Justice Black in *Dennis* refused to sign his name to Justice Douglas's

[45] 319 U.S. 105, 110 (1943).
[46] 337 U.S. 1, 4 (1949).
[47] 341 U.S. 494, 581, 585 (Douglas, J., dissenting).

dissent clearly emerges. By *Dennis*, and probably as early as *Feiner*, Justice Black had made the transition from "preferred position" to absolutism; he accepted the "preferred position" of freedom of speech, but he rejected the idea that it could be limited by the clear and present danger test, or any other test which fluctuating Court majorities can use to set limits to free speech. Soon after *Dennis* Justice Douglas himself joined Justice Black in rejecting forthrightly the clear and present danger test. For himself and Justice Douglas, Justice Black bluntly exclaimed that "courts are without power to appraise and penalize utterances upon their notion that these utterances are dangerous."[48]

Although Justice Black seems to have made the transition to absolutism as early as *Dennis*, he did not specifically use the word "absolute" with reference to speech until a year later. He did acknowledge an absolute right of free thought and belief in *Douds*.[49] But not until *Carlson* v. *Landon* did he explicitly use the word "absolute" in making known his views about the constitutional protection accorded free speech. "I further believe," he said, "that the First Amendment grants an absolute right to believe in any governmental system, discuss all governmental affairs, and argue for desired changes in the existing order."[50] And, six weeks later, he affirmed his now established allegiance to absolutism, this time with added emphasis and with Justice Douglas joining him: "I think the First Amendment, with the Fourteenth, 'absolutely' forbids such laws [abridging the freedom of speech] without any 'ifs' or 'buts' or 'whereases.' Whatever the danger, if any, in such public discussions, it is a danger the Founders deemed outweighed by the danger incident to the stifling of thought and speech."[51]

Absolutism and the Judicial Function

The belief that freedom of speech is absolutely protected by the First Amendment no doubt reflected Justice Black's strong libertarian inclinations in this realm of individual liberty. He had always viewed the First Amendment guarantees "as the foundation upon which our governmental

[48] Wieman v. Updegraff, 344 U.S. 183, 194 (1952) (Black, J., concurring).
[49] *See* notes 9–13 *supra* and accompanying text.
[50] 342 U.S. 524, 555 (1952) (Black, J., dissenting).
[51] Beauharnais v. Illinois, 343 U.S. 250, 275 (1952) (Black, J., dissenting).

structure rests and without which it could not continue to endure as conceived and planned. Freedom to speak and write about public questions," he said, "is as important to the life of our government as is the heart to the human body. . . . If that heart be weakened, the result is debilitation; if it be stilled, the result is death."[52] Of the "unequivocal command" of the First Amendment, he said: "I happen to believe that this was a wise choice and that our free way of life enlists such respect and love that our Nation cannot be imperiled by mere talk. This belief of mine may and I suppose does influence me to protest whenever I think I see even slight encroachments on First Amendment liberties."[53] His devotion to freedom of expression permeates some of his most admirable opinions, written in dissent over the Court's unwillingness to enforce the First Amendment.[54]

The sensitivities of a libertarian like Justice Black were easily aroused during the Cold War period of judicial self-restraint. For example, in *Carlson* v. *Landon*, decided together with *Butterfield* v. *Zydok*,[55] the Court upheld a provision of the Internal Security Act which authorized the attorney general, and through him his subordinates, to hold in jail without bail Communist aliens against whom deportation proceedings had begun. The sole criterion inhibiting the attorney general's complete discretion was that he or his subordinates have reasonable cause to believe that the release of these aliens would endanger the United States; and, at this point in the crusade against communism, being a Communist was sufficient "reasonable cause."

Justice Black dissented for a number of reasons, not the least of which was his view that the provision violated the freedom of speech and association protected by the First Amendment. The case presented to him an illustration of "what is happening." These aliens were "kept in jail solely because a bureau agent thinks that is where Communists should be."[56] Deportation proceedings may last for many years, and under the provision sustained by the Court Communist aliens languished in jail without bail for years simply because of their political association. "[D]espite a patriotic record of which many citizens could well be proud,"

[52] Drivers Union v. Meadowmoor Dairies, 312 U.S. 287, 301–2 (1941) (Black, J., dissenting).

[53] Carlson v. Landon, 342 U.S. 524, 555–56 (1952) (Black, J., dissenting).

[54] *See, e.g.*, Konigsberg v. State Bar, 366 U.S. 36, 56–80 (1961) (Black, J., dissenting); Barenblatt v. United States, 360 U.S. 109, 134–62 (1959) (Black, J., dissenting).

[55] 342 U.S. 524 (1952).

[56] 342 U.S. at 549, 551 (Black, J., dissenting).

Justice Black observed, "[t]his jailing of Zydok . . . is typical of what actually happens when public feelings run high against an unpopular minority."[57] He saw the Cold War "period of fear" as "more ominously dangerous to speech and press than was that of the Alien and Sedition Laws. Suppressive laws and practices are now the fashion."[58]

His sincere commitment to freedom of speech and association and his impatience with the Court's apparent lack of concern were factors that spurred him in the direction of absolutism. But no judge need be an absolutist to cherish and enforce the First Amendment; nor must one embrace that doctrine in order to assure libertarian results in free speech cases. One could have been like the Justice Black of the 1940s, or Justice Douglas in *Dennis*, and still have achieved desirable libertarian results in the 1950s. But Justice Black's absolutism went far beyond any concern for freedom of speech and libertarian results; it was a direct response to the reasoning to which the Court resorted in the early 1950s to sustain seemingly unconstitutional governmental actions.

For instance, Justice Frankfurter based his opinion in *Dennis* on the recognition that Congress sought to preserve the United States by restricting First Amendment freedoms. He asked: "Can we say that the judgment Congress exercised was denied it by the Constitution? Can we establish a constitutional doctrine which forbids the elected representatives of the people to make this choice?"[59] These questions perhaps startled Justice Black, who believed that the answers to his brother justice's queries were firmly and clearly-written in the Constitution. The First Amendment was precisely such a constitutional doctrine; its express purpose was to enjoin Congress from making at least some choices and judgments—specifically those aimed at curtailing freedom of speech and association. The sole question was whether governmental action directly abridged First Amendment freedoms; if so, such action was prohibited by the First Amendment. As Justice Black saw it, Justice Frankfurter was ignoring the commands and restrictions on Congress contained in the First Amendment—the supreme law of the United States. Whether done in the name of judicial self-restraint or humility, a refusal to enforce the First Amendment against Congress was not less than a violation of the judge's

[57] *Id.* at 549.
[58] Wieman v. Updegraff, 344 U.S. 183, 193 (1952) (Black, J., concurring).
[59] 341 U.S. 494, 551 (1951) (Frankfurter, J., concurring).

sworn duty to uphold the Constitution and preserve the meaning of limited government.

Justice Black and the Letter of the Law

Writing before Justice Black advanced his doctrine of absolutism, but after his opinion in *Adamson* v. *California*,[60] Charlotte Williams concluded her case study of Justice Black and the judicial process with the following characterization:

> It is probable that Justice Black belongs to the school of thought which holds that every judge, consciously or unconsciously, writes into his opinions his own economic, social, and political ideas and that the notion of judicial impartiality is little more than a myth. At any rate he has gone to no pains to disguise the fact that he himself has positive ideas of rightness which he believes should be embodied in the law and when he incorporates these in his opinions he feels little necessity for apology or rationalization. Perhaps he no more than others writes his feelings into the law, but does so more candidly.[61]

That, in construing the Constitution, he wrote into it many of his own personal values and beliefs is not denied here, not could it be. But it is to misread his judicial philosophy to conclude that he envisioned the idea of an impartial judge as a "myth," and that he believed judges knowingly (and "should") write their own political, economic, and social policies into their opinions. Justice Black recognized, of course, that complete detachment was impossible, but the quest for objectivity in constitutional law was not a dead end, a "myth," or hopeless case. He believed that judicial policymaking was more the product of willful judges than of some defect inherent in the judicial process. More than any other member of the Court, Justice Black strove persistently throughout his career to find constitutional standards of objectivity which, if followed, would channel the course a judge could take, inhibit judicial legislation, and thereby bring judicial impartiality that much closer to realization.

His primary standards for interpreting the Constitution were the specific terms of the document itself. He believed judicial legislation to be

---

[60] 332 U.S. 46, 68–92 (Black, J., dissenting).
[61] C. WILLIAMS, HUGO L. BLACK: A STUDY IN THE JUDICIAL PROCESS 189–90 (1950).

the result of constitutional adjudication based on judges' own notions of fairness, reasonableness, and justice. He saw the wellspring of judicial lawmaking in the bottomless "due process" clause of both the Fourteenth and Fifth Amendments. As the New Dealer Senator Black from Alabama, he had witnessed the Supreme Court's performance during the heyday of substantive due process, when the Court had sat as ultimate arbiter of national and state legislation the purpose of which was to extricate the nation from the grip of economic depression. Senator Black had described the due process clause as "elastic," a clause "which means one thing to one citizen and another thing to another citizen."[62] As Justice Black, he commented that the due process clause provided the Court with "a blank sheet of paper" on which "to make changes in the Constitution and the Bill of Rights in accordance with [the Court's] idea of civilization's demands."[63]

This was Justice Black in search of objective guidelines in the law—particularly guidelines to replace the void in what was rapidly becoming the most litigated provision of the Constitution. At the same time the intensely libertarian Justice Black wanted to protect individual rights against abuses of state power. In *Barron* v. *Baltimore* (1883) the Court, however, had held that the specific guarantees of the Bill of Rights apply only against the federal government—that the specific rights contained therein do not apply against the states at all. Article I, section 10 of the Constitution specifically limits the states, but such limits have little to do with personal, noneconomic rights, such as the right of expression. Hence the only way, short of constitutional amendment, by which Justice Black could safeguard the fundamental right of free speech, as well as other basic rights, was through the vagaries of the Fourteenth Amendment, which, in only the most general terms, sets limits to state power. His proposed solution to the dilemma confronting him was a remarkable feat for a literalist—uncompromisingly to insist that the elusive language of section 1 of the Fourteenth Amendment was intended by its creators to serve simply as a shorthand embodiment of the Bill of Rights—not just the principles of liberty enshrined therein, but the specific rights and guarantees exactly as written in the first eight amendments. Since the First Amendment said "Congress shall make no law . . . abridging the freedom

[62] Swisher, *History's Panorama and Justice Black's Career*, in HUGO BLACK AND THE SUPREME COURT 6 (Strickland ed. 1967).

[63] Williams v. North Carolina, 325 U.S. 226, 278 (1945) (Black, J., dissenting).

of speech," the due process clause of the Fourteenth Amendment should read in part, "the States shall make no laws . . . abridging the freedom of speech." For a judge openly professing allegiance to a literal construction of the Constitution, this bold move was designed ironically to obviate a literal interpretation of the nebulous due process clause, to make that clause say something other than what it literally says.[64]

Of this clause Judge Benjamin Cardozo had said: "Here is a concept of the greatest generality. Yet it is put before the courts *en bloc*. Liberty is not defined. Its limits are not mapped and charted. How shall they be known?"[65] Justice Black's search for an answer has been called "a vital way-station in the development of his philosophy."[66] Indeed, it was a prodigious accomplishment: the invisible radiations of the due process clause became visible; the maps and charts to guide courts had been found in the language of the Bill of Rights.

Explaining his position in *Adamson*, Justice Black said: "In my judgment . . . history conclusively demonstrates that the language of the first section of the Fourteenth Amendment, taken as a whole, was thought by those responsible for its submission to the people, and by those who opposed its submission, sufficiently explicit to guarantee that thereafter no state could deprive its citizens of the privileges and protections of the Bill of Rights."[67] A student of the Court and Constitution has surveyed the events and arguments surrounding the incorporation controversy and has concluded with a "verdict" which seems to support Justice Black: "[T]here seems little doubt that the Amendment's principal framers and managers, Representative Bingham and Senator Howard, if not every member of the majority in the two houses of Congress, did believe the Bill of Rights to be made generally applicable to the several states via Section 1. And *no* member of that Congress, before he voted on the amendment, contradicted Bingham's and Howard's final statements to that extent."[68]

Still, the evidence contradicting both Justice Black's reading of history and the feasibility of literal and total incorporation seems overwhelming. In the midst of his position are several puzzles that he either could not solve or just ignored. For example, literal incorporation would require

[64] Adamson v. California, 332 U.S. 46, 68–123 (1947) (Black, J., dissenting).
[65] B. Cardozo, The Nature of the Judicial Process 76 (1921).
[66] Reich, *supra* note 38, at 693.
[67] 332 U.S. at 74–75.
[68] H. Abraham, *supra* note 23, at 47–48.

states, via the Seventh Amendment, to provide trial by jury, if requested, in every civil case involving more than twenty dollars. It is not difficult to imagine what this requirement might impose on the legal system. The Fifth Amendment would mandate indictment by grand jury, as opposed to the routine information, in order to initiate state criminal prosecution against the accused. Justice Black's position cannot escape these impossible hindrances on the state legal systems, except, as George D. Braden wrote, "to hedge against such a literal transference."[69] Recognizing this dilemma, Justice Black attempted at least to circumvent it by stating: "Whether this Court ever will, or whether it now should, in the light of past decisions, give full effect to what the [Fourteenth] Amendment was intended to accomplish is not necessarily essential to a decision here."[70]

Moreover, as Justice Frankfurter argued, given the evasive words by which the Fourteenth Amendment supposedly absorbed the Bill of Rights as applicable against the states, "[i]t could hardly have occurred to [the] States that by ratifying the Amendment they uprooted their established methods for prosecuting crime and fastened upon themselves a new prosecutorial system."[71] If the purpose of the Fourteenth Amendment was, in fact, to revolutionize the administration of criminal justice in every state, then it seems strange, as historian Charles Fairman has demonstrated, that very little in the way of state compliance with that amendment can be discerned.[72] After ratification, there were no abrupt changes in the administration of criminal justice in any of the states. Since ratification of a constitutional amendment requires the affirmative vote of three-fourths of the states, one should expect to discover at least some state conformity to the dictates of the newly imposed Bill of Rights.

And then there is, of course, the literalist argument contradicting the literalist Justice Black. Justice Frankfurter, concurring in *Adamson*, argued that "[i]t would be extraordinarily strange for a Constitution to convey such specific commands in such a roundabout and inexplicit way." If one of the avowed purposes of the Fourteenth Amendment was to revolutionize the administration of criminal justice in the states, "it is a strange way of saying it."[73]

---

[69] Braden, *The Search for Objectivity in Constitutional Law*, 47 YALE L. J. 571, 590 (1948).

[70] Adamson v. California, 332 U.S. 46, 75 (1947) (Black, J., dissenting).

[71] *Id.* at 64 (1947) (Frankfurter, J., concurring).

[72] Fairman, *Does the Fourteenth Amendment Incorporate the Bill of Rights? The Original Understanding*, 2 STAN. L. REV. 5 (1949).

[73] 332 U.S. at 63 (Frankfurter, J., concurring).

Perhaps the amendment's sponsors, Senator Jacob M. Howard and Representative John A. Bingham, may have so desired to use the Fourteenth Amendment to bind the states to the Bill of Rights; but they doubtless knew that such an avowed drastic alteration in federal-state relations, as well as abrupt renovations in state criminal justice, might not have gained the requisite state approval. Hence they probably chose the route of generality in the hope that, through judicial construction, the due process clause could, and would, reflect the prevailing principles of liberty and justice. In the words of Robert G. McCloskey: "It is arguable that the Fourteenth Amendment was a kind of license for the Court to proceed at will within broad limits, to make of these phrases what it felt was right and feasible. That is, after all, what the Court had done with other imprecise mandates. If the framers of the Fourteenth Amendment wanted their brainchild to be treated otherwise, nothing would have been easier than for them to say so."[74]

Justice Black's response to critics included the fact that he had been a United States senator from Alabama for ten years—"not a bad way," he countered, "to learn the value of what is said in legislative debates, committee discussions, committee reports, and various other steps taken in the course of passage of bills, resolutions, and proposed constitutional amendments." And, rebutting the view that the language of the Fourteenth Amendment was a peculiar way of restating the Bill of Rights, he said:

> In response to this I can only say that the words "No State shall make or enforce any law which shall abridge the privileges or immunities of citizens of the United States" seems to me an eminently reasonable way of expressing the idea that henceforth the Bill of Rights shall apply to the States. What more precious "privilege" of American citizenship could there be than that privilege to claim the protections of our great Bill of Rights? I suggest that any reading of "privileges or immunities of citizens of the United States" which excludes the Bill of Rights' safeguards renders the words of this section meaningless.[75]

Whatever advantage in terms of insight Justice Black's experience as a senator gave to him over others who have studied the ratification of the Fourteenth Amendment is obscure, if not dubious. The legislative process

[74] R. McCloskey, The American Supreme Court 118 (1960).
[75] Duncan v. Louisiana, 391 U.S. 145, 164–65, 166 (1968) (Black, J., concurring). *See also* H. Black, A Constitutional Faith 31 (1968).

undoubtedly had changed considerably between 1868 and his experience in the Senate. During the interlude occurred the industrial transformation of the United States, World War I, and the Great Depression, events which profoundly affected the reach and practice of American government, including the legislative process. National power was no longer confined in the hands of committee "barons." This is not to say that there were no similarities between congressional behavior in 1868 and that of the 1920s and 1930s, but it is to say that Justice Black's experience as a legislator does not serve to make his reading of history any more valid or conclusive than anyone else's.

Furthermore, if indeed the "privilege and immunities" clause did incorporate the Bill of Rights against the states, it would thereby deny to resident aliens the protection accorded citizens against state infringement of individual liberties. Also, reliance on this clause would nonetheless leave intact the same vague due process clause in which judges could roam at large in the field of policymaking. Perhaps anticipating this very predicament, Justice Black stated his incorporation position in a way so as to solve these problems, but also in a way that made his contention all the less plausible. His reading of history, he said, convinced him that section 1, "separately, and as a whole,"[76] made the guarantees contained in the Bill of Rights applicable to the states. In other words, each of the four clauses in section 1 taken separately, as well as all four taken collectively, were designed to achieve the very same purpose—making the specific guarantees of the Bill of Rights applicable against the states. Rather than stating forthrightly that the provisions of the first eight amendments are hereby made applicable to the states, the framers of the Fourteenth Amendment, according to Justice Black, said just as much in five different ways without once having said so explicitly. To say the least, this is a puzzling method of writing law, especially law that purports, in addition to many other things, to revolutionize the administration of state criminal justice. Justice Black's argument is disconcerting and convoluted, particularly in view of his frequent claim that judicial duty required adherence to the plain and simple words of the constitutional text.

Yet his "separately, and as a whole" contrivance allowed him to accomplish his purposes. He could include aliens among the beneficiaries of the new protection against the states by relying on the due process

---

[76] Adamson v. California, 332 U.S. 46, 71 (Black, J., dissenting).

clause as a vehicle for incorporation. This would also eliminate that clause as "a blank sheet of paper," since it would henceforth mean nothing more or less than the specific provisions of the Bill of Rights. (Apparently Justice Black was not bothered by the fact that complete incorporation would necessarily mean incorporating the Fifth Amendment's due process clause against the states.) And, when confronted with the argument that the due process clause is a strange way of relating the guarantees of the Bill of Rights, he could say that the privileges and immunities clause was explicit enough for him. Thus, by packaging his position in the phrase "separately, and as a whole," he could, in the words of Paul Freund, "achieve to the utmost the objectives" that he wanted.[77]

The transparency of Justice Black's incorporation theory is evident, and critics such as George Braden have attacked it as "collaps[ing], on analysis, into little more than a front for policy-making."[78] Justice Black was no doubt able to implement substantive libertarian values via his maneuver. He stated many times his personal convictions about the liberties contained in the Bill of Rights: "In my judgment the people of no nation can lose their liberty so long as a Bill of Rights like ours survives and its basic purposes are conscientiously interpreted, enforced and respected."[79] But the promotion of his personal libertarian values was not his only aim or goal. A fundamental tenet of his constitutional philosophy was that the federal and state governments were free to govern except where restricted by specific provisions of the Constitution. Striking down a law which violated the First Amendment, or reversing a criminal conviction on the basis of the Fifth Amendment's prohibitions against compulsory self-incrimination, he believed, was altogether different from invalidating a law, or reversing a conviction, because it appeared "unreasonable," "unfair," or "unjust" to a majority of judges. These were terms reminiscent of substantive due process. The dedicated New Dealer, supporter of President Roosevelt's "Court-packing plan," believed that he did not sit on the Court for the purpose of resurrecting the old horrors of what he later called "the McReynolds due process concept."[80]

Like his doctrine of absolutism, Justice Black's incorporation theory

[77] P. FREUND, THE SUPREME COURT OF THE UNITED STATES 47 (1949).
[78] Braden, *supra* note 69, at 593–94.
[79] Adamson v. California, 332 U.S. 46, 89 (1947) (Black, J., dissenting).
[80] Tinker v. Des Moines School District, 393 U.S. 503, 520 (1969) (Black, J., dissenting).

was a synthesis of libertarianism and the search of objectivity. It was in keeping with his conception of the purpose of a written constitution and the limitations it places upon judges. His interpretation of the due process clause of the Fourteenth Amendment was a reaction to the view that the clause was the embodiment of "natural law" or other uncertain standards which he believed "impose no limitations or restrictions whatever on judges, but leave them completely free to decide constitutional questions on the basis of their own policy judgments."[81] Justice Frankfurter, for example, viewed that clause as a guarantee that the states could not act in violation of "those canons of decency and fairness which express the notions of justice of English-speaking peoples."[82] It prohibited governmental behavior, he said, which "shocks the conscience" or runs counter to "the feelings of the American people."[83] He attempted to reassure Justice Black that these standards "do not leave judges at large," because they require "an evaluation based on a distinterested inquiry pursued in the spirit of science."[84]

But such reassurances could not persuade a doubtful Justice Black, for he believed that such "standards" defeated the purpose of a written constitution. He saw the boundaries between individual freedom and governmental power as specifically inscribed in the Constitution; "they are not made of mush." "I do not wish to have to pass on the laws of this country," he explained, "according to the degree of shock I receive! Some people get shocked more readily than others."[85] All standards, such as the natural law formula, that bypass the written provisions of the Constitution were themselves violations of the Constitution, "in that [they] subtly convey to courts, at the expense of legislatures, ultimate power over public policies in fields where no specific provision of the Constitution limits legislative power."[86]

Justice Black derided and ridiculed the collection of vaporous due process standards suggested by his chief jurisprudential antagonists, Justices Frankfurter and Harlan: "If due process means this [here, 'immuta-

[81] H. BLACK, *supra* note 75, at 24.

[82] Adamson v. California, 332 U.S. 46, 67 (1947) (Frankfurter, J., concurring).

[83] Rochin v. California, 342 U.S. 165, 172 (1952) (Frankfurter, J.); Haley v. Ohio, 332 U.S. 596, 607 (1948) (Frankfurter, J., concurring).

[84] Rochin v. California, 342 U.S. 165, 170, 172 (1952) (Frankfurter, J.).

[85] Cahn, *Justice Black and First Amendment "Absolutes": A Public Interview*, 37 N.Y.U. L. REV. 549, 562, 563 (1962).

[86] Adamson v. California, 332 U.S. 46, 75 (1947) (Black, J., dissenting).

ble principles of free government'], the Fourteenth Amendment, in my opinion, might as well have been written that 'no person shall be deprived of life, liberty or property except by laws that the judges of the United States Supreme Court shall find to be consistent with the immutable principles of free government.' "[87] But Justice Black overlooked the fact that he himself bypassed the written words of the due process clause of the Fourteenth Amendment. The short response to his position is: if the due process clause or any other part of the Fourteenth Amendment— "separately, and as a whole"—was intended to mean the Bill of Rights, then the Fourteenth Amendment might as well have been written to say just that! This is the fundamental paradox of his literalism.

His justification was that a look at "history" would transform the limitless domain of the due process clause into the specific prohibitions of the Bill of Rights. One cannot avoid the impression, however, that the compulsion of his historical evidence was of secondary importance in compelling Justice Black to treat that clause as if it were no more, and no less, than the Bill of Rights. Indeed, in defending his position, he seems to have said as much. He appears to have rested his case, not on the strength of historical evidence, but rather on the assertion that his interpretation rejects substantive due process and adheres instead to the strictures already spelled out in a written document:

> Since . . . the cornerstone of my constitutional faith is a basic belief that the Constitution was designed to prevent putting too much uncontrollable power in the hands of any one or more public officials, I cannot subscribe to such a loose interpretation of due process which in effect allows judges, and particularly justices of the United States Supreme Court, to hold unconstitutional laws they do not like. For what else is the meaning of "unreasonable," "arbitrary," or "capricious"—what sort of limitations or restrictions do these phrases put on the power of judges?
>
> I earnestly believe that my due process interpretation is the only one consistent with a written constitution in that it better ensures that constitutional provisions will not be changed except by proper amendment processes.[88]

[87] Duncan v. Louisiana, 391 U.S. 145, 168 (1968) (Black, J., concurring).

[88] H. BLACK, *supra* note 75, at 23–24, 41. A year later he said: "I am firmly and profoundly opposed to construing 'due process' as authorizing this Court to invalidate statutes on such nebulous grounds." Leary v. United States, 395 U.S. 6, 56 (1969) (Black, J., concurring).

Even reading his opinion in *Adamson*, where Justice Black first unfolded his incorporation theory and its historical justification, the reader is struck not so much by his historical arguments, but by his constant, pervasive denunciation of substantive due process and all the evanescent standards elicited to set boundaries around the due process clause. Not long after having witnessed and endured the pains of judge-made law setting aside much legislation designed to cope with the depression of the 1930s, Justice Black said in *Adamson*:

> I fear to see the consequences of the Court's practice of substituting its own concepts of decency and fundamental justice for the language of the Bill of Rights as its point of departure in interpreting and enforcing the Bill of Rights. . . . [T]he natural-law-due-process formula [which he described as "an incongruous excrescence on our Constitution"] . . . has been used in the past, and can be used in the future, to license this Court, in considering regulatory legislation, to roam at large in the broad expanses of policy and morals and to trespass, all too freely, on the legislative domain of the States as well as the Federal Government.[89]

Absolutism, Objectivity, and Balancing

Given Justice Black's vigorous search for specific criteria by which to adjudicate cases, his doctrine of absolutism must be appraised as a corollary to his incorporation theory. If the standard of absolutism is rejected, it means that constitutional rights, part of the highest law of the land, can be subordinated to interests deemed greater or more compelling than the rights themselves. Determining when such circumstances can compel the subordination of constitutional rights is a task which falls upon judges without any objective guidelines except their individual assessments of the values and interests involved. Justice Black rejected any substantive due process standard because it gives the clause "no permanent meaning, but one which is found to shift from time to time in accordance with judges' predilections and understandings of what is best for the country."[90] During the 1950s, the Court transformed the First Amendment—to Justice Black, the most unequivocal and specific command in the

[89] Adamson v. California, 332 U.S. 46, 75, 89 (1947) (Black, J., dissenting).
[90] Duncan v. Louisiana, 391 U.S. 145, 168 (1968) (Black, J., concurring).

Constitution—into a variant of substantive due process. The Court's interpretation of the right of freedom of speech and association was by no means "permanent," for judicial determinations in free speech cases were the product not of the commands of the First Amendment, but of the day-to-day membership of the Court. "Balancing" constitutional rights against competing interests was not much different from the task of putting content into the due process clause. Both processes, in Justice Black's judgment, frustrated the purpose and design of a written constitution.[91] But, unlike his incorporation theory (which was no little paradox for a literalist), his response to the Court's preoccupation with balancing was not built on shaky foundations. At the Court he would thrust repeatedly the express words of the First Amendment: "Congress shall make no law . . . abridging the freedom of speech."

In *Beauharnais* v. *Illinois* (1952) Justice Frankfurter spoke for the Court in upholding a state "group libel" law which made it a crime to publish matter that tended to expose a class of citizens of any race, color, creed, or religion to contempt, derision, or obloquy. Beauharnais, president of the White Circle League of America, was convicted under this statute for distributing a leaflet calling on the people of Chicago to petition the city authorities "to halt the further encroachment, harassment and invasion of white people, their property, neighborhoods and persons, by the Negro." Without ever mentioning the First Amendment (he did not believe that the First Amendment was itself incorporated into the Fourteenth Amendment against the states), Justice Frankfurter wrote an opinion upholding the statute because it was not without reason: "[W]e would deny experience to say that the Illinois legislature was without reason in seeking ways to curb false or malicious defamation of racial and religious groups."[92]

Justice Black dissented from the Court's unwillingness to enforce the strictures of the First Amendment against the reason of the Illinois state legislators: "Today's case degrades First Amendment freedoms to the 'rational basis' level. . . . [S]tate curtailment of these freedoms may be . . . invalidated if a majority of this Court conclude that a particular infringement is 'without reason.' " Attacking the Court's method and reasoning, he said: "I do not agree that the Constitution leaves freedom of petition,

[91] *See* Black, *The Bill of Rights*, 35 N.Y.U. L. REV. 865 (1960); *see also* Cahn, *supra* note 85, at 561–63.

[92] 343 U.S. 250, at 261. Illinois later repealed the statute.

assembly, speech, press or worship at the mercy of a case-by-case, day-by-day majority of this Court. I had supposed that our people could rely for their freedom on the Constitution's commands, rather than on the grace of this Court on an individual case basis."[93] The case was evidence that "the new 'due process' coverall" had been substituted for the specific commands of the First Amendment.[94]

For a brief period in the late 1950s, the Court tried to rectify the imbalance that had resulted from its earlier balances, especially in such free speech cases involving members of the Communist party as *Douds* and *Dennis*. Thus, in *Yates* v. *United States* (1957), for example, the Court sought to restrict its holding in *Dennis*, and thereby to restrict governmental efforts to jail Communists solely because they were Communists, by reconstruing the Smith Act as outlawing not "mere advocacy" of abstract Communist doctrine, but advocacy directed at illegal action.[95] And, in *Sweezy* v. *New Hampshire* (1957), a divided Court reversed the contempt citation of a man who had refused to answer certain questions involving his association with the Progressive party. Justice Frankfurter cast a crucial vote in *Sweezy* by applying the balancing of interests doctrine in favor of the individual. He said: "For a citizen to be made to forego even a part of so basic a liberty as his political autonomy, the subordinating interest of the State must be compelling."[96] (Despite the fact that he balanced "in a spirit of humility,"[97] it remains unclear why humility demanded a more rigid standard for New Hampshire than that accorded Illinois in *Beauharnais* or Congress in *Dennis*.) Also, the Court narrowly construed an act of Congress in order to prevent the secretary of state from refusing to issue passports to American citizens solely because they were allegedly members of the Communist party.[98]

This array of cases in favor of the individual rights of alleged "subversives" presumably was the result of the Court's effort to assert its power in the belief that the "Red Scare" was over. But Congress threatened to diminish the Court's appellate jurisdiction and soon made it known that the crusade was still on. Justices Frankfurter and Harlan, who were both

[93] *Id.* at 269–270, 274–75 (Black, J., dissenting).
[94] *Id.* at 269 (Black, J., dissenting).
[95] 354 U.S. 298.
[96] 354 U.S. 234, 265 (Frankfurter, J., concurring).
[97] *Id.* at 267.
[98] Kent v. Dulles, 357 U.S. 116 (1958); Dayton v. Dulles, 357 U.S. 144 (1958).

instrumental in reversing judicial policy temporarily in favor of individual rights, heeded the government's warning and once again resorted to the balancing doctrine to restrict the free speech rights of Communists and other suspected subversives in favor of official fantasies and illusions about the violent overthrow of the United States.[99] It was during this period of judicial retreat that—as pointed out earlier—Justice Black delivered in dissent his strongest and most memorable opinions advocating absolutism and criticizing the floundering First Amendment policy of the Court.

Whereas in *Beauharnais* the Court refused even to mention the First Amendment in deferring to the Illinois state legislature, in *Konigsberg* v. *State Bar of California* (1961) the Court appears to have bluntly dismissed the command of the First Amendment in its attempt to repudiate Justice Black's absolutism and his biting and relentless attack on the Court's balancing approach. Speaking for the Court majority, Justice Harlan said: "At the outset we reject the view that freedom of speech and association . . ., as protected by the First and Fourteenth Amendments, are 'absolutes,' not only in the undoubted sense that where the constitutional protection exists it must prevail, but also in the sense that the scope of that protection must be gathered solely from a literal reading of the First Amendment."[100] The Court was here seemingly denying that the First Amendment had any binding force against government. As Justice Black lamented in dissent, the Court "necessarily takes the position that even speech that is admittedly protected by the First Amendment is subject to the 'balancing test' and that therefore no kind of speech is to be protected if the Government can assert an interest of sufficient weight to induce this Court to uphold its abridgment."[101]

Justice Black's rejection of substantive due process was prompted by the fact that the empty words of the due process clause required the Court to create nebulous standards—such as "fundamental fairness," conscience-shocking conduct, or "reasonableness"—all of which he believed defeated the purpose of a written constitution. In balancing gov-

---

[99] Less than a decade earlier Justice Frankfurter had explained his virtue of "humility" as one which "presupposes complete disinterestedness." "[I]n the end," he said, "it is right that the Court should be indifferent to public temper and popular wishes. Mr. Dooley's 'th' Supreme Court follows th' iliction returns' expressed the wit of cynicism, not the demand of principle." American Federation of Labor v. American Sash and Door Co., 335 U.S. 538, 557 (1949) (Frankfurter, J., concurring).

[100] 366 U.S. 36, 49 (1961).

[101] 366 U.S. 36, 67 (Black, J., dissenting).

ernmental interests against First Amendment freedoms the Court during the 1950s seemed unmistakably to ignore the rigid bar of that amendment and thus, as Justice Black explained, rewrote the First Amendment into a form of substantive due process in that "neither the First Amendment nor any other provision of the Bill of Rights should be enforced unless the Court believes it *reasonable* to do so."[102] In the realm of substantive due process the Court arrogated to itself the power to strike down laws on the basis of its own notions of fairness or justice; in balancing interests in matters involving free speech the Court "reserved to itself the power to permit or deny abridgment of First Amendment freedoms according to its own view of whether repression or freedom is the wiser governmental policy under the circumstances of each case."[103]

Like substantive due process, balancing precludes consistency, predictability, and objectivity in constitutional law as long as the composition of the Court fluctuates or the context in which the Court functions changes. The Court's retreat in the late 1950s is evidence of this fact. Consistency cannot be expected even in the behavior of individual judges; Justices Harlan's and Frankfurter's surrender to congressional pressure is an indication of this characteristic of the balancing process. Indeed, individual justices apparently cannot even adhere to the same balancing standard from case to case, as witnessed in Justice Frankfurter's use of the "compelling" interest criterion in *Sweezy* rather than his oft-repeated and ostentatiously invoked "reasonableness" test.[104]

Application of both substantive due process and balancing inescapably results in judicial policymaking, but policy made not on the basis of interpreting specific provisions of the Constitution. Balancing, argued Justice Black, "is necessarily tied to the emphasis particular judges give to competing social values. Judges, like everyone else, vary tremendously in their choice of values."[105] He agreed that individual personality necessarily affects the judge's construction even of specific prohibitions in the Bill of Rights. But substantive due process invites "the judge to invalidate

[102] Barenblatt v. United States, 360 U.S. 109, 143 (1959) (Black, J., dissenting). *See also* H. BLACK, *supra* note 75, at 50.

[103] *In re* Anastaplo, 366 U.S. 82, 112 (1961) (Black, J., dissenting).

[104] *See* Uphaus v. Wyman, 360 U.S. 72 (1959), where Justice Frankfurter joined the Court in humbly obliterating *Sweezy*.

[105] Konigsberg v. State Bar, 366 U.S. 36, 75 (1961) (Black, J., dissenting).

statutes because of application of 'natural law' deemed to be above and undefined by the Constitution."[106] In balancing interests—as in substantive due process—judges must resort to criteria above, beyond, or outside the Constitution. To Justice Black it was a wholly different matter for courts to make policy without deriving it from some specific provision of the document itself. What criteria, for example, did the Court enlist to guide its judgment in *Konigsberg* when a majority apparently rejected the absolute command of the First Amendment, even in what was conceded to be "the undoubted sense"? The source of such policy is not the Constitution, but something extraneous to it. And, as Freund has succinctly put it, "the enemy . . . for Justice Black [was] judge-made law as an encrustation on the Constitution."[107]

As Justice Black repeatedly argued, balancing "violate[s] the genius of our *written* constitution."[108] Not only does balancing compel judges to go outside the Constitution in establishing criteria for deciding cases, and not only are constitutional rights guaranteed only on a case-by-case basis; but limited government itself becomes perverted in that government can extend its powers into the realm of individual liberties marked off in the Bill of Rights if the interest in doing so is great enough. Despite the fact that the First Amendment was designed to enclose the powers of Congress, the Court in *Douds* upheld congressional regulation of freedom of belief and association on the ground that Congress's power to regulate interstate commerce was of greater import. The limited powers of the Court itself also become distorted if the Court can dispense with the First Amendment as it seems to have done in the face of determined governmental efforts to suppress a hated political creed.

Absolutism and the Scope of Free Speech

Justice Black's attack on the Court's First Amendment policy during the 1950s and early 1960s was not a utopian delusion of mechanical jurisprudence. It was a powerful denunciation of the balancing of interests doc-

---

[106] Adamson v. California, 332 U.S. 46, 91 (1947) (Black, J., dissenting). *See also* H. BLACK, *supra* note 75, at 35–36.

[107] Freund, *Mr. Justice Black and the Judicial Function*, 14 U.C.L.A. L. REV. 467, 473 (1967).

[108] Barenblatt v. United States, 360 U.S. 109, 143 (1961) (Black, J., dissenting).

trine. "I read 'no law . . . abridging' to *mean no law abridging*,"[109] he said. And, although history seemed to refute his reinterpretation of the uncertain Fourteenth Amendment as shorthand for the certain and specific Bill of Rights, he could reinforce his absolutism with substantial historical evidence pointing to the conclusion that the First Amendment was intended to deny Congress all power to infringe the right of freedom of speech.[110]

Yet the strength of this important approach to the First Amendment seems to have been sapped by Justice Black's compulsive drive for objectivity concerning the meaning of free speech. "No law abridging" does indeed mean no law abridging, but he was unwilling to carry his literalism to the task of answering the question: no law abridging what? For much the same reason that led him to the doctrine of absolutism, he refused to set limits to the meaning of free speech. Impelled by the momentum of his forceful attack on balancing, and by his persistent quest for standards to confine judicial power, he went so far as to hold that neither he, the courts, the Congress, nor anyone was authorized to define the meaning of freedom of speech.[111] For him "the principles of the First Amendment are stated in precise and mandatory terms."[112]

Whereas in the 1940s Justice Black simply assumed that obscenity and libel were not forms of protected—free—speech, after his transition to absolutism, in the wake of his denunciation of judicial policymaking, he simply assumed just the opposite. Since obscenity and libel were forms of speech and press, they were ipso facto free speech and thus absolutely protected. As long as the expression was speech and not outright conduct, the full force of the First Amendment applied.

Justice Black's transition to absolutism appears at first to have been a conversion limited to the view of Alexander Meiklejohn, who believed that expression in the realm of public concern was absolutely protected, since such expression was essential to the workings of democratic self-government.[113] On the other hand, private libel and obscenity Meiklejohn deemed outside the scope of matters of public interest and therefore

---

[109] Smith v. California, 361 U.S. 147, 157 (1959) (Black, J., concurring).

[110] *See* the historical arguments made in ch. II.

[111] Braden v. United States, 365 U.S. 431, 445 (1961) (Black, J., dissenting).

[112] Wilkinson v. United States, 365 U.S. 399, 422 (1961) (Black, J., dissenting).

[113] A. MEIKLEJOHN, FREE SPEECH AND ITS RELATION TO SELF-GOVERNMENT (1948).

outside the reach of Meiklejohn's absolutism. Justice Black seems to have accepted this interpretation in initially transforming himself from advocate of the clear and present danger test to absolutist. For instance, in *Feiner* he spoke of speech involving "matters of public interest"; in *Beauharnais* he stated that the First Amendment absolutely protects expression related to "matters of public concern"; in *Carlson* it was criticism of "governmental affairs"; and in *Wieman* he referred to "questions of current public interest."[114] And, even after he had agreed with Justice Douglas in *Roth* v. *United States* that obscenity is absolutely protected speech, [115] Justice Black reverted continuously to the Meiklejohn theory that the purpose of the First Amendment was to ensure an absolute right for anyone to discuss public affairs. In *Speiser* v. *Randall* (1958), for instance, he echoed the Meiklejohn philosophy: "We should never forget that the freedoms secured by that Amendment—Speech, Press, Religion, Petition and Assembly—are absolutely indispensable for the preservation of a free society in which government is based upon the consent of an informed citizenry and is dedicated to the protection of the rights of all, even the most despised minorities."[116] The fundamental purpose of the First Amendment, he said in 1961, was "to keep this country free by leaving the people free to talk about any kind of change in basic governmental policies they desire to talk about."[117]

He recognized that "the primary purpose of the First Amendment" was specifically to protect "the right of the people to discuss matters of religious or public interest, in the broadest meaning of those terms."[118]

---

[114] These passages are found in Feiner v. New York, 340 U.S. 315, 321 (1951) (Black, J., dissenting); Dennis v. United States, 341 U.S. 494, 580 (1951) (Black, J., dissenting); Beauharnais v. Illinois, 343 U.S. 250, 272 (1952) (Black, J., dissenting); Carlson v. Landon, 342 U.S. 524, 555 (1952) (Black, J., dissenting); Wieman v. Updegraff, 344 U.S. 183, 194 (1952) (Black, J., concurring).

[115] 354 U.S. 476, 514 (1957) (Douglas, J., dissenting). It should be recalled that in *Dennis* Justice Douglas had expressly repudiated the idea that obscenity was protected speech and the view that the First Amendment is an absolute.

[116] 337 U.S. 513, 530. In Yates v. United States, 354 U.S. 298, 340 (1957) (Black, J., concurring in part, dissenting in part), Justice Black cited Professor Meiklejohn's work.

[117] Communist Party v. Subversive Activities Control Board, 367 U.S. 1, 164 (1961) (Black, J., dissenting). *See also* Gregory v. Chicago, 394 U.S. 111, 113–26 (1969) (Black, J., concurring); New York Times v. United States, 403 U.S. 713, 714–20 (1971) (Black, J., concurring).

[118] Konigsberg v. State Bar of California, 366 U.S. 36, 64 (1961) (Black, J., dissenting).

The central purpose of the Bill of Rights was to ensure "complete religious and political freedom."[119] Of course, he would have been rightly ridiculed had he attempted to defend his broad conception of free expression by arguing that in writing the First Amendment the framers wanted to protect pornography and deliberate lies calculated to ruin the reputation of an innocent individual.[120] But, unlike the absolutist Meiklejohn, the absolutist Justice Black nonetheless proceeded to insist that even hard-core pornography and maliciously false defamation are free speech worthy of absolute protection.[121] He seems to have offered three justifications for his view.

First, he sought to validate the inclusion of libel and obscenity within the meaning of free speech on the basis of a literal reading of the First Amendment. "Since the language of the Amendment contains no exceptions," he argued, "I have continuously voted to strike down all laws dealing with so-called obscene materials. . . . Just as with obscenity laws, I believe the First Amendment compels the striking down of all libel laws."[122] But, as was argued earlier, the First Amendment's freedom of speech contains no definitions from which exceptions can be made. In fact, one could maintain that the word "freedom" is as devoid of specific meaning as the word "liberty" in the due process clause. Moreover, if the language of the First Amendment contains no exceptions, according to Justice Black, bigamy laws should be struck down as infringements on the absolute right of Mormons freely to exercise their religion. On the basis of this reasoning any law should be invalidated that prohibits "the free exercise of religion," a right protected by constitutional language containing no exceptions.

His second argument was that the meaning of obscenity or libel is so vague that consequently government officials could punish public criticism merely by calling it obscenity or libel or slander. "For example, it is said that Augustus punished people for criticizing the Emperor by the simple device of calling such criticism obscene. So far as I am concerned, I do not believe there is any halfway ground for protecting freedom of speech and press. If you say it is half free, you can rest assured that it will

---

[119] Communist Party v. Subversive Activities Control Board, 367 U.S. 1, 163 (1961) (Black, J., dissenting).

[120] *See* the discussion of the historical meaning of freedom of speech in ch. II, *supra.*

[121] *See* Cahn, *supra* note 85, at 557, 559.

[122] H. BLACK, *supra* note 75, at 46, 48.

not remain as much as half free."[123] Obscenity is an "elastic phrase" which he believed "can, and most likely will, be synonymous with the political and maybe with the religious unorthodoxy of tomorrow."[124] This is an important point, even with respect to libel.[125] But it is doubtful that such importance warrants the conclusion that deliberate lies which destroy innocent victims must be absolutely protected because the English language or any other language is not mathematics. And it is not enough to justify the complete refusal to distinguish between art properly dealing with sex and commercially exploitive stag films. Indeed, the refusal to distinguish solely because of this reasoning conjures up an image of judicial irresponsibility.

His third rationale is an extension of the second and stems directly from Justice Black's judicial philosophy. It perhaps best explains why he treated libel and obscenity on par with political speech as free expression deserving of absolute protection. If obscenity and libel are "elastic" phrases, judicial attempts to define those terms could not square with his resolute conception of the judicial function. The task of reconciling obscenity with the principles of the First Amendment, in view of the fact that materials which deal with sex are not always obscene, cannot avoid a case-by-case appraisal of the merits and value of a particular publication, film or photograph unless one resorts to blanket protection for all such expression. And this process of judgment, as Justice Black well knew, means that

> every member of the Court must exercise his own judgment as to how bad a picture [or any publication] is, a judgment which is ultimately based at least in large part on his own standard of what is immoral. The end result of such decisions seems to me to be a purely personal determination by individual Justices as to whether a particular picture [or book, etc.] viewed is too bad to allow it to be seen by the public. Such an individualized determination cannot be guided by reasonably fixed and certain standards.[126]

The Court, in other words, becomes a censor lost in metatextual considerations that necessarily depend for the most part on the personal

---

[123] *Id.* at 47.

[124] Smith v. California, 361 U.S. 147, 160 (1959) (Black, J., concurring).

[125] *See, e.g.*, the facts and the opinions, especially Justice Black's, in New York Times v. Sullivan, 376 U.S. 254 (1964).

[126] Kingsley Pictures Corp. v. Board of Regents, 360 U.S. 684, 690–91 (1959) (Black, J., concurring).

values and predilections of each member of the Court. Justice Black expressed the same idea concerning judicial efforts to define constitutionally protected libel: "No one, including this Court, can know what is or is not constitutionally obscene or libelous under this Court's ruling. . . . In fact, the Court is suggesting various experimental expedients in libel cases, all of which boil down to a determination of how offensive to this Court a particular judgment may be."[127]

The parallels between his disgust with balancing and substantive due process are readily apparent: judges assume the role of policymakers, making policy guided only by their own moral and social values. The echoes of his attack on substantive due process can be heard: "When this Court makes particularized rules on what people can see and read, it determines which policies are reasonable and right, and thereby performs the classical function of legislative bodies directly responsible to the people."[128] Of the Court's primary criterion for determinations of obscenity in the late 1960s—"utterly without redeeming social value"—he said: "This element seems to me to be as uncertain, if not even more uncertain, than is the unknown substance of the Milky Way."[129]

For the same reasons why he rejected balancing and substantive due process, Justice Black included libel and obscenity within the scope of free speech. Balancing "plainly encourages and actually invites judges to choose for themselves between conflicting values."[130] Substantive due process sets judges adrift in the realm of policymaking without any specific guidelines but their own values and predilections. And the implementation of any legal definition of obscenity is almost surely the product of something little more concrete than individual, personal moral standards. Any definition of obscenity, and even libel, is uncertain, and "uncertainty," he said, "cannot easily be reconciled with the rule of law which our Constitution envisages." To put it briefly, defining obscenity is simply not the business of the judiciary: "In my judgment this Court should not permit itself to get into the very center of such policy controversies, which have so little in common with lawsuits."[131]

[127] Curtis Publishing Co. v. Butts, 388 U.S. 130, 171–72 (1967) (Black, J., dissenting).
[128] Mishkin v. New York, 383 U.S. 501, 516 (1966) (Black, J., dissenting).
[129] Ginzburg v. United States, 383 U.S. 463, 480 (1966) (Black, J., dissenting).
[130] Time, Inc. v. Hill, 385 U.S. 374, 399 (1967) (Black, J., concurring).
[131] Kingsley Pictures Corp. v. Board of Regents, 360 U.S. 684, 691 (1959) (Black, J., concurring).

"It seems plausible," writes a perceptive observer of Justice Black's judicial career, "that Justice Black's absolutist approach to the first amendment is ultimately a result of his conception of the judge's interpretative role, not his admitted personal support for the freedoms which the provision protects."[132] Since he could not isolate libel and obscenity with precise, objective lines ("the rule of law"), the absolutist Justice Black decided that all expression short of outright conduct must be protected absolutely by the First Amendment. Seeking to avert a policymaking role with only his own values as guidelines, his decision was itself a policy choice—one, if carried out, which would entail massive repercussions within the body politic—derived from his own beliefs and values which he developed into a judicial philosophy. For neither history nor language requires his interpretation of the scope of free speech.

CONCLUSION

Writing toward the end of the second period of Justice Black's long tenure on the Supreme Court, Charles Black, Jr., sought to explain why the justice promoted the doctrine of absolutism when, after all, "[t]here are no absolutes, not even in the construction of the word 'absolute' when it is used by a sensible man." Black made "a safe conjecture that what is really on the scale is *attitude.* Attitude is what is at stake between Mr. Justice Black and his adversaries."[133] That is, the justice was more sensitive to the central importance of free expression in a democratic society than was the prevailing majority on the Court. His libertarianism was intense; and by thrusting his views in absolutist language at his more cautious colleagues, he could thereby prod them into accepting a much more generous reading of the First Amendment. Black views Justice Black's doctrine of absolutism, and his First Amendment posture in general, as an expedient vehicle for goading the less libertarian majority (during the 1950s) into a more libertarian disposition.

Justice Black continuously tried to encourage a more libertarian outlook on the Court, but libertarianism alone does not explain his resort to absolutism and the expansive scope of free expression that he advocated. If

[132] Yarbrough, *Mr. Justice Black and Legal Positivism,* 57 VA. L. REV. 375, 395 (1971).
[133] Black, Jr., *Mr. Justice Black, the Supreme Court, and the Bill of Rights,* 222 HARPER'S 63, 68 (February 1961).

libertarian results were his only goal, he could just as well, and perhaps more successfully, have endeavored to impel the Court along a more libertarian path without resorting to absolutism, and thus without incurring the endless criticism of his position. (Sidney Hook, for instance, has commented that Justice Black was trying to "be liberal without being intelligent."[134] If his concern were solely to generate libertarian results in the free speech cases during the Cold War period, Justice Black could simply have, and quite justifiably, denounced the Court's prevailing interpretation of the First Amendment as too hollow; or he could have argued, with an abundance of evidence, that the balancing of interests doctrine as employed by the Court at that time was a sham.[135] The submission to absolutism (and its numerous dilemmas)[136] was unnecessary if his only goal were to give First Amendment freedoms the respect they deserve in a free society.

Furthermore, if Charles Black dismisses the notion of absolutism as an unrealistic standard in a society of multiple interests, why should Justice Black's brethren on the Court have been persuaded to move in the direction of that absolutism? "A judge who has not Justice Black's principles," wrote Alexander Bickel in reply to his colleague Black, "will not read his literal absolutes."[137] In fact, an ardent free speech advocate complained that Justice Black's frequent and unilluminating insistence that the First Amendment "means what it says" made it easier for the other members of the Court and his critics to ignore his arguments.[138] Moreover, Black implied that Justice Black himself did not believe in absolutes. Hence, why should anyone else?

There is a good deal more to the doctrine of absolutism than a libertarian's concern for freedom of speech. Of course Justice Black was dedicated to the task of protecting the freedom he believed to be the cornerstone of self-government; and absolutism served him to that end in the 1950s and early 1960s. But the doctrine was as much an outgrowth of his rejection of substantive due process, his rejection of judge-made law narrowing or expanding the written Constitution. Absolutism reflects his

---

[134] Hook, Book Review, 46 The New Leader 11, 15 (May 13, 1963).

[135] *See, e.g.*, Alfange, Jr., *The Balancing of Interests in Free Speech Cases: In Defense of an Abused Doctrine*, 2 L. Transition Q. 35 (1965).

[136] *See* ch. V *infra*.

[137] A. Bickel, The Least Dangerous Branch 97 (1962).

[138] Frantz, *The First Amendment in the Balance*, 71 Yale L. J. 1424, 1432 (1962).

constant search for objectivity and certainty in constitutional law—his pursuit of the "rule of law" in a written constitution, one that sets limits to judicial, as well as legislative or executive, power.[139] During his last term on the Court, he stated the belief underlying his constitutional jurisprudence:

> [U]nbounded authority in any group of politically appointed or elected judges would unquestionably be sufficient to classify our Nation as a government of men, not the government of laws of which we can boast. With a "shock the conscience" test of constitutionality, citizens must guess what is the law, guess what a majority of nine judges will believe fair and reasonable. Such a test wilfully throws away the certainty and security that lies in a written constitution, one that does not alter with a judge's health, belief, or his politics.[140]

A leading critic of Justice Black, Wallace Mendelson, poses this question about the justice: "[I]s he a great judge?" In answer, he says: "Many, of course, insist that he is. This view comes easily, if one is a liberal humanitarian—caring only for the policy outcome of a case. . . . Those, however—whether liberal or conservative—who care about method, who cannot dismiss law entirely as a myth, are not so easily persuaded." Mendelson himself remains unpersuaded that Justice Black was, according to the former's criteria, a great judge because "Mr. Justice Black has seemed so unhampered by 'rules'—so inspired by *ad hoc* or cadi justice— that one might have found him a dedicated practitioner of 'American legal realism.' "[141] He places Justice Black in the company of Justices Stephen J. Field, Rufus W. Peckham, George Sutherland, and Chief Justices John Marshall and Melville W. Fuller, all of whom shared the view that "judicial legislation is not incidental, it is the heart of the judicial process." "Obviously, for Mr. Justice Black law is largely an instrument in the service of his ideals."[142] Reflecting on Justice Black's voting behavior in

---

[139] *See* Howard, *Mr. Justice Black: The Negro Protest Movement and the Rule of Law*, 53 Va. L. Rev. 1030 (1967).

[140] Boddie v. Connecticut, 401 U.S. 371, 393 (1971) (Black, J., dissenting).

[141] Mendelson, *Hugo Black and Judicial Discretion*, 83 Pol. Sci. Q. 17, 35–36 (1970).

[142] Inspired by a mystical admiration for Mr. Justice Frankfurter—Justice Black's chief jurisprudential antagonist on the Court—Professor Mendelson seems to have devoted his scholarly talents to a singularly unsuccessful effort to discredit Justice Black. For example, against overwhelming and convincing evidence to the contrary, he has nonetheless written that "Mr. Justice Black seems as thoroughly activist in economic cases as in those pertaining

numerous areas of constitutional law, he aserts that "Mr. Justice Black's votes were highly predictable in terms that have little to do with the law." Instead, "[h]is background may provide a clue."[143]

As will be suggested in the next chapter, there are several serious weaknesses in Justice Black's absolutism, especially the many unruly dilemmas that confronted him in the 1960s. And, through his jurisprudence, he could, and often did, promote some of his personal values regarding the powers of government and the freedom of individuals. But, of Justice Black and his participation on the Court, Mendelson contrives a distorted image. "Mr. Justice Black tends to focus on the needs of the specific case, as distinct from the demands of legal principles."[144] Of course Justice Black was not unconcerned with the specific result of each case. As Mr. Justice Jackson once implied, dispassionate judges are as real as Easter Bunnies.[145] But Mendelson greatly exaggerates the justice's concern for the result in individual cases. He ignores Justice Black's constant search for objectivity in the law and the impact that objective

---

to civil liberty." MENDELSON, *supra* note 12, at 34. Indeed, he has even berated Justice Black for adhering to a judicial posture which Mendelson has approvingly called "humilitarian" when practiced by his hero, Justice Frankfurter. The Frankfurter doctrine of judicial deference to legislative judgment is for Mendelson the humble recognition of the dispersion of power in our political system. When Justice Black subscribes to that doctrine, as he did in Southern Pacific v. Arizona, 325 U.S. 761 (1945), he is ridiculed as creating "an absolute rule which the Court has never accepted as law." Mendelson, *The First Amendment and the Judicial Process*, 17 VAND. L. REV. 479, 482 & n.18 (1964); *see also* W. MENDELSON, CAPITALISM, DEMOCRACY, AND THE SUPREME COURT 99–102 (1960). In *Southern Pacific* Justice Black believed that the interests involved in regulating the length of trains in interstate transportation should be balanced, but by legislatures, not courts. There the Supreme Court, with Justice Frankfurter in the majority, struck down Arizona's law regulating the length of trains as an unconstitutional burden on the free flow of interstate commerce. Justice Black dissented, adhering to a position which was essentially the same as Justice Frankfurter's refusal to invalidate the Smith Act in *Dennis*. Thus, in attempting to avoid accidents in Arizona resulting from long trains, the Arizona legislature, unlike the Congress which sought to prosecute Communists in spite of the First Amendment, was presumably for Justice Frankfurter devoid of reason. This humility, according to Mendelson, is the virtue of a good judge who believes that the " 'sovereign prerogative of choice' is not for judges." W. MENDELSON, *supra* note 31, at 130–31. But for Justice Black, Mendelson unabashedly claims, the heart of the judicial process is judicial lawmaking.

[143] Mendelson, *supra* note 141, at 34.
[144] W. MENDELSON, *supra* note 31, at 110.
[145] United States v. Ballard, 322 U.S. 78, 94 (1944) (Jackson, J., dissenting).

standards had in curbing judicial discretion.[146] Consequently, Mendelson's portrait of his subject is inaccurate and grossly misleading.[147]

[146] Cases in which Justice Black did not reach the "just" result, which supposedly could have been predicted from his concern for the underdog, are relegated to a footnote by Mendelson, where they are written off as "surprises." Mendelson, *supra* note 141, at 34 & n.65.

[147] In a later article, however, Mendelson appears to concede what he has long denied: that Justice Black's constitutional jurisprudence had at least some control over judicial discretion. *See* Mendelson, *From Warren to Burger: The Rise and Decline of Substantive Equal Protection*, 66 AM. POL. SCI. REV. 1226, 1232–33 (1972).

For example, he does not place Justice Black among "today's judicial activists" who find the strictures of the Bill of Rights "too confining." *Id.* at 1232. He appears to praise Justice Black for "[b]elieving deeply in government by law and not by men." The justice "could not abide doctrines that allow judges to impose their own predilections upon a reluctant community." Referring to the latter's distaste for judicial lawmaking through the vehicle of the Fourteenth Amendment, Mendelson sees the "target" of Justice Black's jurisprudence as "judicial free-wheeling." *Id.* His idea of democracy, Mendelson says, was this: "The people must be free to formulate their own policies on poverty, birth control, and other social issues—however wise or unwise they may seem to judges. It comes at last to this: Courts must protect 'fundamental' interests, but in determining what is fundamental they must look to the Constitution." *Id.* at 1232–33. This appears to be a "sea-change" from statements, made just two years earlier, that Justice Black was a freewheeler "so inspired by *ad hoc* or cadi justice." *See* note 141 *supra*. *See also* Mendelson, *A Response to Professor Goldman*, 39 J. POL. 159, 164 (1977).

CHAPTER V

Judicial Behavior and Judicial Philosophy: The Dilemmas of an Absolutist

THE GREAT DIVIDE

After nearly a quarter of a century of distinguished service, in 1962 Mr. Justice Frankfurter retired from the Supreme Court. The addition of his replacement, Mr. Justice Arthur Goldberg, changed the voting alignment of the Court once more, this time sufficiently to place Justice Black in a libertarian majority. This marks the beginning of the third and last period of his long and influential career on the Court. Furthermore, it might be appropriately called the beginning of the Warren Court Revolution in many fields of constitutional law—a period characterized by increased judicial activism in new dimensions of public policy. At this point Justice Black's unalterable commitment to an absolutist construction of the First Amendment was firmly established. The Justice Black of the 1940s, who had applied the clear and present danger test in conjunction with the "preferred position" doctrine, by the very early 1950s had transformed himself into a vigorous absolutist no longer willing to entrust the protection of freedom of speech to the application of judicial tests because he had witnessed firsthand the fact that such tests are susceptible to judicial manipulation and thus, for judges less libertarian than he, "standing invitation[s] to abridge" the freedom of speech. "This is nowhere more clearly indicated," he lamented, "than by the sudden transformation of the 'clear and present danger test' in *Dennis* v. *United States.*"[1]

In the 1960s a new political and social context emerged within which First Amendment policy continued to unfold and to which previous policy was required to adapt. The campaign against communism at home had largely dissipated, and this new libertarian majority on the Court helped to restore the First Amendment rights of political dissidents.[2] But other First Amendment issues surfaced from the intense political protest that grew up against American military involvement abroad and the too obvious racial, political, social, and economic inequalities at home. A major instrument of dissent utilized by those for whom traditional modes of expression were presumed inadequate, and for whom the powerful means of communication were usually inaccessible, was no longer just speech and association, but symbolic, demonstrative conduct designed to convey the plight and frustration of sundry minority groups dissatisfied with the course of American life and politics. Justice Black carried his constitutional jurisprudence and personal predilections into this era of protest, into a social and political milieu far different from that which earlier had helped solidify and intensify his judicial philosophy. He would soon be called upon to apply his absolutist interpretation of the First Amendment to a new wave of political dissent.

A most important value at the core of his jurisprudence was predictability and certainty in the law.[3] Yet in this last decade of his judicial career, to this whirlwind of social and political protest that found its way to the Supreme Court in the form of free speech claims, Justice Black's response was unanticipated by many of his longtime critics and especially by many admirers to whom his impassioned libertarian opinions of the previous twenty years had established him as the hero of American liberalism.[4]

---

[1] Konigsberg v. State Bar of California, 366 U.S. 36, 63–64 (1961) (Black, J., dissenting).

[2] *See, e.g.*, United States v. Robel, 389 U.S. 258 (1967).

[3] *See* H. BALL, THE VISION AND THE DREAM OF JUSTICE HUGO L. BLACK: AN EXAMINATION OF A JUDICIAL PHILOSOPHY 1–15 (1975).

[4] Wallace Mendelson claims to have witnessed "a sea-change in the thrust of the judge's votes" in the mid to late 1960s. Mendelson, *Hugo Black and Judicial Discretion*, 85 POL. SCI. Q. 17, 38 (1970). Harry Kalven, a longtime admirer of Justice Black, could not understand why the ardent proponent of free expression could have been "so impatient with this kind of communication [symbolic conduct]." Kalven, *Upon Rereading Mr. Justice Black on the First Amendment*, 14 U.C.L.A. L. REV. 428, 449 (1967). However, John P. Frank, one of Justice Black's former law clerks and consistent admirers, professes to be an exception in saying that

Many observers—but certainly not all—have concluded that from 1964 until his death in 1971, Justice Black grew increasingly less libertarian and more reflective of the conservative reaction to the Warren Court's onward march into problems of social and economic, as well as political and racial, inequality.[5] A major issue which impelled his alleged retreat was the spiraling use of symbolic conduct—for example, sit-ins, mass demonstrations, and the wearing of black armbands—as a means of communication and expression.[6] Whereas many of his dissenting opinions in free speech cases involving the Communist party or suspected subversives during the 1950s are replete with deeply felt libertarian beliefs and feelings, many of his dissents in symbolic speech cases in the 1960s seemed inspired by a hard-line, caustic, almost reactionary attitude toward the protesters and demonstrators and the methods by which they chose to convey their dissent.[7]

In other areas of individual freedom Justice Black appeared to make further retreats. In the notable Connecticut Birth Control Case he refused to join most of his colleagues in finding a right to marital privacy emanating from the constitutional text, however fundamental such a right might seem to be:

The Court talks about a constitutional "right of privacy" as though there is some provision or provisions forbidding any law ever to be passed which might abridge the "privacy" of individuals. But there is not. . . . I get nowhere in this case by talk about a constitutional "right of privacy" as an emanation from one or more constitutional provisions. I like my privacy as well as the next one, but I am nevertheless compelled

---

on the basis of earlier voting patterns on the Court, "Black's position on racial 'sit-ins' has been predictable." Frank, *The New Court and the New Deal*, in Hugo Black and the Supreme Court 70 (Strickland ed. 1967).

[5] *See, e.g.*, G. Schubert, The Constitutional Polity 118–129 (1970). Snowiss, *The Legacy of Justice Black*, 1973 Sup. Ct. Rev. 187; Ulmer, *The Longitudinal Behavior of Hugo Lafayette Black: Parabolic Support of Civil Liberties, 1937–1971*, 1 Fla. St. U. L. Rev. 131 (1973).

[6] *See, e.g.*, Tinker v. Des Moines School District, 393 U.S. 503, 515–26 (1969) (Black, J., dissenting); Brown v. Louisiana, 383 U.S. 131, 151–68 (1966) (Black, J. dissenting); Adderley v. Florida, 385 U.S. 39 (1966) (Black, J., speaking for the Court).

[7] *Compare In re* Anastaplo, 366 U.S. 82, 97–116 (1961) (Black, J., dissenting) and Barenblatt v. United States, 360 U.S. 109, 134–62 (1959) (Black, J., dissenting) *with* Brown v. Louisiana, 383 U.S. 131, 151–68 (1966) (Black, J., dissenting) and Bell v. Maryland, 378 U.S. 226, 318–46 (1964) (Black, J., dissenting).

to admit that government has a right to invade it unless prohibited by some specific constitutional provision.[8]

In another dimension of the right of privacy he rejected the Court's inclusion of wiretapping and electronic surveillance within the strictures of the Fourth Amendment's prohibitions against "unreasonable searches and seizures." Disowning any claim of authority to adjust by constitutional interpretation the language of that document, Justice Black argued in dissent that the words of the Fourth Amendment confine its reach to physical searches of tangible items.[9] Thus, on the privacy front of individual rights, Justice Black's voting record disappointed a number of his erstwhile libertarian admirers.

Surprise or frustration following Justice Black's votes on these privacy matters, however, should have visited only those observers who declined to treat seriously the extent to which the justice sought to bind himself to the strictures of his constitutional jurisprudence, particularly the demand of consistency. He never gave the Fourth Amendment much force, and his stringent interpretation could be traced as far back as 1948 when he had agreed in dissent with the view that "[t]he Fourth Amendment is to be construed in light of what was deemed an unreasonable search and seizure when it was adopted."[10] Explaining his position later, he said: "The Fourth Amendment was aimed directly at the abhorred practice of breaking in, ransacking and searching homes and other buildings and seizing people's personal belongings without warrants issued by magistrates."[11] It had little to do, in other words, with eavesdropping; and he refused to update the Constitution so as to extend the Fourth Amendment's protection to circumscribe governmental snooping and wiretapping.

Likewise, his response in the Connecticut Birth Control Case finds its roots in Justice Black's important dissent in *Adamson v. California* (1947),

---

[8] Griswold v. Connecticut, 381 U.S. 479, 508, 509–10 (1965) (Black, J., dissenting).

[9] Katz v. United States, 389 U.S. 347, 367 (1967) (Black, J., dissenting). This narrow construction of the Fourth Amendment was not unique to Justice Black. The Court itself adhered to such a view, Olmstead v. United States, 277 U.S. 438 (1928), a holding not directly overruled until *Katz*.

[10] Trupiano v. United States, 334 U.S. 699, 716 (1948) (Vinson, C. J., dissenting), *quoting from* Carroll v. United States, 267 U.S. 132, 149 (1925). Justice Black had joined the dissenting opinion of the chief justice in rejecting the privacy claim advanced in *Trupiano*.

[11] Katz v. United States, 389 U.S. 347, 367 (1967) (Black, J., dissenting).

where he outlined his incorporationist theory of the Fourteenth Amendment. Paul Freund's pertinent and incisive observation is worth quoting here at length:

> The integrity of Justice Black's philosophy of judicial review was demonstrated vividly when, in the Connecticut birth control case, he found it impossible to recognize privacy as a constitutional right. His dissent puzzled and confounded those observers who had simply been counting judicial votes and ignoring judicial opinions. For the usual agreement in result between Justice Black and a number of his colleagues could not conceal a difference in approach, one that could and did become decisive. Only those forecasters, unhappily all too fashionable, who reduce judicial positions to the binary system of the computer should have been astonished at the cleavage. As far back as *Adamson* v. *California*, Justice Black made it clear that the Bill of Rights sets limits as well as horizons for him, while others on the Court were unwilling to make this commitment and chose to regard the Bill of Rights as furnishing a minimal, not a preemptive, content to the fourteenth amendment.[12]

But it was mainly Justice Black's response to symbolic expression that moved both sympathetic and acerbic critics to inquire why the champion of free speech, the absolutist, reacted so harshly to symbolic conduct and removed that form of expression from the reach of his absolutism. After all, he had felt compelled to give libel and pornography absolute protection, but he appeared to give none at all to symbolic conduct. Much has been written in the effort to uncover and explain the motivations prompting his seeming retreat from liberal judicial activism in cases involving the symbolic protest of the 1960s.[13] Some friendly observers have advanced the "rule of law" explanation; they have concluded that Justice Black objected to the particular methods or extravagances of the protesters who

[12] Freund, *Mr. Justice Black and the Judicial Function*, 14 U.C.L.A. L. REV. 467, 468–69 (1967).

[13] *See, e.g.*, H. BALL, *supra* note 3, at 183–96; Ash, *The Growth of Justice Black's Philosophy on Freedom of Speech: 1962–1966*, 1967 WIS. L. REV. 840; Howard, *Mr. Justice Black: The Negro Protest Movement and the Rule of Law*, 53 VA. L. REV. 1030 (1967); Krislov, *Mr. Justice Black Reopens the Free Speech Debate*, 11 U.C.L.A. L. REV. 189 (1964); McBride, *Mr. Justice Black and His Qualified Absolutes*, 2 LOY. L. A. L. REV. 37 (1969); Rice, *Justice Black, The Demonstrators, and a Constitutional Rule of Law*, 14 U.C.L.A. L. REV. 454 (1967); Yarbrough, *Justice Black and His Critics on Speech-Plus and Symbolic Speech*, 52 TEX. L. REV. 257 (1974); *see also* authorities cited in note 5 *supra*.

ignored recourse to the ordinary channels of political change and, instead, seemed bent on encroaching on other people's rights through sit-ins, demonstrations, and other modes of dissent offensive to some members of the community.[14]

Rejecting this idea, Glendon Schubert, a leading political scientist in the field of empirical judicial behavior, offers an alternative derived from his scientific investigations: Justice Black's "reaction" was not confined to a particular dislike of the peculiar modes of dissent employed by the protesters; instead, his "reaction" was "generic." Age had besieged the elderly jurist, degenerating the great liberal of another era into a senile old man; his reaction to symbolic protest was only the catalyst to a grueling metamorphosis of his disposition on all issues that set him, like the anti-New Deal justices before him, on "the road to reaction." Schubert suggests, then, "a sociopsychological explanation of cultural obsolescence and . . . a biological explanation of psychophysiological senescence."[15] (It has been said that Schubert "stood almost as alone in conclusion as he did in vocabulary.")[16]

Schubert assigns no weight at all to Justice Black's constitutional jurisprudence; he seems willing to explore any hypothesis under the sun before he attaches any significance to Justice Black's determination to adhere to the strictures and doctrines that he synthesized into a judicial philosophy. Indeed, among the paltry fragments of nearly nonexistent evidence mustered to support his stunning conclusion, Schubert includes the justice's well-known and consistently narrow approach to claims of privacy and his rejection of the general right to privacy in the Birth Control Case; presumably, consistent application of a doctrine, where egregious invasions of privacy are involved, indicates cultural dissonance and senility. Such evidence refutes rather than supports his conclusion. Moreover, Schubert appears genuinely puzzled by the fact that Justice Black was determined to stick to the tenets of his judicial philosophy—to restrain, as well as to exercise, the judicial power; to achieve "conservative," as well as libertarian, results:

As we have seen, Black's retreat has had little impact upon the Court's civil liberties policy, because in all except a very few instances there were enough votes, in the new Warren majority, to make decisions

[14] *See* Howard, *supra* note 13, and Rice, *supra* note 13.
[15] Schubert, *supra* note 5, at 118–29.
[16] G. DUNNE, HUGO BLACK AND THE JUDICIAL REVOLUTION 419 (1977).

without the support of either Black or Douglas. But this makes Black's behavior the more interesting, because his articulation of his new conservative faith has come almost completely in dissenting opinions— it has been, that is to say, largely nonfunctional, so far as concerns the Court's policy output. Why, then, did he do it?[17]

(Of course, Justice Black's "liberal" faith had survived in the 1950s almost completely through dissenting opinions; his absolutism and belief in total incorporation of the Bill of Rights into the Fourteenth Amendment were made almost completely in dissent, at least until the retirement of Justice Frankfurter in 1962. "Why, then, did he do it?")

Schubert's unsupported conjectures flow from an undisguised dislike of the results that Justice Black derived, in the late 1960s, from his literalist construction of the Constitution. When it resulted in the promotion of libertarian values, as it did in free speech cases and in those involving the application of the Bill of Rights against the states, it was acceptable to Schubert as a palatable constitutional approach. But once the libertarian values infused in such an approach had finally become largely accepted by the Court of the 1960s, and once further application of it tended to result in a form of judicial self-restraint, adherence to it becomes unsound social policy, and the adherent must be explained away as no longer capable of effectively serving on the United States Supreme Court. In Schubert's blunt words, Justice Black's jurisprudence represented "a poor fit for the needs of our day," and Justice Black's "problem" was that he was "too old for the job."[18]

Justice Black's personal values of liberty, order, and justice were not subdued by the "objectivity" that he claimed to find in the letter of the law and in history. Such a proposition is as unrealistic and dubious as Schubert's presumption that Justice Black's judicial philosophy explains nothing. Nor is it contended that his voting record in the 1960s, or at any other time in his judicial career, was the consequence of nothing more than a literal reading of the Constitution.[19] Rather, Justice Black's judicial

---

[17] Schubert, *supra* note 5, at 125–26.

[18] *Id.* at 122, 129.

[19] For instance, Justice Douglas claimed also to adhere strictly to a literal construction of the Fourth Amendment; yet he concluded with a view which is almost the exact opposite of that of Justice Black. Whereas the latter held that electronic surveillance does not fall within the purview of that amendment, Justice Douglas said that "[e]lectronic surveillance is the greatest leveler of human privacy ever known. How most forms of it can be held 'reasonable' within the meaning of the Fourth Amendment is a mystery . . . . [A] 'strict construction' of

philosophy is inextricably and intimately bound up with his judicial behavior, and it is therefore important to an understanding of that behavior because, by the 1960s, Justice Black was willing—in fact, determined—to follow, often relentlessly, the standards and strictures that he had set for himself.

Probably more than any other member of the Supreme Court, both past and present, Justice Black strove continuously for internal consistency in his opinions and voting record. Consistency was another face of objectivity, and, for him, an omnipresent check on judicial discretion. He was unable to discern a right of privacy in the Constitution. He was joined by his colleague Justice Potter Stewart, who also wrote a ringing dissent chiding the Court majority for writing its own social policies into the Constitution: "With all deference, I can find no such general right of privacy in the Bill of Rights, in any other part of the Constitution, or in any case ever before decided by this Court." "It is the essence of judicial duty," he warned, "to subordinate our own personal views, our own ideas of what legislation is wise and what is not."[20] Eight years later Justice Stewart discarded his "self-restraint" to find in the vagaries of the due process clause of the Fourteenth Amendment a constitutional right of privacy, at least for women—a right of a pregnant woman to terminate her pregnancy prematurely through abortion.[21]

Justice Black developed his constitutional jurisprudence as a reaction to the Supreme Court during the 1920s and 1930s, when that tribunal believed it desirable for the judiciary to regulate the economy through uncertain phrases in the Constitution, and during the 1950s, when a majority of justices felt it the better part of wisdom to sacrifice the Communist party, its sympathizers, and the First Amendment to the winds of public opinion and official suppression. He was determined to adhere to the mandates of his jurisprudence, once developed and however contrived or unsupported, in order to circumscribe the sort of arbitrariness which characterizes the behavior of Justice Stewart. One of the very purposes of a written constitution, Justice Black so often repeated, was to preclude, or at least confine, the arbitrariness of those whose solemn duty

---

the Fourth Amendment is necessary if every man's liberty and privacy are to be constitutionally honored." United States v. White, 401 U.S. 745, 756 (1971) (Douglas, J., dissenting).

[20] Griswold v. Connecticut, 381 U.S. 479, 530–31 (1965) (Stewart, J., dissenting).

[21] Roe v. Wade, 410 U.S. 113, 167–71 (1973) (Stewart, J., concurring).

it is "to say what the law is."[22] As was argued previously, his desire to rewrite the words of the Fourteenth Amendment, so as to be read as shorthand for the Bill of Rights, was impelled not so much by the force of historical evidence, as by what he saw as the need to set limits to the potentially limitless domain of the "liberty . . . without due process" clause of the Fourteenth Amendment—the font of most major rulings in constitutional law. His rendition of the meaning of this clause, however unfounded historically and contrary to the clause as written, was not merely a plan to advance libertarian values but also a design to constrain judicial policymaking by forcing judges to interpret and protect only the rights outlined specifically in the constitutional text.

This is not to say, however, that Justice Black successfully synthesized into a consistent whole more than three decades of constitutional adjudication. A generation in time provides unforeseen constitutional issues, and judicial responses to them, with ample opportunity to emerge, develop, change, and fade away. And a generation on the Court provides even the most detached judge with a panorama of events salient enough to affect his disposition toward liberty and order. A change in Justice Black's attitude toward dissent and protest no doubt occurred sometime during the 1960s. For instance, he had dissented in the *Feiner* case in which the Court upheld the power of police to stop a man who was delivering a racially inflammatory speech to a mixed crowd of whites and blacks on a busy street corner in Syracuse, New York. Justice Black denounced the Court's decision, saying: "I will have no part or parcel in this holding which I view as a long step toward totalitarian authority."[23] This statement was made at the height of his libertarian concern for freedom of expression, in the year in which he converted to absolutism. But when the facts of Dick Gregory's civil rights march in Chicago were before the Supreme Court for review in 1969, Justice Black treated them as evidence of what can happen when political views clash in the streets: "These facts disclosed by the record point unerringly to one conclusion, namely, that when groups with diametrically opposed, deep-seated views are permitted to air their emotional grievances, side-by-side, on city streets, tranquility and order cannot be maintained even by the joint efforts of the finest and best officers

---

[22] Judicial arbitrariness was a main target of Justice Black's constitutional jurisprudence. *See, e.g.*, Green v. United States, 356 U.S. 165, 193–219 (1958) (Black, J., dissenting).

[23] Feiner v. New York, 340 U.S. 315, 323 (1951) (Black, J., dissenting).

and of those who desire to be the most law-abiding protestors of their grievances."[24]

His attitude toward the conflict between public order and freedom of expression was undoubtedly tempered by witnessing the turbulence, violence, and upheaval that seemed to characterize the politics of the late 1960s. It is not enough to explain his disposition in terms of a consistent dedication to the "rule of law."[25] Certainly he believed strongly in the rule of law; it was the foundation on which he erected his constitutional faith. But there are marked differences in his understanding of that concept before and after the protests and dissents that often went up in flames during the 1960s. Concluding his examination of Justice Black's response to the civil rights protest movement, law professor A. E. Dick Howard, a sympathetic critic and former law clerk to Justice Black, says that the latter believed in "a rule of law for the people at large: an appeal to channel grievances into lawful processes and not to take the law into their own hands, lest the undermining of order be the undoing of liberty."[26] Wrongs, in other words, should be remedied through the rule of law rather than sit-ins and mass demonstrations. But soon after his conversion to absolutism, Justice Black joined Justice Douglas's dissenting opinion, where the two agreed that "when a legislature undertakes to proscribe the exercise of a citizen's constitutional right to free speech, it acts lawlessly; and the citizen can take matters in his own hands and proceed on the basis that such a law is no law at all."[27] This is not the sentiment of respect for the rule of law that resounded throughout many of the biting dissents which Justice Black wrote in the 1960s.[28]

Justice Black's disposition toward protest and dissent did become increasingly more cautious and conservative during the last years of his life, and this change in attitude affected his voting behavior on this issue during his last years on the Court. Nevertheless, to concentrate analysis

[24] Gregory v. Chicago, 394 U.S. 111, 117 (1969) (Black, J., concurring). Sylvia Snowiss makes this same observation in *The Legacy of Justice Black, supra* note 5, at 234.

[25] Howard, *supra* note 13, and Rice, *supra* note 13.

[26] Howard, *supra* note 13, at 1086. Howard underestimates the change in Justice Black's attitude, but he carefully takes into consideration the crucial importance of the Justice's judicial philosophy. *Id.* at 1052–70.

[27] Poulos v. New Hampshire, 345 U.S. 395, 423 (1953) (Douglas, J., dissenting).

[28] *See, e.g.*, Brown v. Louisiana, 383 U.S. 131, 151–68 (1966) (Black, J., dissenting); *see also* Tinker v. Des Moines School District, 393 U.S. 503 (1969); Bell v. Maryland, 378 U.S. 226 (1964).

only on such a change—whether brought on by uneasiness, fear, or even old age—is erroneously to underestimate Justice Black's allegiance to the demands of his judicial philosophy, which he had painstakingly sought to develop and enforce. "No one can read . . . Justice Hugo Black's opinions," writes Sidney Hook, "without becoming aware of the overriding importance of his philosophy."[29]

There were, of course, numerous internal contradictions in his constitutional jurisprudence, as there were in his changing attitude toward political protest. These juridical inconsistencies, which will be discussed presently, derive from the inevitable difficulties and dilemmas that challenge an absolutist who disavows a previous commitment to balancing and still desires to appear consistent over time. To point out the holes and contradictions in the web of consistency that Justice Black conscientiously attempted to create, however, is insufficient evidence to dismiss his jurisprudence as irrelevant, a façade, or unimportant in explaining his judicial behavior. Schubert enlists Justice Black's repeated rejection of privacy claims to support the conclusion that something had gone awry with the justice and his values. But that a jurist for more than twenty years adhered to a narrow and restrictive conception of the Fourth Amendment is a fact which ought to be assigned a most prominent place in any realistic and serious examination of his treatment of that amendment during his last years; and this is especially true of Justice Black. Drawing attention to the weaknesses, defects, and dangers of such an approach to the important issue of privacy is insufficient to sustain the expectation that Justice Black would not therefore seriously have followed it. His professions of literalism and absolutism, his desire to abide by the standards and principles embodied in his constitutional jurisprudence, are important factors that cannot be ignored in the effort to explain his judicial behavior. Justice Black was most conspicuous in his endeavor to maintain consistency by adhering, at times almost dogmatically, to the dictates that he evolved into his constitutional faith.

SYMBOLIC CONDUCT AND THE FIRST AMENDMENT

Perhaps his doctrine of absolutism was one well suited to the claims of freedom of speech and association as they were raised in the context of the

[29] Hook, *A Philosopher Dissents in the Case of Absolutes*, in Free Speech and Political Protest 78 (Summers ed. 1967).

1950s. His absolutist stance was a libertarian's reaction to the Court's willingness to accommodate First Amendment freedoms to facilitate the official effort to exterminate a despised and feared political ideology. It does not exaggerate the purpose of the First Amendment to interpret it as a rigid bar against official attempts to suppress an unorthodox political creed and to make life intolerable for those who commit the sin of ever having been even remotely associated with it. But after the anti-Communist crusade had burned itself out, the demand for constitutional protection began shifting emphasis to matters beyond belief, speech, and association to public assembly and symbolic conduct as expressions of protest and dissent. Incumbent on Justice Black was the task of explaining and adapting the reach of his absolutist interpretation of the First Amendment. The problem for him now was to articulate the freedoms that the First Amendment (and through the Fourteenth) places wholly beyond the reach of government.

Symbolic conduct very often conveys legitimate ideas on important public issues. In the words of Mr. Justice Jackson:

Symbolism is a primitive but effective way of communicating ideas. The use of an emblem or flag to symbolize some system, idea, institution, or personality, is a short cut from mind to mind. Causes and nations, political parties, lodges, and ecclesiastical groups seek to knit the loyalty of their followings to a flag or banner, a color or design. The State announces rank, function, and authority through crowns and maces, uniforms and black rrobes; the Church speaks through the Cross, the Crucifix, the altar and shrine, and clerical raimant. Symbols of State often convey political ideas just as religious symbols come to convey theological ones. Associated with many of these symbols are appropriate gestures of acceptance or respect: a salute, a bowed or bared head, a bended knee. A person gets from a symbol the meaning he puts into it, and what is one man's comfort and inspiration is another's jest and scorn.[30]

Remaining faithful to the major tenets of his jurisprudence—such as the doctrine of absolutism—lest obvious inconsistency reduce his jurisprudence to a sham or a hoax, was a primary preoccupation of Justice Black in the 1960s. His response to the issue of symbolic conduct during this period must be examined as that of a confirmed, often doctrinaire,

[30] West Virginia Board of Education v. Barnette, 319 U.S. 624, 632–33 (1943) (Jackson, J.).

absolutist struggling to resolve a complex jurisprudential dilemma: How to control the effects of an absolutist construction of the First Amendment without destroying the concept or plausibility of absolutism; how to apply an absolutist interpretation of that amendment to a form of expression which in practice cannot be accorded absolute protection.

The symbolic protest of the 1960s conveyed social problems and ideas that are much more deserving of First Amendment protection than the ideas, if any, that radiate from hard-core pornography or the ideas that attend the ruin of innocent victims of calculated lies. Yet Justice Black, who protected absolutely both malicious defamation and hard-core pornography by reading such "speech" into the meaning of free speech and press guaranteed by the First Amendment, attempted a solution to his jurisprudential dilemma by withdrawing symbolic conduct from the purview of constitutionally protected expression. "In giving absolute protection to free speech," he explained, "I have always been careful to draw a line between speech and conduct."[31]

As an absolutist, he was, of course, compelled to remove conduct, such as picketing, marching, and sit-ins, from the reach of the First Amendment's guarantee of freedom of expression. Not even one prepared to extend absolute constitutional protection to pornography and libel was prepared to argue that the First Amendment extends to people an absolute right to mobilize, picket, and march for their causes, however noble. Had he included such conduct, or other symbolic expression, within the domain of freedom of expression, he would have had either to foster a constitutional and commonsense absurdity by granting absolute protection to any conduct that manifests an idea or to deny absolutism altogether and thus repudiate a view of the First Amendment, and one of the pillars of his jurisprudence, which he had defended for more than a decade. The absolutist Justice Black was thus caught in the grips of Justice Frankfurter's foreboding in the *Dennis* case that "[a]bsolute rules would eventually lead to absolute exceptions, and such exceptions would eventually corrode the rules."[32]

Justice Black sought to make it clear that the distinction between

---

[31] H. Black, A Constitutional Faith 53 (1968).

[32] Dennis v. United States, 341 U.S. 494, 524 (1951) (Frankfurter, J., concurring). Justice Frankfurter's criticism of absolutism was probably leveled against Alexander Meiklejohn, another proponent of that doctrine. See A. Meiklejohn, Free Speech and Its Relation to Self-Government (1948).

speech and conduct was not a makeshift fabrication to save his absolutism, but instead a corollary to his continuous denunciation of substantive due process and the judges who depart from the Constitution as written when construing that document. "I want to emphasize that in harmony with my general views of faithful interpretation of the Constitution as written," he maintained, "I am vigorously opposed to efforts to extend the First Amendment's freedom of speech beyond speech . . . ." Such expansion, he argued, compels judges to substitute their own words and values for those fixed by the First Amendment. To those who spoke "many loose words . . . about an alleged right to picket, demonstrate, or march," Justice Black responded by saying that "[m]arching back and forth [or any other form of symbolic conduct], though utilized to communicate ideas, is not speech and therefore is not protected by the First Amendment."[33] To him, the meaning of freedom of speech was distinct and clear: "that government shall not do anything to the people . . . either for the views they have or the views they express or the words they speak or write."[34] The free speech guarantee protects speech; conduct beyond speech is not protected.

However, in constructing this dichotomy he was not asserting that no constitutional protection for peaceful symbolic expression could be found within the broad expanses of the First Amendment's freedom of speech. Categorically to deny that symbolic expression was at least an indirect beneficiary of First Amendment protection would have been to repudiate a series of cases in which the nonabsolutist Justice Black of the 1940s readily found constitutional support for conduct apart from pure speech.[35] Thus, he erected still another dichotomy, this one "subtle and difficult to articulate, yet profound," writes Tinsley E. Yarbrough in defense of Justice Black[36]—the distinction between "direct" and "indirect" abridgments of freedom of speech. Governmental legislation aimed directly at suppressing expression, even that enmeshed in symbolic conduct, is absolutely forbidden; but laws that purport to regulate conduct, and only indirectly impinge on ideas or expression, are not prohibited by the First Amendment so long as such laws are not discriminatory, not

[33] H. BLACK, *supra* note 31, at 44–45, 54.

[34] *Id.* at 45.

[35] *See, e.g.*, Martin v. Struthers, 318 U.S. 141 (1943) (Black, J.); Drivers Union v. Meadowmoor Co., 312 U.S. 287, 299–317 (1941) (Black, J., dissenting); Thornhill v. Alabama, 310 U.S. 88 (1940).

[36] Yarbrough, *supra* note 13, at 276.

overboard, and are clearly and specifically drawn. Indeed, he went so far as to suggest that all picketing, marching, and patrolling could be constitutionally prohibited under a law which meets all these standards.[37]

Justice Black explained that a law which had the "effect" of indirectly infringing on freedom of speech would be subjected to a balancing test; that is, "it would be unconstitutional if under the circumstances it appeared that the State's interest in suppressing the conduct was not sufficient to outweigh the individual's interest in engaging in conduct closely involving his First Amendment freedoms."[38] Yet, Patrick McBride has commented that Justice Black never really partook of such balancing in symbolic conduct cases; or, if he did, he discussed all the important interests of government in regulating such conduct but found "nothing at all on the free expression side of the scales."[39] Responding to McBride's claim, Yarbrough contends that "[c]ontrols over the types of activities involved in the [symbolic] protest cases were valid per se," in Justice Black's view, "so long as they were nondiscriminatory and free of the vices of vagueness and over-breadth."[40] Yarbrough's explication seems to reflect the approach that Justice Black actually took in symbolic conduct cases during the 1960s.[41] Still, such an approach was not truly a balancing test in that Justice Black never squarely raised or answered the question, as he clearly did in such cases in the 1940s,[42] whether the social interest in symbolic expression outweighed the social interest in regulating it. Perhaps he used the word "balancing" in describing his approach in the 1960s to build a bridge of consistency—an effort to make it appear that his constrained and confined approach to free speech cases in that period was merely the application of the approach he had embraced in the 1940s, when the nonabsolutist Justice Black could, and did, freely balance interests in all free speech cases.

---

[37] Cox v. Louisiana, 379 U.S. 536, 581 (1965) (Black, J., concurring in part, dissenting in part).

[38] *Id.* at 577.

[39] McBride, *supra* note 13, at 65.

[40] Yarbrough, *supra* note 13, at 279.

[41] *See, e.g.*, Coates v. Cincinnati, 402 U.S. 611, 616–17 (1971) (Black, J., dissenting); Schacht v. United States, 398 U.S. 58 (1970) (Black, J.); Gregory v. Chicago, 394 U.S. 111, 113–26 (1969) (Black, J., concurring); Cox v. Louisiana, 379 U.S. 536, 575–84 (1965) (Black, J., concurring in part, dissenting in part).

[42] *See, e.g.*, West Virginia Board of Education v. Barnette, 319 U.S. 624, 643–44 (1943) (Black, J., concurring).

Justice Black and His Dichotomies

The juridical distinction between speech and conduct is a valid, literal response to the view that symbolic conduct is constitutionally protected "speech." A majority of the Court in 1969, for example, held that the wearing of black armbands as a means of public protest is expression "closely akin to 'pure speech.' "[43] Justice Black's reply that such conduct is not pure "speech" is sustainable by a literal reading of the word "speech" in the First Amendment. As a juridical concept, this dichotomy theoretically extricated Justice Black and his absolutism from the dilemma of applying the First Amendment's command to a form of expression which cannot be accorded absolute protection. However, as a discernible and intelligible distinction for adjudicating concrete constitutional cases, the line between speech and conduct that he created was extremely confusing.

The problem of implementation is not so much in drawing a line between pure speech and everything beyond it. Harry Kalven, for instance, raised this criticism, contending that the distinction "will not work," for "all speech is necessarily 'speech plus.' If it is oral, it is noise and may interrupt someone else; if it is written, it may be litter."[44] His argument was that the free speech guarantee must protect something more than speech—some conduct—if only to protect pure speech. But Justice Black was not claiming that the First Amendment, or even the free speech guarantee by itself, does not protect any conduct beyond pure speech. He spoke of "activity specifically protected by the First Amendment."[45] Many of the free speech cases of the 1950s, moreover, in some of which he articulated the doctrine of absolutism, were cases that did not involve pure speech, but rather the freedom of association—a right clearly implicit in the First Amendment, although a freedom involving behavior other than speech.[46]

The difficulty in implementing the dichotomy between speech and conduct is thus not in the line distinguishing pure speech from speech-plus, although this is nonetheless a valid critism of a dichotomy purportedly grounded in "literalism." Instead, the practical difficulty is in find-

---

[43] Tinker v. Des Moines School District, 393 U.S. 503, 505 (1969).

[44] H. KALVEN, THE NEGRO AND THE FIRST AMENDMENT 200–201 (1965).

[45] Gregory v. Chicago, 394 U.S. 111, 119 (1969) (Black, J., concurring).

[46] *See, e.g.*, Barenblatt v. United States, 360 U.S. 109 (1959); Yates v. United States, 354 U.S. 298 (1957); Adler v. Board of Education, 342 U.S. 485 (1952); Wieman v. Updegraff, 344 U.S. 183 (1952); Dennis v. United States, 341 U.S. 494 (1951).

[159]

ing the line that must distinguish constitutionally protected speech freedoms from unprotected conduct. Had Justice Black truly drawn the line
"vigorously" and "carefully" between pure speech and everything beyond
speech, as he insisted that he had always done, his later attempts to isolate
the "freedom of speech" entitled to absolutism might have been intelligible
and consistent, rather than reflecting disingenuous attempts to make it
seem that as both absolutist and nonabsolutist he had, in fact, been
consistent.

The line between speech and conduct, which he claimed always to
have observed and articulated while on the Court, is so circuitous and
elusive as to be practically and constitutionally meaningless. This is not
the place comprehensively to survey Justice Black's application of the
speech-conduct dichotomy during the more than three decades of his
service on the Supreme Court. To illustrate the nature of the difficulty
inherent in the dichotomy, and the confusion compounded by Justice
Black's treatment of it, it is enough to focus on a few examples. One such
example is *Thornhill* v. *Alabama* (1940).[47]

Byron Thornhill was arrested for peacefully picketing the premises of
the Brown Wood Preserving Company. Speaking for all except Justice
James C. McReynolds, who dissented without opinion, Justice Murphy
invalidated on its face as unconstitutional the following state statute under
which Thornhill was convicted:

Any person or persons, who, without a just cause or legal excuse
therefor, go near to or loiter about the premises or place of business of
any other person, firm, corporation, or association of people, engaged
in a lawful business, for the purpose, or with the intent of influencing,
or inducing other persons not to trade with, buy from, sell to, have
business dealings with, or be employed by such persons, firm, corporation, or association, or who picket the works or place of business of such
other persons, firms, corporations, or association of persons, for the
purpose of hindering, delaying, or interfering with or injuring any
lawful business or enterprise of another shall be guilty of a misdemeanor; but nothing herein shall prevent any person from soliciting
trade or business from a competitive business.[48]

Seeking to make his agreement in *Thornhill* consistent with his later
view compelled by absolutism that picketing, however peaceful, is con-

[47] 310 U.S. 88.
[48] *Id.* at 91–92.

duct unprotected by the First Amendment, Justice Black insisted that *Thornhill* had "held the Alabama law against picketing unconstitutional not as a violation of the First Amendment, but denied enforcement because of its overbroadness and vagueness."[49] To be sure, the Court did strike the statute down because it was overbroad, but not for the reasons implicit in Justice Black's explanation. In the eyes of the Court in *Thornhill*, the statute was too broad in that it seemed clearly to punish as criminal not just violent or en masse picketing but communicative conduct which the Court held was protected by the First Amendment—here, peaceful picketing publicizing the facts of a labor dispute. A year later Justice Black referred to the *Thornhill* case as one involving "curtailment of free expression."[50] The statute was so sweeping in its proscriptions that it amounted to an unconstitutional prior restraint of freedom of expression. As J. Woodford Howard, one of Justice Murphy's biographers, has explained: "The basic flaw [of the statute], by common consensus, was its absolute character, its failure to distinguish the coercive aspects of picketing from harmless forms; and toward the final phase of drafting [the Court's opinion], greater attention was focused on this aspect of the case."[51]

The Court invoked the clear and present danger test in resolving the issue in *Thornhill*. The state of Alabama no doubt was empowered to take adequate steps to ensure the preservation of peace and the protection of privacy, lives, and property. But here the state had gone too far:

> [N]o clear and present danger of destruction of life or property, or invasion of the right of privacy, or breach of the peace can be thought to be inherent in the activities of every person who approaches the premises of an employer and publicizes the facts of a labor dispute involving the latter. We are not now concerned with picketing *en masse* or otherwise conducted which might occasion such imminent and aggravated danger to these interests as to justify a statute narrowly drawn to cover the precise situation giving rise to the danger. . . . [The statute] in question here does not aim specifically at serious encroachments of these interests and does not evidence any such care in balancing these interests against the interest of the community and that of the individual in freedom of discussion on matters of public concern.[52]

[49] H. BLACK, *supra* note 31, at 57.
[50] Carpenters Union v. Ritter's Cafe, 315 U.S. 722, 731 (1942) (Black, J., dissenting).
[51] J. HOWARD, MR. JUSTICE MURPHY: A POLITICAL BIOGRAPHY 246 (1968).
[52] 310 U.S. at 105.

The constitutional defect of Alabama's law, therefore, was its failure to distinguish between protected and unprotected picketing. Rather than holding that the First Amendment did not protect picketing at all, the opinion reads as a treatise on freedom of expression, an opinion in which "Justice Murphy launched one of the Court's boldest and most controversial experiments with freedom of expression—the doctrine that constitutional guarantees of free communication include peaceful picketing. . . . The *Thornhill* decision thus not only enlarged the concept of free speech but also fertilized 'the voice of labor,' and made picketing a matter of constitutional import, all at the expense of traditional state rules." And, as Justice Murphy's opinion circulated among his brethren for their approval, excluding Justice McReynolds who dissented, "[o]nly Justice Stone raised serious criticism and even his was not directed against the basic premise that Thornhill's conduct was speech and therefore constitutionally protected."[53]

Giboney v. *Empire Storage and Ice Company* (1949) is the case perhaps most often cited by Justice Black and his defenders to provide tangible evidence that he had always observed a line between speech and conduct, such as picketing, in adjudicating First Amendment cases.[54] Of course, he had always set limits to what could be done in the name of free speech; certain conduct, however closely involving First Amendment freedoms, cannot find a place among First Amendment values. But *Giboney* had nearly nothing to do with the delineation between "speech" and "conduct" in the sense in which Justice Black used those terms in the 1960s. In fact, as with *Thornhill*, the reasoning employed in *Giboney* by the Court, through Justice Black himself, seems to refute the conclusion that he later attributed to that case.

Giboney and other union members and officials were enjoined from peacefully picketing the place of business of the Empire Storage and Ice Company. Through such picketing the union sought to induce Empire to refuse to sell ice to nonunion peddlers. But the company would not be induced and, in view of the fact that its business was diminished by nearly

---

[53] J. HOWARD, *supra* note 51, 238, 239, 247.

[54] 336 U.S. 490 (1949). In defending his speech-conduct dichotomy, Justice Black frequently referred to *Giboney. See* H. BLACK, *supra* note 31, at 56–57. His defenders have also referred to this case. See Howard, *supra* note 13, at 1076–77; Yarbrough, *supra* note 13, at 254–66.

85 percent, sought a court order to restrain the union from continuing its picketing. The company "charged that the concerted efforts of union members to restrain Empire from selling to nonunion members was a violation of the anti-trade-restraint [state] statute and that an agreement by Empire to refuse to make such sales would violate the same statute." The contention made by the union that is relevant here was "that the injunction against [the] picketing . . . is an unconstitutional abridgment of free speech because the picketers were attempting peacefully to publicize truthful facts about a labor dispute."[55] Both the trial and state supreme courts agreed with Empire, and Giboney and the union appealed to the Supreme Court.

Speaking for a unanimous Court, Justice Black resorted to a candid balancing of competing interests and consequently concluded that the state's interests, under the circumstances of the case, outweighed the interests of Giboney and the union in picketing the premises of Empire's business in order to publicize the facts of a labor dispute.[56] Missouri had a valid interest in preventing the restraint of trade, and it passed a valid anti-trade-restraint law to protect that interest. And the injunction issued against the union to enforce that interest did not violate the First Amendment, the Court argued, because the union's "publicizing" via picketing could not be treated "in isolation."

For the placards were to effectuate the purposes of an unlawful combination, and their sole, unlawful immediate objective was to induce Empire to violate the Missouri law by acquiescing in unlawful demands to agree not to sell ice to nonunion peddlers. It is true that the agreements and course of conduct here were as in most instances brought about through speaking or writing. But it has never been deemed an abridgment of freedom of speech or press to make a course of conduct illegal merely because the conduct was in part initiated, evidenced, or carried out by means of language, either spoken, written, or printed. . . . Such an expansive interpretation of the constitutional guarantees of speech and press would make it practically impossible ever to enforce laws against agreements in restraint of trade as well as many other agreements and conspiracies deemed injurious to society.[57]

[55] 336 U.S. at 493, 497–98.
[56] *Id.* at 501.
[57] *Id.* at 498, 502.

"In this situation," Justice Black reasoned, "the injunction did no more than enjoin an offense against Missouri law, a felony."[58]

Thus the illegal "conduct" at which the injunction was aimed was not the picketing element apart from speech, but the consequences of the continuation of the union's "publicizing," consequences that eventually would have produced a violation of Missouri's anti-trade-restraint law. Indeed, Justice Black in *Giboney*, as he and the Court had earlier in *Thornhill*, treated interchangeably the picketing and the speech intrinsically involved in the pickets and placards. Rejecting the union's free speech claim, Justice Black said: "It rarely has been suggested that the constitutional freedom for speech and press extends its immunity to speech or writing used as an integral part of conduct in violation of a valid criminal statute."[59] The union's behavior in "publicizing" through picketing was regarded by Justice Black as the speech that nevertheless could not immunize illegal conduct—here, the violation of Missouri's law—merely because such speech was an integral part of that conduct.

There are several interesting observations that follow from *Giboney* and the reasoning advanced by Justice Black therein to uphold the state court's injunction. First, not only is this a case which does not elaborate and substantiate the distinction between speech and all conduct beyond speech, such as picketing; it is also a case which, if it does not demonstrably refute the proposition that Justice Black had always adhered to such a dichotomy, at least serves immeasurably to blur whatever line he insisted that he had drawn. This is not to suggest that he once treated picketing as pure speech. Rather, in *Thornhill*, *Giboney*, and other picketing cases it is apparent that he viewed peaceful picketing to publicize ideas as constitutional freedom within the meaning of "freedom of speech." It was a freedom not absolute; it could be regulated, as, of course, it must be. In *Giboney* he no doubt recognized "that appellants were doing more than exercising a right of free speech or press. . . . They were exercising their economic power together with that of their allies to compel Empire to abide by union rather than by state regulation of trade." But this is a speech-plus distinction entirely unrelated to the one he would later pursue between speech and conduct such as picketing, because in *Giboney* the

[58] *Id.* at 498.
[59] *Id.*

speech was simply presumed to be "the display of placards by peaceful picketers."[60]

Second, what prompted the issuance of the injunction was the effect of the ideas that the union had sought to publicize on Empire's business. The purpose of "the placards," Justice Black explained, "was to induce Empire to violate the Missouri law by acquiescing in unlawful demands to agree not to sell ice to nonunion peddlers." In other words, the state's injunction had the direct effect of suppressing the content of the placards—the speech itself—state action that Justice Black would later argue is absolutely forbidden. But in *Giboney*, after recognizing "the essential importance to our society of a vigilant protection of freedom of speech and press," and that "[s]tates cannot consistently with our Constitution abridge those freedoms to obviate slight inconveniences or annoyances," Justice Black stated: "But placards used as an essential and inseparable part of a grave offense against important public law cannot immunize that unlawful conduct from state control."[61] Here is a rejection of the absolutism and the dichotomies he would later espouse, for Justice Black was here saying that when the consequences of speech (here the peaceful picketing) result in a clear violation of valid state law, that expression can be balanced against the interests of the state, as was done in *Giboney*. Or perhaps the state injunction was, as Justice Black's defenders have assumed without explanation, only an indirect abridgment of the First Amendment—an abridgment that did not have the effect of directly suppressing ideas.[62] If so, it becomes all the more impossible to determine what kind of state action would have that effect; it makes the direct-indirect dichotomy that much more nebulous, vaporous, and useless as an aid to judges who must adjudicate real cases.

Finally, aside from certainly confusing, if not squarely refuting, both the line Justice Black claimed always to have drawn between speech and conduct such as picketing and any coherent distinction between direct and indirect effects, the rationale put forth in *Giboney* could be read further to repudiate Justice Black's later claim that government is absolutely forbid-

---

[60] *Id.* at 503, 498.

[61] *Id.* at 501–2.

[62] Both Howard and Yarbrough treat the state action in *Giboney* as having had an "indirect" effect on speech. Howard, *supra* note 13, at 1076–77; Yarbrough, *supra* note 13, at 264–66.

den, consistent with the First and Fourteenth Amendments, to pass any defamation laws to protect the innocent from injurious lies. Surely a state has a legitimate and valid interest in protecting its citizens against the calculated destruction of their privacy, reputations, liberty, and even their lives, resulting from defamatory falsehoods—a state interest indisputably as great as that sanctioned in *Giboney*. And certainly the free speech interest in lies is less than that in knowing the truthful facts about a labor dispute. Upholding an award in damages against one who maliciously defames another in violation of a state libel law, a state judge might rely on the reasoning in *Giboney*, concluding perhaps as follows:

> Maliciously destroying an innocent individual's reputation, and the consequences which follow that destruction, is a "grave offense against an important public law." Although such "illegal conduct" was accomplished through speech and press, "the record does not permit this publicizing to be treated in isolation." The lies published about this person were an "essential and inseparable part of a course of conduct which is in violation of state law." And "[i]t rarely has been suggested that the constitutional freedom of speech and press extends its immunity to speech or writing used as an integral part of conduct in violation of a valid criminal [or civil] statute. We reject that contention now."

The disposition and judicial reasoning that Justice Black attributed to *Thornhill* and *Giboney* are not there. The speech-conduct and direct-indirect dichotomies, as Justice Black explained them, cannot be found in either case because neither the Court nor Justice Black adjudicated free speech cases with such dichotomies as standards to guide them. Of course conduct, such as willfully destroying another's property, was never protected in the name of freedom of expression, but not because such a conclusion derived from any dichotomy; the denial of such protection is common sense. Picketing was never regarded as an absolute—not because of calculations based on dichotomies, but again because of common sense. The speech-conduct distinction advocated by Justice Black in the 1960s was one which separated freedom of speech from conduct such as picketing, marching, demonstrating—conduct obviously requiring regulation, but conduct that the Justice Black of another period could and did protect. In the 1940s he needed and resorted to no dichotomies because he was a judge who could balance interests freely, uninhibited by the dilemmas of absolutism.

In still another case in the 1940s, though one not involving labor picketing, Justice Black once more failed to mark the mysterious and inscrutable line separating speech from conduct. This case is more revealing than either *Thornhill* or *Giboney* (although one never much discussed either by Justice Black or his defenders); in this case he seems unmistakably to have rejected not only the need or desirability but also the possibility of such a distinction. In *United Public Workers* v. *Mitchell* (1947) the Supreme Court upheld a section of the Hatch Act which prohibited a certain class of federal employees from taking "any active part in political management or in political campaigns." The act did not, however, forbid such employees to "express their opinions on all political subjects and candidates."[63]

Justice Black dissented. "Since under our common political practices most causes and candidates are espoused by political parties," he said, "the result is that, because [these federal employees] are paid out of the public treasury, all these citizens who engage in public work can take no really effective part in campaigns that may bring about changes in their lives, their fortunes, and their happiness." He found a "hopeless contradiction" in the fact that the act purported to leave an employee's right of free expression unfettered, while it nevertheless prohibited political participation in campaigns. Here was Congress by statute attempting to draw the line between speech and conduct. But Justice Black viewed it as hopelessly contradictory and undesirable: "The right to vote and privately to express an opinion on political matters, important though they be, are but parts of the broad freedoms which our Constitution has provided as bulwark of our free political institutions. Popular government, to be effective, must permit and encourage much wider political activity by all the people."[64]

Not only was the line between speech and conduct drawn by the Hatch Act undesirable because it ran counter to the meaning of popular government; it was a line impossible constitutionally to sustain because of conflict with the First Amendment itself:

I think the Constitution prohibits legislation which prevents millions of citizens from contributing their arguments, complaints, and suggestions to the political debates which are the essence of our democracy; prevents them from engaging in organizational activity to urge others to vote and take an interest in political affairs; bars them from performing the interested citizen's duty of insuring that his and his fellow citizens'

[63] 330 U.S. 75.
[64] *Id.* at 106–7, 108–110 (Black, J., dissenting).

votes are counted. Such drastic limitations on the right of all the people to express political opinions and take political action would be inconsistent with the First Amendment's guaranty of freedom of speech, press, assembly, and petition.

"That Amendment," he concluded, "unless I misunderstand its meaning, includes a command that the Government must, in order to promote its own interest, leave the people at liberty to speak their own thoughts about government, advocate their own favored governmental causes, and work for their own political candidates and parties."[65]

It is not very clear from Justice Black's opinion in *United Public Workers* at which point constitutionally protected "political action" ceases and unprotected "conduct" begins. Certainly door-to-door solicitation for the purpose of encouraging citizens to vote or publicizing a favored candidate's name and beliefs, and even bouncing basketballs or juggling eggs in the streets to raise funds for his support, is "political action" within the meaning of Justice Black's dissenting opinion. But, then, it is only by raw judicial fiat (the enemy of Justice Black's judicial philosophy) that he could later insist on the conclusion that a public demonstration, peaceful picketing, a sit-in, or the wearing of black armbands is conduct, not speech, and therefore outside the reach of his absolutism.

Justice Black frequently spoke of the First Amendment as written in "plain words, easily understood," even by "a rather backward country fellow," as he described himself.[66] First Amendment freedoms, he exclaimed, were outlined in "principles . . . precisely stated," "for all who care to see."[67] He praised the framers of the First Amendment for casting its guarantees in language that "could never be misunderstood."[68] His law clerks have pointed out his earnest desire to clarify and simplify the law and his "belief that the law and its ways ought to be as intelligible to the citizenry of Clay County, Alabama, as to the law faculty of a great University."[69] Thus, it is no little irony that, for Justice Black, the adjudication of free speech cases should take place within the intersection

[65] *Id.* at 111, 114.
[66] Cahn, *Justice Black and First Amendment "Absolutes": A Public Interview*, 37 N.Y.U. L. REV. 549, 553–54 (1962).
[67] Wilkinson v. United States, 365 U.S. 399, 422 (1961) (Black, J., dissenting).
[68] New York Times v. United States, 403 U.S. 713, 717 (1971) (Black, J., concurring).
[69] Howard, *supra* note 13, at 1052.

of two ambivalent and nebulous dichotomies. Freund, for instance, thought it "somewhat surprising" that Justice Black resorted to the direct-indirect dichotomy. "In the field of national power over matters affecting commerce," Freund explained, "it proved to be so artificial and eventually discredited a criterion that one might hesitate long before reviving it in the vital area of the first amendment."[70]

The problem of ascertaining the distinction between direct and indirect abridgments is complicated enough by the fact that only infrequently does a government forthrightly acknowledge that the goal of its legislation is directly to suppress freedom of expression. Rather than to demarcate the line and to disclose the judicial procedure for detecting it, even during the last years of his life Justice Black's own search for the distinction served, once again, only to confound the problem even more.

Two cases, *Street* v. *New York* (1969) and *Cohen* v. *California* (1971), involved issues of symbolic expression.[71] In *Street*, a man distraught over the shooting of civil rights figure James Meredith took to a street corner and publicly burned in protest an American flag which he owned. He was subsequently arrested and convicted for violating a state law making it a crime "publicly [to] mutilate, deface, defile, or defy, trample upon, or cast contempt upon either by words or act" an American flag. Speaking for the Court, Justice Harlan reversed Street's conviction and remanded the case to the lower court because the verdict rendered by the trial judge had been too general, thus making it impossible to discern whether Street had been convicted for what he had done to the flag or for what he said about it while burning it. Justice Black dissented, arguing that it was clear that the offense for which Street had been convicted "was the burning of the flag and not the making of any statements about it."[72] Arguably, then, this was an indirect infringement on the expression of ideas implicit in Street's symbolic conduct.[73] He added, however, that he would have had no trouble reversing this or any other conviction had it rested on a direct abridgment of freedom of speech. "If I could agree," he explained, "with the Court's interpretation of the record as to the possibility of the conviction's resting on these spoken words [which Street had uttered while he

---

[70] Freund, *supra* note 12, at 472.
[71] 394 U.S. 576; 403 U.S. 15.
[72] 394 U.S. at 609 (Black, J., dissenting).
[73] *But cf.* Spence v. Washington, 418 U.S. 405 (1974).

had burned the flag], I would firmly and automatically agree that the law is unconstitutional."[74]

Two years later, in *Cohen* v. *California*, Justice Black was presented with the opportunity "automatically" to reverse such a conviction and further clarify the boundaries between direct and indirect abridgments of freedom of expression and between speech and conduct. Paul Cohen walked into Los Angeles County Courthouse wearing a jacket bearing the words "Fuck the Draft." He was arrested, convicted, and sentenced to thirty days in jail for violating a state statute making it a criminal offense "maliciously and willfully [to] disturb the peace or quiet of any neighborhood or person . . . by . . . offensive conduct." Speaking for the Court once again, Justice Harlan reversed Cohen's conviction. The issue, he said, "stands out in bold relief. It is whether California can excise, as 'offensive conduct,' one particular scurrilous epithet from the public discourse, either upon the theory of the court below that its use is inherently likely to cause violent reaction or upon a more general assertion that the States, acting as guardians of public morality, may properly remove this offensive word from the public vocabulary." The Court majority found the state's interests clearly insufficient constitutionally to sustain the attempt to "make the simple public display here involved of this single four-letter expletive a criminal offense," and hence reversed the conviction.[75]

In the context of Justice Black's dichotomies, the Court treated the issue as a direct abridgment of expression—a matter of offensive speech, not offensive conduct apart from speech. But Justice Black disagreed, joining the brief dissenting opinion of Justice Blackmun, where "Cohen's absurd and immature antic" was viewed as "mainly conduct and little speech."[76] Presumably for Justice Black the abridgment was only indirect and thus outside the pale of the First Amendment's protection. But, had Cohen entered the courthouse without the expletive inscribed on his jacket, he surely would not have been convicted because he obviously would not have been arrested. Apparently, the addition of the "speech" made Cohen's behavior "conduct" and therefore beyond the purview of freedom of speech! To say the least, this is bizarre reasoning by which to make "the law and its ways . . . intelligible to the citizenry of Clay County, Alabama, . . . the law faculty of a great University," or anybody. It

[74] 394 U.S. at 609.
[75] 403 U.S. at 22–23, 26 (1971).
[76] 403 U.S. at 27 (Blackmun, J., dissenting).

succeeds only in adding more confusion to that already stultifying the attempt to draw the nebulous and artificial lines which create the dichotomies. Cohen's conviction was clearly based on the offensiveness of the words by which he chose to express his emotions and feelings about military conscription during America's intervention in Indochina—the same words which, if printed in a book or uttered in a motion picture, would have found a protecting hand in Justice Black's First Amendment on the assumption that the words in either of these contexts are "speech" or "press" absolutely protected. But in Cohen's case the use of the expletive was "mainly conduct and little speech."

The practical difficulty of implementing Justice Black's dichotomies becomes clear when one speculates how the justice might have employed his distinctions to resolve some hypothetical problems. Punishment for perjury, like punishment for libel, is certainly aimed directly at "spoken words." Perjury, like libel, consists of lies—"mere words." Thus, by the logic of his opinion in *Street* and consistent with his position on libel, Justice Black would have had "automatically" to reverse convictions for perjury. But, too, he could have relied on the rationale of *Giboney*, thereby sustaining such convictions since words, like "placards," cannot make otherwise illegal conduct—here, obstructing the fair administration of justice, a "grave offense"—constitutionally immune. Or, with equal persuasiveness, he could have called perjury itself "mainly conduct and little speech," and have been done with the matter.

The last opinion which Justice Black wrote as a member of the Supreme Court was in the celebrated Pentagon Papers Case, where he said: "In the First Amendment the Founding Fathers gave the free press the protection it must have to fulfill its essential role in our democracy. . . . The press was protected so that it could bare the secrets of government and inform the people."[77] But consider the possibility of an agent of the government who has official knowledge of national security and military secrets and who subsequently decides to "bare the secrets of government" to inform the country's foreign rivals and enemies as well as its own people. How does a judge distinguish between saying and doing, between "mere words" and mere treason?

Or imagine the following hypothetical set of facts: Local government officials requested a local playwright and producer to stage a public play

[77] New York Times Co. v. United States, 403 U.S. 713, 717 (1971) (Black, J., concurring).

about *Human Life in the Twenty-First Century.* The play was to be performed for the public on an outdoor stage in a public park on a Sunday
afternoon. But during the performance local officials abruptly halted its
continued showing because the participants on the stage, according to
script, actually engaged in overt sexual acts before hundreds of families
gathered in the audience. How would a judge who is locked into Justice
Black's matrix of dichotomies treat this situation were it brought before
him in the context of a free speech case?

Justice Black would have ruled against the government had the case
involved a movie version of the play, since such "speech"—or "press"?—he
had insisted was absolutely protected.[78] He could have held, then, that
the play is the technological and thus constitutional equivalent of the
movie, and likewise absolutely protected. After all, such protection for the
play would more accurately reflect the intent of the framers since they
could not have foreseen the invention of movies, though they enjoyed
plays; and, if the film is protected by "plain words, easily understood," as
Justice Black said, then the play must obviously be so protected. Yet, on
the other hand, he might have concluded that the play was "mainly
conduct and little speech." since, in fact, it was mainly conduct and little
speech. But, then again, even if conduct, the effect of the injunction was
directly to suppress expression that local officials did not like; thus the
injunction should have been absolutely forbidden.

Rather than illuminating the essential task for judges, and instead of
making "the law and its ways . . . intelligible," judicial reasoning based on
Justice Black's ethereal dichotomies brings to mind Felix Cohen's poignant criticism of jurists of an earlier generation who articulated a good
deal of "nonsense" to weave their symmetries, to preserve their syl-
logisms, and to avoid grounding their decisions in candid considerations of
social policy and its consequences. A judge afflicted with the dilemmas
that Justice Black created for himself cannot resolve the difficulties, but
perforce takes refuge by escaping to the world of fictions and ambiguity-
-to the heaven of legal concepts where, as depicted in the jurist Jhering's
dream, there exists "a dialectic-hydraulic-interpretation press, which
could press an indefinite number of meanings out of any text or statute, an
apparatus for constructing fictions, and a hair-splitting machine that could

---

[78] *See, e.g.,* Kingsley Pictures Corp. v. Regents, 360 U.S. 684, 690–91 (1959) (Black, J.,
concurring).

divide a single hair into 999,999 equal parts and, when operated by the most expert jurists, could split each of these parts again into 999,999 equal parts."[79]

The First Amendment and the Letter of the Law

The edifice of elusive dichotomies and distinctions collapsed when the literalist was compelled to take his absolutism beyond the boundaries of "the freedom of speech, or of the press," and into those establishing a "right of the people peaceably to assemble, and to petition the Government for a redress of their grievances." The foundation of Justice Black's absolutism in the area of the First Amendment freedoms was the literal command "Congress shall make no law"—a prohibition which casts its shield over all First Amendment freedoms, not just speech and press.

Apparently attributing to Justice Black the indefensible view that the First Amendment does not protect at all any conduct, Patrick McBride has written: "No matter how often and adamantly Black may repeat his formula that the Amendment protects 'speech' and not 'conduct,' it is hard to see how any sensible reading of the English language could comprehend a 'right of the people peaceably to assemble' to be something apart from 'conduct.' "[80] However, the speech-conduct dichotomy was one confined to the interpretation of the free speech guarantee. Justice Black did not say, as he never could have consistent with the language of the First Amendment, that the amendment protects no conduct; he said, instead, that it holds no protection for "conduct which is more than 'speech,' more than 'press,' more than 'assembly,' and more than 'petition,' as those terms are used in the First Amendment."[81] The problem for Justice Black on the issue of assembly, then, was to define that right absolutely protected by the First Amendment.

A public and peaceful demonstration or marching in the streets in protest of some governmental policy, although not literally "speech"—but certainly expression—might be deemed "assembly" or "petition" within the meaning of the First Amendment. In fact the Court, including Justice Black, so described a civil rights march and peaceful demonstration by

---

[79] Cohen, *Transcendental Nonsense and the Functional Approach*, 35 COLUM. L. REV. 809, 809 (1935).

[80] McBride, *supra* note 13, at 47.

[81] Gregory v. Chicago, 394 U.S. 111, 124 (1969) (Black, J., concurring).

nearly two hundred people on South Carolina's state house grounds. Speaking for all but Justice Clark, who dissented, Justice Stewart concluded "that in arresting, convicting, and punishing the petitioners under the circumstances disclosed by this record [showing no danger of a breach of the peace], South Carolina infringed the petitioners' constitutionally protected rights of free speech, free assembly, and freedom to petition for redress of their grievances." This case involved "an exercise of these basic constitutional rights in their most pristine and classic form. The petitioners . . . peaceably assembled at the site of the State Government and there peaceably expressed their grievances 'to the citizens of South Carolina, along with the Legislative Bodies of South Carolina.' "[82]

Marching and demonstrating in protest, perhaps even picketing, can thus be adjudged "assembly"—a right, when exercised peaceably, protected by the First Amendment. The very "conduct" that in the 1960s Justice Black insisted was not "speech" and therefore outside the scope of the free speech guarantee can literally find its way back into the reach of the absolute prohibition "Congress shall make no law." Of course, not all or any conduct fits within the meaning of assembly, and hence is absolutely protected. But, as the Court argued, surely a civil rights march or demonstration can be so called. Moreover, conduct necessarily requiring regulation that is "more than 'assembly,' " in Justice Black's view, can nevertheless be viewed as "petition"—a right equally placed wholly beyond the reach of government under Justice Black's construction of the First Amendment. For instance, four members of the Court viewed as "petition" the peaceful gathering outside a city jail to protest policies of racial segregation and discrimination. Writing in dissent for himself, Justices Abe Fortas and William J. Brennan, Jr., and Chief Justice Warren, Justice Douglas said:

> The right to petition for the redress of grievances has an ancient history and is not limited to writing a letter or sending a telegram to a congressman; it is not confined to appearing before the local city council, or writing letters to the President or Governor or Mayor. . . . Those who do not control television and radio, those who cannot afford to advertise in newspapers or circulate elaborate pamphlets may have only a more limited type of access to public officials. Their methods should not be

[82] Edwards v. South Carolina, 372 U.S. 229, 235 (1963).

condemned as tactics of obstruction and harassment as long as the assembly and petition are peaceable, as these were.[83]

In defining the rights of assembly and petition, Justice Black, of course, held the prerogative of excluding such conduct from the meaning of assembly. Whatever it might mean, he conceivably could have said that it is a right which involves none of these things, such as picketing, patrolling, marching, or demonstrating. A distinguished authority on the First Amendment, Thomas I. Emerson, concludes (as apparently does McBride) that Justice Black accepted this extremely constrictive view of assembly and petition, saying that "Justice Black's position . . . takes 'conduct,' as distinct from 'speech,' completely outside the First Amendment. 'Conduct' is defined as including 'standing,' 'patrolling,' and 'marching.' " Emerson argues that "[o]n [Justice Black's] formulation there is very little left to the right of assembly or petition."[84]

Indeed, Justice Black appears to have advanced such a view when he said: "It is not difficult to understand why the Founders believed that the peace and tranquility of society absolutely compel the . . . distinction between constitutionally protected freedom of religion, speech and press, and nonconstitutionally protected conduct like picketing and street marching."[85] Of course, such conduct must be regulated in the interests of peace and order. But, however carefully he tried to make it appear that such conduct falls outside the purview of the amendment, he did not, as he clearly could not, treat assembly as anything but the sort of conduct to which Emerson refers—the very conduct which Justice Black sought to exclude from the reach of absolutism.

Although he called picketing and marching "nonconstitutionally protected conduct," it is clear from the foregoing passage that the distinction which Justice Black made does not apply to assembly or petition, as those rights are not even mentioned in this passage. In explaining his position he hardly mentioned them at all; the first step in his attempt to resolve his

---

[83] Adderley v. Florida, 385 U.S. 39, 49–51 (1966) (Douglas, J., dissenting). Such rights are, however, not absolute: "[I]t may be necessary to adjust the right to petition for redress of grievances to other interests inhering in the uses to which the public property is normally put." *Id.* at 54. This balancing may seem somewhat strange for Justice Douglas, a professed First Amendment absolutist. But, unlike Justice Black, Justice Douglas was a libertarian absolutist not disposed to be concerned with the constraints of consistency or the dilemmas of absolutism.

[84] T. EMERSON, THE SYSTEM OF FREEDOM OF EXPRESSION 298 (1970).

[85] H. BLACK, *supra* note 31, at 55.

dilemmas was, indeed, to avoid them. For example, in *Cox* v. *Louisiana* (1965), wherein he delivered a lengthy exposition of his First Amendment posture during the 1960s, he stated the distinction between speech and conduct. "I have no doubt," he explained, "about the general power of Louisiana to bar all picketing on its streets and highways. Standing, patrolling, or marching back and forth on streets is conduct, not speech, and as conduct can be regulated or prohibited." And, earlier in his opinion in *Cox*, he again ignored the right of assembly and the problems that such a right creates for absolutism and the speech-conduct dichotomy:

> A [nondiscriminatory and narrowly drawn] state statute . . . regulating *conduct*—patrolling and marching—as distinguished from *speech*, would in my judgment be constitutional, subject only to the condition that if such a law had the effect of indirectly impinging on freedom of speech, press, or religion, it would be unconstitutional if under the circumstances it appeared that the State's interest in suppressing the conduct was not sufficient to outweigh the individual's interest in engaging in conduct closely involving his First Amendment freedoms.

Finally, he said, "when passing on the validity of a regulation of conduct, which may *indirectly* infringe on free speech, this Court does, and I agree that it should, 'weigh the circumstances' in order to protect, not to destroy, freedom of speech, press, and religion."[86]

It is difficult to mistake the fact that Justice Black's absolute right of assembly is deliberately ignored in his discussions of the speech-conduct dichotomy.[87] But it is not difficult to understand why: Not only can the regulation of conduct such as marching and demonstrating on public streets indirectly affect expression; such regulation might be aimed directly at the exercise of a constitutional right, since such conduct, although not "speech," might itself be "assembly"—not just "conduct closely involving . . . First Amendment freedoms." And any law, Justice Black insisted, that directly encroaches on First Amendment rights is absolutely forbidden by that amendment. Since assembly can be construed to include the very conduct which Justice Black correctly maintained must be regulated "directly," in arguing that such regulation is constitutional he ignored the right of assembly.

---

[86] 379 U.S. 536, 581, 577, 578 (Black, J., concurring in part, dissenting in part).

[87] In his Carpentier Lecture on the First Amendment, Justice Black ignored the right of assembly in at least nine places where he attempted to explain the distinction between constitutionally protected and unprotected behavior. *See* H. BLACK, *supra* note 31, at 44–61.

Yet he accepted the view that such conduct does fall within the meaning of "assembly." To gather and organize on public streets, he said, is "to assemble."[88] And he frankly acknowledged that a peaceful march and demonstration along city streets is clearly within the meaning of free assembly. In *Gregory* v. *Chicago* (1969), the Court unanimously reversed the convictions of Dick Gregory and his fellow civil rights demonstrators who marched along the streets of Chicago protesting governmental policies that they considered racially discriminatory. Speaking for the Court, Chief Justice Warren said that "[p]etitioner's march, if peaceful and orderly, falls well within the sphere of conduct protected by the First Amendment."[89] Justice Black agreed:

> And it must be remembered that only the tiniest bit of petitioners' conduct could possibly be thought illegal here—that is, what they did after the policeman's order to leave the area. The right "peaceably to assemble, and to petition the Government for a redress of grievances" is specifically protected by the First Amendment. For the entire five-mile march, the walking by petitioners in a group, the language, and the chants and songs were all treated by the city's assistant attorney and its specially detailed policeman as lawful, not lawless, conduct.[90]

The fundamental dilemma posed by absolutism thus became insoluble for Justice Black: If he were realistically to continue to adhere to the doctrine of absolutism as a jurisprudential concept, he could not in practice apply it to the conduct that comprises the right of assembly; on the other hand, the literalist Justice Black could not treat "assembly" as anything but conduct necessarily requiring governmental regulation and control, even if peaceful and orderly. It is a constitutional right which, to be protected at all, must be balanced against other societal interests. But balancing an admitted constitutional right against competing social interests is the antithesis of absolutism. Having attempted, unsuccessfully, to seem consistent by insisting that he had always and carefully distinguished between "speech" and all else in enforcing the free speech guarantee, there remained for Justice Black the formidable task of stating his case for an absolute right of assembly. After having ignored that right wherever possible in explaining his reconstruction of the First Amendment, he

---

[88] Cox v. Louisiana, 379 U.S. 536, 581 (1965) (Black, J., concurring in part, dissenting in part).

[89] 394 U.S. 111,112.

[90] 394 U.S. at 119 (Black, J., concurring).

ultimately confronted it and the insoluble juridical dilemma that attached to it.

It is important at this point to recall the essence of Justice Black's conception of the judicial function. If a right were not protected by the Constitution as written, or at least derivable from a liberal reading of language, Justice Black would refuse, as he did in the Connecticut Birth Control Case, to create such a right by adjusting constitutional language. To rewrite the Constitution was to violate his oath of office. Conversely, if a right plainly did exist in the Constitution, it was his sworn duty to enforce it, not to balance it against conflicting values and interests. Commenting on this aspect of Justice Black's judicial philosophy, Freund has said that one of the "consequences of Justice Black's insistence on natural meaning" is that "the rights enumerated will receive extremely generous protection."[91] And Justice Black stated that the right of assembly was no exception. "The First and Fourteenth Amendments," he said, "take away from government . . . all power to restrict freedom of speech, press, and assembly. . . ."[92] But, in resolving his dilemma, he was faced with a Hobson's choice of abolishing absolutism or the right of assembly, and it was the latter which he sacrificed, for he could not deny that "no law" means no law. Retaining a place in the theory and rhetoric of absolutism, the constitutional right of assembly was reduced to a privilege which, subject only to restraints of writing clear, specific, nondiscriminatory laws, government may withhold, extend, or withdraw.

His solution was clear and simple. People have an absolute right of assembly, he said, but only *"where people have a right to be for such purposes."*[93] Constitutional rights cannot be exercised on private property against the will of the owner. "The right to freedom of expression is a right to express views," he explained, "not a right to force other people to supply a platform or a pulpit."[94] With this much few would disagree, for people do not have an absolute right to exercise their constitutional rights however and wherever they choose. But, if private property is not the place to exercise the right of assembly, according to Justice Black, neither is public property, unless government agrees to provide a place. Thus his dilemma

[91] Freund, *supra* note 12, at 468.

[92] Cox v. Louisiana, 379 U.S. 536, 578 (1965) (Black, J., concurring in part, dissenting in part).

[93] *Id.*

[94] Bell v. Maryland, 378 U.S. 226, 345 (1964) (Black, J., dissenting).

vanished as the constitutional right of assembly evaporated: The people have an absolute right of assembly whenever the government so allows. Transcending the middle of an insoluble dilemma, Justice Black found himself promoting a contradiction in terms.

To support this, the literalist Justice Black once again resorted to the language of the First Amendment. "That language," he argued, "deals not with supplying people a place to speak, write, or assemble, but only with the right to speak, write, or assemble. . . . Nor does a grant to the people of the right to assemble, to speak, or to write carry any inference that the government must provide streets, buildings, or places to do the speaking, writing, or assembling."[95]

Aside from the fact that an absolute right conditioned upon government's willingness to grant it makes no sense at all (indeed, to make such a statement is to refute it), Justice Black's conclusion neither is consistent with his past behavior and beliefs nor comports with his enforcement of other constitutional rights. In 1939 the Court invalidated local ordinances that prohibited the distribution of printed matter, and holding of public meetings without permits, in the streets and other public places. Announcing the judgment of the Court in an opinion in which only Justice Black joined, Justice Roberts said: "Wherever the title of streets and parks may rest, they have immemorially been held in trust for the use of the public and, time out of mind, have been used for purposes of assembly, communicating thoughts between citizens, and discussing public questions. Such use of the streets and public places has, from ancient times, been a part of the privileges, immunities, rights, and liberties of citizens."[96] Three years later, a unanimous Court, speaking again through Justice Roberts, voiced the same conclusion about the use of the streets: "The Court has unequivocally held that the streets are proper places for the exercise of the freedom of communicating information and disseminating opinion and that, though the states and municipalities may appropriately regulate the privilege in the public interest, they may not unduly burden or proscribe its employment in these public thoroughfares."[97]

Another explicit rejection of the view that government is not constitutionally required to provide a place to exercise First Amendment freedoms came from Justice Black himself in 1946, when he led the Court in an

[95] H. BLACK, *supra* note 31, at 58.
[96] Hague v. Committee for Industrial Organization, 307 U.S. 496, 515 (1939).
[97] Valentine v. Chrestensen, 316 U.S. 52, 54 (1942).

[179]

opinion invalidating a town regulation (as enforced through a state tres-pass law) which flatly prohibited the distribution of literature anywhere on the town premises. This opinion is doubly interesting in view of the fact that the town (Chicasaw, Alabama) was company-owned—private property. Reversing the conviction of a Jehovah's Witness for distributing religious literature in violation of the regulation, Justice Black said:

> Had the title to Chicasaw belonged not to a private but to a municipal corporation and had the appellant been arrested for violating a mu-nicipal ordinance rather than a ruling by those appointed by the cor-poration to manage a company town it would have been clear that appellant's conviction must be reversed. Under our decision[s] . . . , neither a state nor a municipality can completely bar the distribution of literature containing religious or political ideas on its streets, sidewalks and public places . . . .

No town, whether private or not, has "sufficient power to pass an ordi-nance completely barring the distribution of religious literature."[98]

The fact that the town was private property was not dispositive, he said: "Ownership does not always mean absolute dominion. The more an owner, for his advantage, opens up his property for use by the public in general, the more do his rights become circumscribed by the statutory and constitutional rights of those who use it." Unencumbered by the strictures and dilemmas of absolutism, Justice Black balanced the interests of private property against First Amendment freedoms: "When we balance the Constitutional rights of owners of property against those of the people to enjoy freedom of press and religion, as we must here, we remain mindful of the fact that the latter occupy a preferred position."[99] Another Justice Black would later reject such balancing; he would also hold a rather different view of private property. "We must never forget," he warned those who would allow protesters to stage sit-ins at public libraries and restaurants, "that the Fourteenth Amendment protects 'life, liberty, and property' of all people generally, not just some people's 'liberty,' and some kinds of 'property.' "[100] This clause of the Fourteenth Amendment, which he earlier had sought to rewrite in the form of the Bill of Rights so as to eliminate substantive due process and the sanctity of private property,

[98] Marsh v. Alabama, 326 U.S. 501, 504, 505 (1946).
[99] *Id.* at 506, 509. *See also* Jamison v. Texas, 318 U.S. 413 (1943) (Black, J.).
[100] Bell v. Maryland, 378 U.S. 226, 332 (1964) (Black, J., dissenting).

would thus be later revisited by a Justice Black in search of a check on his absolutism and a resolution of his dilemmas.

Finally, Justice Black's assertion that government is not required to provide the citizens of the United States with a place to exercise their absolute constitutional right of assembly is contrary to his enforcement of other constitutional rights, particularly the Sixth Amendment right to counsel. The First Amendment, to be sure, does not expressly stipulate that the government must provide a place to exercise such rights of assembly; but, as Justice Black and the rest of the Court of the 1940s assumed, the streets and other public places are the appropriate and lawful places to assemble. The provision creating the right to counsel does not anywhere specify that those criminal defendants too poor to hire counsel are entitled, nonetheless, to counsel at government expense. In fact, the original purpose of the Sixth Amendment's right to counsel was merely to guarantee that the criminally accused would not be prohibited from retaining or employing their own counsel.[101] But it was Justice Black who spearheaded the argument, ultimately triumphantly, that for the indigent defendants unable to employ their own counsel that right remains a hollow guarantee unless they are furnished with public assistance.[102] But what could be more irrelevant, a more meaningless constitutional guarantee, than an absolute right to assemble, but only in midair?[103] This desperate construction of the constitutional right of assembly could be propounded only by a judge eager to seem consistent without advocating a position which would be absurd—yet, if indeed he were consistent with his past behavior, a position which would seem compelled by his literalism and his absolutism. The resort to unintelligible and nebulous dichotomies and the creation of an insubstantial (but absolute!) right of assembly were the options available to a judge preoccupied with the appearance of consistency and deadlocked by a dogma.

[101] *See* W. BEANEY, THE RIGHT TO COUNSEL IN AMERICAN COURTS (1955); W. MENDELSON, CAPITALISM, DEMOCRACY, AND THE SUPREME COURT 106 (1960).

[102] *See* Gideon v. Wainwright, 372 U.S. 335 (1963) (Black, J.); Betts v. Brady, 316 U.S. 455, 474–77 (1942) (Black, J., dissenting).

[103] *See Mr. Justice Black and the Bill of Rights, CBS Reports*, December 3, 1968, where Eric Sevareid asked Justice Black to explain such a right.

CHAPTER VI

Conclusion

In an essay published three years after the death of Justice Black, Tinsley Yarbrough painstakingly endeavors to document lines of consistency linking the justice's treatment of symbolic conduct in the 1960s with his earlier approach to free speech cases. Finding what he deems to be that consistency, he contends that "the tenor of Black's opinions did change over time," but those "differences in tone . . . are attributable to something other than a basic change in Justice Black's constitutional philosophy."[1]

The linchpin that held together the major tenets of his judicial philosophy remained intact throughout Justice Black's long service on the Supreme Court; the premise of his constitutional faith remained unchanged—that legislators, not judges, are empowered to set social and economic policy subject to the specific constitutional restrictions which it is the duty of the courts to enforce. But Yarbrough takes his case further, suggesting something beyond this underlying, general consistency. He claims that "[t]hroughout his distinguished career on the United States Supreme Court," Justice Black's construction of the First Amendment remained unaltered: that the speech-conduct and direct-indirect

---

[1] Yarbrough, *Justice Black and His Critics on Speech-Plus and Symbolic Speech*, 52 Tex. L. Rev. 257, 262 (1974).

dichotomies—and, presumably, the doctrine of absolutism—had always been the mainstays of his approach to free speech cases.[2]

Justice Black, however, had not always adhered to such dichotomies, nor had he always been an absolutist. The transition to absolutism in the 1950s was a major turning point in the development of his constitutional jurisprudence—"a basic change," indeed. The nonabsolutist of the 1940s had balanced constitutional rights not only against countervailing governmental claims but also against each other when they conflicted in the context of a concrete case—for example, in *Marsh* v. *Alabama* (1946), when he weighed "the Constitutional rights of owners of property against those of the people to enjoy freedom of the press and religion."[3] As an absolutist he denigrated and repeatedly condemned, as a device to destroy the Constitution, this process of constitutional adjudication.

His undisguised record as a balancer who had protected some forms of symbolic expression (especially labor picketing), his later desire at least to seem consistent with this past, and the practical need to restrict the reaches of his absolutism are all factors that help to explain why in the 1960s Justice Black sought refuge in the hidden meaning of his unarticulated dichotomies. They were created to set practical limits to his newly acquired absolutist stance on First Amendment issues; they were concepts devised to manipulate and manage this absolutism through a web of unanticipated problems and also to establish some basis for the belief that his doctrinal approach to free speech cases had never changed.

Strangely enough, Yarbrough acknowledges as much when he asserts that the resort to "facile" dichotomies "actually was the only position that [Justice Black] could have adopted and still remain faithful to his absolutist first amendment philosophy"—that the dichotomies were developed "in order to retain absolutism in certain first amendment contexts." In fact, Yarbrough's major conclusion is that the dichotomies "enabled [Justice Black] to reject . . . untenable alternatives"—either abandoning absolutism altogether or protecting absolutely any conduct that expresses an idea.[4]

Yarbrough's anaylsis, however, overlooks a crucial fact: that Justice Black was not an absolutist in the 1940s, that he freely—with no reaľ attachment to any dichotomies—balanced interests in all free speech cases. The transition from balancer to absolutist was for Justice Black of pro-

[2] *Id.* at 257 and *passim.*
[3] 326 U.S. 501, 509 (Black, J.).
[4] Yarbrough, *supra* note 1, at 273, 275, 283.

found jurisprudential significance, at least insofar as it generated a host of juridical dilemmas that he could not resolve. In his effort to defend Justice Black against the critics' charges of inconsistency, Yarbrough has put forth the claim of consistency that the Justice contrived in his own defense—a consistency more apparent than real.

A jurist who commits himself to the doctrine which holds that there are absolute constitutional rights must inevitably encounter at least some of the difficulties and dilemmas which beset Justice Black. The problems for the latter were compounded by the language from which he derived his absolutism: "Congress shall make no law," a command which arches over all the rights contained in that amendment. The problems abound from the fact that the First Amendment is introduced by an absolute standard which, in a society without anarchy, cannot realistically be applied to all the rights as written in that amendment. His problematic treatment of the right of assembly betrays the nature of his predicaments and belies the assumption that the routine tasks of a literalist are easy—even when construing "plain words, easily understood." The consignment of the right of assembly to the unsure, contradictory status of an absolute right conditioned upon the government's willingness to grant it was all the recourse available to the absolutist Justice Black.

Freedom of assembly was not the only First Amendment guarantee that raised such a problem for him. The "free exercise of religion" was also scuttled in the endeavor to preserve his absolutism as a plausible and practical doctrine. The exercise of religion can be literally interpreted to include conduct that is not very conducive to absolutism, at least not in an organized society. Indeed, as long as the right means anything, it would be difficult to conclude that it does not protect some conduct. Hence that right was destined to share a fate similar to that which was bestowed by Justice Black upon the right of assembly. The element of conduct implicit in the free exercise guarantee was removed as Justice Black asserted his position, once more, as the result of plain language: "[I]n harmony with my general views of faithful interpretation of the Constitution as written, . . . I am vigorously opposed to efforts to extend the First Amendment's . . . freedom of religion beyond religious beliefs."[5]

However, it does not follow at all from the language of the amendment that the free exercise clause guarantees no more than mere believing. In

---

[5] H. BLACK, A CONSTITUTIONAL FAITH 44–45 (1968).

1972 the Court affirmed that past "decisions have rejected the idea that religiously grounded conduct is always outside the protection of the Free Exercise Clause."[6] In the 1940s Justice Black had also construed the right to include more than freedom of belief, agreeing that freedom of religion has "a double aspect—freedom of thought and freedom of action."[7] He had insisted, for instance, that door-to-door distribution of literature is a constitutional right which "widely established religious organizations have used . . . [in] disseminating their doctrines."[8]

As a practical matter, however, freedom of religion as conduct is a constitutional right which, like assembly, cannot be enforced except through a process of balancing or accommodating conflicting interests. The community has legitimate social interests that frequently require the subordination of the individual's interest in engaging in conduct which the tenets of his or her faith may encourage or command. "But to agree that religiously grounded conduct must often be subject to the broad police power of the State," the Court has held, "is not to deny that there are areas of conduct protected by the Free Exercise Clause and thus beyond the power of the State to control, even under regulations of general applicability."[9] Delineating protected from unprotected conduct involves the Court in appraising conflicting values.

Pursuing objective, textual standards for the resolution of First Amendment problems, Justice Black allowed himself to be trapped by his absolutism, confined to an essentially all or nothing approach in this crucial realm of constitutional adjudication. He included libel and obscenity within the sweep of his absolutism because he said the First Amendment's language permits no exceptions. Of course, he could just as well have said that since the free exercise of religion clause contains no exceptions, all laws impeding religious activity are absolutely prohibited. But the rights of the First Amendment that comprise conduct he could hardly

---

[6] Wisconsin v. Yoder, 406 U.S. 205, 219–20.

[7] Jones v. Opelika, 316 U.S. 584, 618 (1942) (Murphy, J., dissenting, joined by Justice Black). *See also* Cantwell v. Connecticut, 310 U.S. 296, 303–4 (1940), where Justice Roberts for a unanimous Court said: "[T]he [First] Amendment embraces two concepts,—freedom to believe and freedom to act. The first is absolute but, in the nature of things, the second cannot be." *See also* United States v. Ballard, 322 U.S. 78, 86 (1944), where the Court again referred to this "dual aspect" of the freedom of religion.

[8] Martin v. Struthers, 319 U.S. 141, 145 (1943) (Black, J.).

[9] Wisconsin v. Yoder, 406 U.S. 205, 220 (1972). *See also* Justice Douglas's partial dissent, 406 U.S. at 247–49.

protect at all, because he could not protect them absolutely.[10] Instead, to retain the viability of absolutism (and so to maintain the integrity and consistency of his constitutional jurisprudence) he was forced ultimately to reduce the scope and importance of a number of "first freedoms."

His narrow construction of free exercise of religion also provided him with a theoretical escape from still another dilemma intrinsic to his absolutist version of the First Amendment. The justices of the Supreme Court have noted many times the mutual incompatibility of the two religion clauses of that amendment.[11] In providing chaplains and chapels for members of the armed services, for example, the government is to some degree "respecting an establishment of religion"; and the First Amendment says "Congress shall make no law respecting an establishment of religion." But to deny these people such a means of practicing their faith is—again, to some extent—to collide with the free exercise clause, particularly the rights of those who want to worship but whose service in the military is not volunteered. Or to provide police and fire protection to religious organizations (almost all of which are exempt from the payment of property taxes) is conceivably to respect an establishment of religion; but to withhold such necessary protection is undoubtedly to place obstacles before the free exercise of those who belong to these organizations.

Countless similar conflicts arise when either clause is regarded as an absolute prohibition. Thus, if government is absolutely forbidden to respect an establishment of religion—that is, if a "wall of separation" is to be erected, as Justice Black insisted[12]—the government's complete (absolute) observance of that limitation can easily be translated into a violation

---

[10] In explaining and defending his interpretation of the "free exercise" clause, Justice Black cited Reynolds v. United States, 98 U.S. 145 (1878), where the Supreme Court upheld a federal law making polygamy a crime over the objection of Mormons that such conduct is part of their religion. Justice Black seems to have assumed that since polygamy is not within the meaning of "free exercise," no conduct is. It seems, however, that such a conclusion merely begs the question. *See* H. BLACK, *supra* note 5, at 55–56.

[11] The Court has recently stated: "Our prior holdings do not call for total separation between Church and State; total separation is not possible in an absolute sense. Some relationship between government and religious organizations is inevitable." Lemon v. Kurtzman, 403 U.S. 602, 614 (1971); *see also* Wisconsin v. Yoder, 406 U.S. 205, *passim* (1972); Sherbert v. Verner, 374 U.S. 398, 413–18 (1963) (Stewart, J., concurring).

[12] *See* Engel v. Vitale, 370 U.S. 421 (1962); Everson v. Board of Education, 330 U.S. 1 (1947).

of the free exercise clause. Since the textual source of his absolutism was "Congress shall make no law," Justice Black could not avoid being the proponent of the perplexing and enigmatic position that both religion clauses are absolute. Only by reducing the scope of one or the other clause could he have averted the possibility of a collision of absolutes. He could maintain a "wall of separation" without encroaching on free exercise as long as the latter was construed to constitute only religious beliefs. People, including soldiers on the battlefield, could do all their believing internally—by themselves, without any governmental intrusions or aid which might breach the wall.

Still, as Sidney Hook has written in his indictment of Justice Black's First Amendment posture, "[o]ne of the commonest experiences in life is the conflict of rights. But if rights are absolute, how can there be more than one of them?"[13] As argued in Chapter I, Hook is among those critics who have misread absolutism as a doctrine which purports to define the scope or meaning of constitutional rights rather than as merely a standard for enforcing those rights, whatever their meaning or scope. But the conflict of rights is real and ever present, as the Justice Black of the 1940s had witnessed and had resolved through the process of balancing such rights against each other.[14] The absolutist, on the other hand, insisted that such resolution is to be found in the Constitution: "Where conflicting values exist in the field of individual liberties protected by the Constitution, that document settles the conflict." Through the words of that document— with Justice Black's help—a collision of absolutes between the two religion clauses was avoided. But, in 1966, he was faced with a case presenting a clash between the absolute freedom of the press and the Sixth Amendment's guarantee of a trial by an impartial jury—a right stated, he said, "in terms both definite and absolute."[15] In *Sheppard* v. *Maxwell* the Supreme Court, with only one dissenter, reversed the conviction of Dr. Sam Sheppard, who had been found guilty in a lower court of having murdered his wife.[16] The Court held that press coverage of the episode (before and during the trial) had been so pervasive and egregious as to constitute a

---

[13] Hook, *A Philosopher Dissents in the Case of Absolutes*, FREE SPEECH AND POLITICAL PROTEST 79 (Summers ed. 1967).

[14] Marsh v. Alabama, 326 U.S. 501 (1946).

[15] Black, *The Bill of Rights*, 35 N.Y.U. L. REV. 865, 879, 872 (1960).

[16] 384 U.S. 333 (1966).

deprivation of the defendant's right to a fair trial by an impartial jury. Justice Black was the lone dissenter. But it is uncertain whether or how "that document settle[d] the conflict" for him, because he registered his dissent without the support of an opinion explaining why. His dissent at least reinforces the argument that he was committed to following a dogma (although here he had a choice of absolutes) no matter how unfair or absurd the consequences.

Justice Black's jurisprudential contribution to the development of the First Amendment must be appraised in conjunction with the substantive achievements he helped make in protecting, strengthening, and weakening First Amendment freedoms, for the latter were inextricably tied to the former. This is evident in view of what remained of the rights of assembly and free exercise as a result of Justice Black's protecting them absolutely. One would ordinarily expect absolute constitutional rights to be substantial, enforceable, and strong. But one of the ironies of Justice Black's absolutism is that such rights are all but eliminated inasmuch as they can be construed as conduct, the absolute protection of which would be dangerous and utterly impractical. Moreover, when absolute rights are in conflict with each other, apparently one is sacrificed completely for the sake of the other. On the other hand, he read free speech and press as protecting absolutely even libel and slander—including those lies the very purpose of which is the deliberate ruin of an individual's life. If such perverse results are the consequences of a plain reading of the Constitution, they would symbolize the triumph of law over the life of a free society. But these results were derived less from the First Amendment and more from Justice Black's search for objectivity and the concomitant inability to resolve the insoluble dilemmas that attached to his absolutism.

Despite the weaknesses, contradictions, inconsistencies, and occasionally perverted priorities of his constitutional jurisprudence, Justice Black's dedication to the protection of constitutional liberties (as he understood them) reflected his stern commitment to the belief that the Bill of Rights was designed to protect individuals from governmental powers, and that courts are authorized—indeed, required—to enforce its many guarantees. "Under our constitutional system," he said in moving words for the Court in 1940, "courts stand against any winds that blow as havens of refuge for those who might otherwise suffer because they are helpless, weak, outnumbered, or because they are non-conforming victims of prejudice and public excitement." The judiciary has "[n]o higher duty, no more solemn responsibility."[17] His defense of First Amendment freedoms during the ravages of the Cold War and McCarthyism depicts the courage of his convictions. He sincerely believed that the American Constitution had established a limited government and that the very purpose of the First Amendment was to prevent the harassment and punishment of political dissidents which were in vogue in the United States during that period. With tenacious spirit he defied both a determined government, which sought to suppress Communists and their sympathizers, and a timid Court majority, who sustained such an effort on the disputable claim that the First Amendment was not being violated, or on the tenuous assertion that national self-preservation hung in the balance, or because such action was "reasonable."

In the 1950s he repeatedly objected to the government's practice, through such means as legislative investigations, of exposing suspected Communists "for the sake of exposure"—that is, so as to subject them to public opinion whipped up by hatred and fear. Public disclosure through congressional investigations was the goal of many inquisitive legislators. One Barenblatt was brought before the House Un-American Activities Committee; he was a college instructor, and the questions put to him were, for the record, designed to uncover the extent of subversion in American education. But, in practice, the purpose was to publicize the names of Communists and what became known as "Fifth Amendment Communists" in order to expose them to hostile public reaction, a fate which tended to result in loss of job and social ostracism. Barenblatt refused to answer a number of questions, and the Supreme Court in 1959 upheld his conviction for contempt of Congress.

Dissenting, Justice Black recognized that "[s]uch publicity is clearly punishment." "The punishment imposed is generally punishment by humiliation and public shame. There is nothing strange or novel about this kind of punishment. It is in fact one of the oldest forms of governmental punishment known to mankind; branding, the pillory, ostracism and subjection to public hatred being but a few examples of it."[18] "In my judgment," he had told a graduating class of Swarthmore College in 1955,

---

[17] *Chambers v. Florida*, 309 U.S. 227, 241 (Black, J.).
[18] *Barenblatt v. United States*, 360 U.S. 109, 159, 153–54 (Black, J., dissenting).

"the very heart of the Bill of Rights is the First Amendment. Unless people can freely exercise those liberties, without loss of good name, job, property, liberty or life, a good society cannot exist. That is my faith."[19]

And so it was. His votes and opinions during this era confirm his consistent allegiance to that faith; his eloquent and moving defense of basic First Amendment rights doubtless stirred some pessimistic and disillusioned libertarians into the hope that the stricken rights would nonetheless survive and be restored, as Justice Black had hoped as early as *Dennis* v. *United States* (1951), "to the high preferred place where they belong in a free society."[20]

But Justice Black's libertarian faith would ultimately be forced to comport with his search for a justification for that libertarianism—a constitutional standard transcending his merely personal values and beliefs. For here was a jurist who felt it incumbent upon him to justify all constitutional decisions through the written document; and he sincerely believed that he could. To what he perceived as the Court's unjustifiable propensity to balance the First Amendment out of existence, Justice Black responded with the doctrine of absolutism. And, as far as it held that the First Amendment prohibits governmental punishment of unorthodox political views, it was a powerful response; to the Court's frequent concessions that the governmental actions which it upheld were no doubt invasions of First Amendment liberties, his absolutist stance was a most pertinent reply. But he would not confine the application of that doctrine only to the political dissent which the Court subordinated to the national security claims of the 1950s. His libertarianism also had to compete with his drive for objectivity in constitutional adjudication. Law professor G. Edward White writes: "Black, in constitutional law cases, was concerned more with the preservation of his theory of adjudication than with the results it produced."[21]

Justice Black pursued the goal of objectivity to the degree to which he refused to delineate the necessarily difficult, and almost always subjective, lines setting free speech apart from other expression, such as defamatory lies and obscene publications. Moreover, his absolutism prevented him from giving peaceful symbolic expression its proper constitutional protection at the same time that he felt obligated to protect expression which

[19] Commencement Address by Justice Black at Swarthmore College, June 6, 1955.
[20] 341 U.S. 494, 581 (Black, J., dissenting).
[21] G. White, The American Judicial Tradition 362 (1976).

seems, even from a libertarian standpoint, undeserving of that protection. In this vein Sidney Hook has derided Justice Black's position: "The truth is that if [Justice Black's] views became the law of the land, and the citizens of our republic could libel and slander each other with impunity, democratic self-government would be impossible and the entire structure of our freedoms would go down in dust and turmoil . . . ." "The very foundations of civil society . . . would collapse."[22]

Hook's gloomy visions of doom and catastrophe would not likely materialize if Justice Black's absolutism became the law of the land. But the consequences of implementing his position would not fare well for the health of a society which respects and desires to protect many freedoms and values. If his dissent in Dr. Sheppard's case is any indication, one such debilitating effect would be that a criminal defendant's fundamental right to a fair trial would depend on the attitude of the local press; a defendant like Sam Sheppard, who is disliked by the press, would be unable constitutionally to obtain a fair trial—despite any pronouncements that such a right is absolute. Moreover, Justice Black's resolve absolutely to protect obscene and defamatory publications, no matter how ruinous and malicious the libelous utterances might be, together with his equally firm unwillingness to accord free speech status to peaceful symbolic protest, constitute something of an absurdity in his position—something which no free society would long tolerate.

The denouement of applying his absolutist version of the First Amendment takes the form of something short of Hook's dire predictions, but it displays an irony which seems to shatter the libertarian purpose of the First Amendment and the spirit that initially helped to induce Justice Black to promote his generous reading of free speech and association. The ultimate fruition of the application of his position might well be the suppression of the very right to dissent from political orthodoxy which, according to his every belief, was the heart of a free society and the central purpose of the First Amendment.

"History should teach us . . . ," Justice Black said movingly in his dissenting opinion in the *Barenblatt* case,

> that in times of high emotional excitement minority parties and groups which advocate extremely unpopular social or governmental innovations will always be typed as criminal gangs and attempts will always be

---

[22] Hook, *supra* note 13, at 84, 78.

made to drive them out. It was knowledge of this fact, and of its great dangers, that caused the founders of our land to enact the First Amendment as a guarantee that neither Congress nor the people would do anything to hinder or destroy the capacity of individuals or groups to seek converts and votes for any cause, however radical or unpalatable their principles might seem under the accepted notions of the time.[23]

He believed that his view of the First Amendment would ensure this right insofar as government could neither punish unorthodox believers nor "expose" them "for the sake of exposure."

But the First Amendment does not bind "the people"; it does not prevent the people from "exposing" dissidents "for the sake of exposure," despite Justice Black's assertions in *Barenblatt*. On the contrary, his First Amendment would provide immunity for individuals who would expose others—with either truths or falsehoods—"for the sake of exposure." By including libel and slander within the realm of free discussion, Justice Black's position fostered an absolute constitutional right of individuals deliberately and maliciously to defame each other, to spread rumors about each other, and consequently to punish each other. And no government and no court could prevent this from happening; neither the government nor the courts could safeguard the right freely to dissent "without loss of good name, job, property, liberty" and conceivably "the life" of an alleged or real Communist, or any other hated dissident, who might be the victim of a malicious lie published or rumored about for the very purpose of provoking hostile public reaction. An absolute license to defame, rumor, or expose would shield all utterances from government suppression and so would protect no one from their consequences. During such periods of public paranoia as the 1950s, none would be above suspicion; social repression would work its way particularly hard on the few who would dare openly to dissent from conformity—the very individuals Justice Black sought to protect, and whom the First Amendment was designed to protect. Of course, one would have the absolute right to respond to his accusers. But, in such times, it is more likely that would-be political dissenters would be driven to self-censorship; at any rate, it is doubtful that many others would listen, lest they too become suspected of having committed the sin of heresy. Resort to the courts, even to the Supreme Court of the United States, would be unavailing, notwithstanding Justice

---

[23] 360 U.S. 109, 151 (1959) (Black, J., dissenting).

Black's avowed and sincere belief that the highest, most solemn duty of courts is to stand as havens of refuge for "non-conforming victims of prejudice and public excitement." For the majority's right to assure compliance with the tenets and practices of political orthodoxy, through the effective strategy of social pressure via the tactics of libel and rumor, would be enshrined absolutely in the highest law of the land.

This is the denouement in the long line of sundry and ironic dilemmas that afflicted Justice Black's constitutional jurisprudence.

One year before the deaths of Justices Murphy and Rutledge—one year before the passing of the "preferred position" doctrine of the First Amendment—the Supreme Court announced the doctrine of "divisible divorce," whereby an ex parte divorce would be given "full faith and credit" (according to the requirements of Article IV of the Constitution) for some purposes, but not for others. As Justice Jackson said in dissent, the Court was treating the divorce as half good and half bad despite the "full" faith and credit clause. But the Court majority was impelled by the recognition of legitimate interests and the desire to accommodate the claims of both sides to the dispute. Speaking for that majority and explaining its rationale, Justice Douglas spoke these words (with which his soon-to-become fellow absolutist Justice Black agreed) depicting the essence of the judicial process in the realm of constitutional law: "An absolutist might quarrel with the result and demand a rule that once a divorce is granted, the whole of the marriage relation is dissolved, leaving no roots or tendrils of any kind. But there are few areas of the law in black and white. The greys are dominant and even among them the shades are innumerable. For the eternal problem of the law is one of accommodations between conflicting interests."[24]

But soon thereafter Justice Black recognized too frequently that the eternal problem of the law had its own problem, as another Court majority exploited the subjectivity intrinsic to the balancing of interests doctrine. He dissented from the Court's abuse of that doctrine to weaken rather than strengthen First Amendment rights. In the 1940s, with the support of his libertarian colleagues, he approvingly utilized the balancing process to promote the rights he believed essential to a good society. When that decade had come to a close, and as another began, he was in a minority as he watched in dissent a majority of justices, in his words, balance the First

[24] Estin v. Estin, 334 U.S. 541, 545 (1948).

Amendment away. His ultimate response was his absolutism, the culmination of his constitutional jurisprudence, his solution to "the eternal problem of the law."

No justice of the Court conscientiously and persistently endeavored, as much as Justice Black did, to establish consistent standards of objectivity for adjudicating constitutional issues. Throughout his influential, long, and dedicated service on the Supreme Court, believing firmly, as he did, in the rule of law, he tried to find those standards primarily in the language of the Constitution. His diligence, perseverance, and his purpose were laudable: He wanted to limit the capacity of life-appointed judges to establish social policy as the product of their own ideas and values—their politics; he wanted to prevent courts from balancing away precious constitutional guarantees. But Justice Black was in search of an objectivity which does not exist, at least not in the field of constitutional interpretation and adjudication. The dilemmas, contradictions, and ironies that followed from his efforts confirm the admonition of the poet Goethe: "For what he weaves no weaver knows." Justice Black's efforts were admirable; but they nonetheless coldly illustrate the difficulties.

Bibliography

Indexes

Bibliography

ABRAHAM, Henry J. *Freedom and the Court: Civil Rights and Liberties in the United States*. 3d ed. New York: Oxford University Press, 1977.

——. *Justices and Presidents*. New York: Oxford University Press, 1974.

ALFANGE, Dean, Jr. "The Balancing of Interests in Free Speech Cases: In Defense of an Abused Doctrine," 2 *Law in Transition Quarterly* 35 (1965).

ANASTAPLO, George. Book Review, 39 *New York University Law Review* 735 (1964).

ANNALS OF CONGRESS, 1st Congress (1789–91).

ANTIEAU, Chester J. "Judicial Delimitation of the First Amendment Freedoms," 34 *Marquette Law Review* 57 (1950).

ASH, Michael. "The Growth of Justice Black's Philosophy on Freedom of Speech, 1962–1966," 1967 *Wisconsin Law Review* 840.

BALL, Howard. *The Vision and the Dream of Justice Hugo L. Black: An Examination of a Judicial Philosphy*. University: University of Alabama Press, 1975.

BEANEY, William M. *The Right to Counsel in American Courts*. Ann Arbor: University of Michigan Press,, 1955.

BEARD, Charles A. *An Economic Interpretation of the Constitution of the United States*. New York: The Macmillan Co., 1913.

BERNS, Walter. *Freedom, Virtue, and the First Amendment*. Baton Rouge: Louisiana State University Press, 1957.

BICKEL, Alexander M. *The Least Dangerous Branch*. Indianapolis: Bobbs-Merrill Co., 1962.

——. *The Supreme Court and the Idea of Progress*. New York: Harper Torchbook, 1970.

BLACK, Charles L., Jr. "Mr. Justice Black, the Supreme Court, and the Bill of Rights," 222 *Harper's* 63 (Feb. 1961).

BLACK, Hugo L. Commencement Address at Swarthmore College, June 6, 1955.

——. "The Bill of Rights," 35 *New York University Law Review* 865 (1960).

——. *A Constitutional Faith*. New York: Alfred A. Knopf, 1968.

BLACK, Hugo, Jr. *My Father: A Remembrance*. New York: Random House, 1975.

BOORSTIN, Daniel J. *The Genius of American Politics*. Chicago: University of Chicago Press, 1953.

BOYD, Julian P., ed. *The Papers of Thomas Jefferson*, vol. 14. Princeton, N.J.: Princeton University Press, 1958.

BRADEN, George D. "The Search for Objectivity in Constitutional Law," 57 *Yale Law Journal* 571 (1948).

CAHN, Edmond. "The Firstness of the First Amendment," 65 *Yale Law Journal* 464 (1956).

——. "Justice Black and First Amendment 'Absolutes': A Public Interview," 37 *New York University Law Review* 549 (1962).

CAPPON, Lester J., ed. *The Adams-Jefferson Letters*, vol. 1. Chapel Hill: University of North Carolina Press, 1959.

CARDOZO, Benjamin N. *The Nature of the Judicial Process*. New Haven: Yale University Press, 1921.

CHAFEE, Zechariah, Jr. *Free Speech in the United States*. Cambridge: Harvard University Press, 1941.

——. Book Review, 62 *Harvard Law Review* 891 (1949).

CHASE, Harold W. *Federal Judges: The Appointing Process*. Minneapolis: University of Minnesota Press, 1972.

CLOR, Harry M. *Obscenity and Public Morality: Censorship in a Liberal Society*. Chicago: University of Chicago Press, 1969.

COHEN, Felix S. "Transcendental Nonsense and the Functional Approach," 35 *Columbia Law Review* 809 (1935).

CORWIN, Edward S. "Freedom of Speech and Press Under the First Amendment: A Résumé," 30 *Yale Law Journal* 48 (1920).

DENNIS, Everette E., et al., eds. *Justice Hugo Black and the First Amendment*. Ames: Iowa State University Press, 1978.

DILLIARD, Irving. "Hugo Black and the Importance of Freedom," 10 *The American University Law Review* 7 (1961).

DOUGLAS, William O. "Mr. Justice Black: A Foreword," 65 *Yale Law Journal* 449 (1956).

DUNNE, Gerald T. *Hugo Black and the Judicial Revolution*. New York: Simon and Schuster, 1977.

EMERSON, Thomas I. *The System of Freedom of Expression*. New York: Random House, 1970.

——. *Toward a General Theory of the First Amendment*. New York: Random House, 1966.

FAIRMAN, Charles. "Does the Fourteenth Amendment Incorporate the Bill of Rights? The Original Understanding," 2 *Stanford Law Review* 5 (1949).

FRANK, John P. *Mr. Justice Black: The Man and His Opinions*. New York: Alfred A. Knopf, 1949.

FRANTZ, Laurent B. "The First Amendment in the Balance," 71 *Yale Law Journal* 1424 (1962).

——. "Is the First Amendment Law?—A Reply to Professor Mendelson," 51 *California Law Review* 729 (1963).

FREUND, Paul A. "Mr. Justice Black and the Judicial Function," 14 *U.C.L.A. Law Review* 467 (1967).

——. *The Supreme Court of the United States*. Gloucester, Mass.: Peter Smith, 1972.

GORDON, Rosalie. *Nine Men Against America*. New York: Devlin-Adair Co., 1958.

GRAHAM, Fred. P. *The Due Process Revolution*. New York: Hayden, 1970.

GRISWOLD, Erwin N. "Absolute Is in the Dark," 8 *Utah Law Review* 167 (1963).

HAND, Learned. *The Spirit of Liberty*. Ed. Irving Dilliard. 2d ed. New York: Alfred A. Knopf, 1954.

——. *The Bill of Rights*. New York: Atheneum, 1968.

HART, Fred B. "Power of Government over Speech and Press," 29 *Yale Law Journal* 410 (1920).

HENKIN, Louis. "Morals and the Constitution: The Sin of Obscenity," 63 *Columbia Law Review* 391 (1963).

——. "Some Reflections on Current Constitutional Controversy," 109 *University of Pennsylvania Law Review* 637 (1961).

HOFSTADTER, Richard. "Beard and the Constitution: The History of an Idea," 2 *American Quarterly* 195 (1950).

HOOK, Sidney. *The Paradoxes of Freedom*. Berkeley: University of California Press, 1962.

——. Book Review, 46 *The New Leader* 11 (1963).

——. "A Philosopher Dissents in the Case of Absolutes," in Marvin Summers, ed. *Free Speech and Political Protest*. Boston: D. C. Heath & Co., 1967.

HOWARD, A. E. Dick. "Mr. Justice Black: The Negro Protest Movement and the Rule of Law," 53 *Virginia Law Review* 1030 (1967).

HOWARD, J. Woodford. *Mr. Justice Murphy: A Political Biography*. Princeton, N. J.: Princeton University Press, 1968.

HOWE, Irving, and COSER, Lewis. *The American Communist Party*. New York: Praeger, 1962.

KALVEN, Harry, Jr. "The Metaphysics of the Law of Obscenity," 1960 *Supreme Court Review* 1.

——. "The New York Times Case: A Note on the 'Central Meaning of the First Amendment,' " 1964 *Supreme Court Review* 191.

——. *The Negro and the First Amendment*. Chicago: University of Chicago Press, 1965.

——. "The Reasonable Man and the First Amendment: Hill, Butts, and Walker," 1967 *Supreme Court Review* 267.

——. "Upon Rereading Mr. Justice Black on the First Amendment," 14 *U.C.L.A. Law Review* 428 (1967).

KARST, Kenneth. "The First Amendment and Harry Kalven: An Appreciative Comment on the Advantages of Thinking Small," 13 *U.C.L.A. Law Review* 1 (1965).

KATCHER, Leo. *Earl Warren: A Political Biography*. New York: McGraw-Hill, 1967.

KELLY, Alfred H., and HARBISON, Winfred A. *The American Constitution*. 4th ed. New York: W. W. Norton & Co., 1970.

KOCH, Adrienne, and PEDEN, William, eds. *The Life and Selected Writings of Thomas Jefferson*. New York: Modern Library, 1944.

KRISLOV, Samuel. "Mr. Justice Black Reopens the Free Speech Debate," 11 *U.C.L.A. Law Review* 189 (1964).

KURLAND, Philip. Book Review, 30 *University of Chicago Law Review* 191 (1962).

LEUCHTENBURG, William. "A Klansman Joins the Court: The Appointment of Hugo Lafayette Black," 41 *University of Chicago Law Review* 1 (1973).

LEVY, Leonard W. *Legacy of Suppression: Freedom of Speech and Press in Early American History*. Cambridge: Harvard University Press, 1960.

McBRIDE, Patrick. "Mr. Justice Black and His Qualified Absolutes," 2 *Loyola University (L.A.) Law Review* 37 (1969).

McCLOSKEY, Herbert. "Consensus and Ideology in American Politics," 58 *American Political Science Review* 361 (1964).

McCLOSKEY, Robert G. *The American Supreme Court*. Chicago: University of Chicago Press, 1960.

McDONALD, Forrest. *We the People: The Economic Origins of the Constitution*. Chicago: University of Chicago Press, 1958.

McILWAIN, Charles H. *The American Revolution: A Constitutional Interpretation*. Ithaca, N. Y.: Great Seal Books, 1923.

MARCUSE, Herbert. "Repressive Tolerance," in Robert Paul Wolff et al. *A Critique of Pure Tolerance*. Boston: Beacon Press, 1965.

MASON, Alpheus T. *The States' Rights Debate: Antifederalism and the Constitution*. Englewood Cliffs, N. J.: Prentice-Hall, 1964.

——. *Free Government in the Making*. 3d ed. New York: Oxford University Press, 1965.

MEIKLEJOHN, Alexander. *Free Speech and Its Relation to Self-Government.* New York: Harper & Row, 1948.

——. *Political Freedom: The Constitutional Powers of the People.* New York: Harper & Row, 1960.

——. "The First Amendment Is an Absolute," 1961 *Supreme Court Review* 245.

MENDELSON, Wallace. *Capitalism, Democracy, and the Supreme Court.* New York: Appleton-Century-Crofts, 1960.

——. *Justices Black and Frankfurter: Conflict in the Court.* 2d ed. Chicago: University of Chicago Press, 1966.

——. "On the Meaning of the First Amendment: Absolutes in the Balance," 50 *California Law Review* 821 (1962).

——. "The First Amendment and the Judicial Process: A Reply to Mr. Frantz," 17 *Vanderbilt Law Review* 479 (1964).

——. ed. *The Supreme Court: Law and Discretion.* Indianapolis: Bobbs-Merrill, 1967.

——. "Hugo Black and Judicial Discretion," 85 *Political Science Quarterly* 17 (1970).

——. "From Warren to Burger: The Rise and Decline of Substantive Equal Protection," 66 *American Political Science Review* 1226 (1972).

"Mr. Justice Black and the Bill of Rights," "CBS Reports," Dec. 3, 1968.

MURPHY, Walter F. *Congress and the Court.* Chicago: University of Chicago Press, 1962.

POWELL, Thomas Reed. *Vagaries and Varieties in Constitutional Interpretation.* New York: Columbia University Press, 1956.

PRESTON, William, Jr. "The 1940s: The Way We Really Were," 2 *The Civil Liberties Review* 4 (1975).

PRITCHETT, C. Herman. *Civil Liberties and the Vinson Court.* Chicago: University of Chicago Press, 1954.

——. *Congress Versus the Supreme Court, 1957–1960.* Minneapolis: University of Minnesota Press, 1961.

REICH, Charles. "Mr. Justice Black and the Living Constitution," 76 *Harvard Law Review* 673 (1963).

RICE, Charles E. "Justice Black, the Demonstrators, and a Constitutional Rule of Law," 14 *U.C.L.A. Law Review* 454 (1967).

ROCHE, John P. "The Founding Fathers: A Reform Caucus in Action," 55 *American Political Science Review* 799 (1961).

——, and LEVY, Leonard, eds. *The Judiciary.* New York: Harcourt, Brace and World, 1964.

ROSSITER, Clinton, ed. *The Federalist Papers.* New York: New American Library of World Literature, 1961.

Rostow, Eugene V. "The Japanese American Cases—A Disaster," 54 *Yale Law Journal* 489 (1945).

——. "The Democratic Character of Judicial Review," 45 *Harvard Law Review* 193 (1952).

——. "Mr. Justice Black: Some Introductory Observations," 65 *Yale Law Journal* 451 (1956).

——. *The Sovereign Prerogative: The Supreme Court and the Quest for Law.* New Haven: Yale University Press, 1962.

Rutland , Robert A. *The Birth of the Bill of Rights.* Chapel Hill: University of North Carolina Press, 1955.

Scammon, Richard, and Wattenberg, Ben. *The Real Majority.* New York: Coward, McCann & Geoghegan, Inc., 1970.

Schubert, Glendon. *Judicial Policy-Making.* Glenview, Ill.: Scott, Foresman and Co., 1965.

——. *The Constitutional Polity.* Boston: Boston University Press, 1970.

Shapiro, Martin. *Freedom of Speech: The Supreme Court and Judicial Review.* Englewood Cliffs, N. J.: Prentice-Hall, 1966.

Simon, James. *In His Own Image.* New York: McKay, 1973.

Snowiss, Sylvia. "The Legacy of Justice Black," 1973 *The Supreme Court Review* 187.

Soles, James R. "Mr. Justice Black and the Defendant's Constitutional Rights." Ph.D. dissertation, University of Virginia, 1968.

Spaeth, Harold J. "The Judicial Restraint of Mr. Justice Frankfurter: Myth or Reality," 8 *Midwest Journal of Political Science* 22 (1964).

Strickland, Stephen P., ed. *Hugo Black and the Supreme Court.* Indianapolis: Bobbs-Merrill, 1967.

Ulmer, S. Sidney. "The Longitudinal Behavior of Hugo Lafayette Black: Parabolic Support for Civil Liberties, 1937–1971," 1 *Florida State University Law Review* 131 (1973).

Vance, W. R. "Freedom of Speech and of the Press," 2 *Minnesota Law Review* 239 (1918).

White, G. Edward. *The American Judicial Tradition: Profiles of Leading American Judges.* New York: Oxford University Press, 1976.

Williams, Charlotte. *Hugo L. Black: A Study in the Judicial Process.* Baltimore: Johns Hopkins University Press, 1950.

Yarbrough, Tinsley E. "Mr. Justice Black and Legal Positivism," 57 *Virginia Law Review* 375 (1971).

——. "Justices Black and Douglas: The Judicial Function and the Scope of Constitutional Liberties," 1973 *Duke Law Journal* 441.

——. "Justice Black and His Critics on Speech-Plus and Symbolic Speech," 52 *Texas Law Review* 257 (1974).

General Index

Absolutism, 38, 61–62; as an absurdity, 7; attack on, 8, 131; defined, 6–7, 21, 81; dilemma of, 8–14, 177; and freedom of the press, 54; inseparable from literalism, 15; as response to balancing, 11

Alien and Sedition Laws, 118. *See also* Sedition Act, 1789

Alien Registration Act. *See* Smith Act

American Revolution, 34–35, 53

Antifederalists, 47

Authentic view, 33–35. *See also* Constitution

Balancing of interests doctrine, 11–17, 25–26, 29, 32, 38, 67, 71, 73, 81, 86, 88–89, 92, 97–98, 129, 133, 138, 163, 177, 193

Bill of Rights, 8–14, 38–40, 47–48; absolute rights, 8, 38; address, *see* James Madison Address; federal application of, 121; limits of, 148; vagueness of, 9, 11, 16, 18, 27

Carpentier Lecture, 176n

Classification Act (1879), 95

Clear and present danger test, 32, 52, 69, 82–86, 88, 90, 91, 92, 93, 106, 107, 108, 110, 112, 113–15, 144–45, 161; as a balancing test, 88, 93

Cold war, 3–4, 98, 101, 110, 117–18, 140, 189

Communism, 65, 66, 67, 98, 100–101, 102, 105, 106, 110–11, 117, 131, 189

Communist party, 3, 65, 77n, 100–103, 104, 106, 107, 110, 130, 146, 151, 155, 189

Conflict of rights, 68, 186–88

Compelled testimony, 78

Congress, First, 47

Constitution: Article I, 37, 120; Article IV, 193; challenge to, 10; compared with British Parliament, 34; historical determination of meaning, 13, 34, 38, 48–58; importance of written, 19–20; supremacy of, 33, 34, 35

Constitutional adjudication: role of history in, 16, 29–48, 66–67; Roche on, 30–31

Constitutional Convention (1787), 30–31, 47; Mendelson on, 39; Roche on, 30–31

Cruel and unusual punishment, 15, 16–17, 18, 20, 21

Death penalty, 17

Demonstrations. *See* Symbolic expression

Direct/indirect abridgments, 86, 89, 92, 159–73

Divisible divorce, 193

Double jeopardy, 9, 78–79

Draft, 31

Eighth Amendment, 21

Electronic surveillance, 15, 147, 150n

The Federalist, 37

Fifth Amendment: double jeopardy, 9; due process clause, 17, 71, 74, 78, 120, 125

First Amendment, 60–63, 104, 131–33; future of, 4; preferred position of, 64, 80–82, 92, 99, 105, 190, 193; purpose of, 2, 52–54; refused en-

First Amendment (*cont.*)
forcement of, 101, 102–3; right of assembly, 130, 173–75, 176; right to petition, 129, 173–74; vagueness of, 10–11, 24–25, 50, 59, 136
Fourteenth Amendment, 75, 77, 91, 94, 123–24, 143; due process clause, 61, 120–21, 122, 123, 125, 126, 127, 128, 151, 152; historical view of, 120, 125–26; privilege and immunities clause, 123, 124, 125
Fourth Amendment, 16, 21, 147
Freedom of assembly, 184; only enforced by balancing, 185
Freedom of contract, 20
Freedom of expression, 1–5, 28, 54, 57–58, 60–61, 65; historical view of, 48–59. *See also* Freedom of speech
Freedom of the press, 23–26, 45, 48, 49, 50–53, 58, 60–61, 171; Blackstone on, 51
Freedom of religion, 9, 24–25, 55, 184–85, 186–87; only enforced by balancing, 185
Freedom of speech, 1–3, 21–28, 45, 49, 51–58, 60–61, 81, 92, 93, 94–95, 113, 170; limits of, 21–24, 29, 87
Fundamentalist theological approach, 9. *See also* Mechanical jurisprudence

Hatch Act, 167
House Un-American Activities Committee, 4, 189

Inciteful speech, 7, 54
Indirect abridgments, 89, 165. *See also* Direct/indirect abridgments
Indochina war, 4, 171
Internal Security Act, 117
Involuntary servitude, 31

James Madison Address (Bill of Rights Address), 8, 13, 15–16, 21, 32, 71, 74, 82
Japanese relocation, 42, 59n, 69–71
Jehovah's Witness, 24n, 67, 95n, 180

"Judge X," 71–73, 79, 82; thought to be Frankfurter, 72
Judge-made law, 10, 20, 26, 124, 125, 128, 133, 138, 143, 151–52
Judicial function, 46, 47, 109, 119
Judicial restraint, 12, 13, 42, 117, 118. *See also* Test of reasonableness
Judicial review, 39, 45–46

Legislative reapportionment, 66
Legislative supremacy, 32, 35, 37, 42, 53
Libel and slander, 23, 28, 54–58, 66, 94, 96–97, 129, 139, 188; Cahn on Black's position on, 27; distinguishing problem between, 7; seditious libel, 56–57, 58
Literalism, 21–28; attack on, 8; defined, 15; and free speech, 18; and judicial function, 14–20; simplistic literalism charge, 11
Los Angeles Times, 83–84
Loyalty oath, 101–2, 103, 104

McCarthyism, 98, 189. *See also name index*
Madison Address. *See* James Madison Address
Majority rule, 40, 41, 42, 44–45
Mechanical jurisprudence, 9, 11, 14, 19, 133
Minority rights, 40–46

National conscription, 31
National Labor Relations Board, 101, 102
Necessary and proper clause, 37–38, 72
New Deal, 10, 19

Obscenity and pornography, 7, 22–23, 28, 54, 57–61, 66, 136; distinguishing problem between, 7, 139

Parchment barriers, 35, 40, 44–46
Perjury, 171
Polygamy, 136, 186

Pornography. *See* Obscenity and pornography

Preferred position, 64, 80, 81, 82, 84–85, 92, 93, 100, 115, 190; as balancing test, 112; passing of, 65, 99, 100, 104, 105, 107, 110, 111, 193. *See also* First Amendment

Prior restraint, 50

Privileges and immunities clause, 124–25

Progressive party, 130

Right to petition, 174–75

Right to privacy, 15, 74, 146–47, 148, 151

Rule of law, 148

Search and seizure, 15, 16, 18, 20, 21, 147

Sedition Act of 1798: denounced by Madison, 56

Seditious libel, 50, 51, 52, 53, 54n, 58, 60, 63

Sixth Amendment: right to counsel, 181; trial by jury, 8, 122, 187

Slander. *See* Libel and slander

Smith Act (Alien Registration Act), 42, 105–6, 107, 109, 110, 130, 142

Soviet Union, 100

Speech/conduct dichotomy, 22, 92, 159–73

States' rights, 46–48, 57, 60, 120, 122, 123, 124

Substantive due process, 125, 128–29, 131–33, 138, 140

Supreme Court: balancing of, 129–33; judicial revolution of 1937, 10, 19; libertarian wing, 64, 66, 80

Swarthmore College: commencement address, 189–90

Symbolic expression, 4, 66, 145, 146, 148, 154–58, 159; in *Giboney*, 162–66

Taft-Hartley Act, 101, 103

Tenth Amendment, 60

Test of reasonableness, 41, 42, 76, 108, 132, 141

Thirteenth Amendment, 31

Wall of separation, 186–87

Warren Court, 66, 149–50; revolution of, 144, 146

Wiretapping. *See* Electronic surveillance

Name Index

Anastaplo, George, 53n

Beard, Charles A., 30

Berns, Walter, 43

Bickel, Alexander, 13, 16, 17, 27
  on Black, 9–10, 11, 18, 140
  on Roberts, 10

Black, Charles L., Jr.
  on Bill of Rights Address, 21
  on Black's absolutism, 139, 140

Black, Hugo Lafayette
  absolutism of, 5, 6, 13, 14, 77, 91, 98,
    128, 187–88
    as absolutist, 6, 144
    origins of, 59, 65, 75, 116, 183
    as response to balancing, 11, 193–94
    trapped by, 28, 177–78, 184, 185
  appointed to the Supreme Court, 5,
    64
  balancing, 12–13, 22, 32, 71–73, 78,
    82, 86–87, 89, 129, 131, 132, 133,
    158, 187
    as balancer, 12n, 67, 73, 85, 86, 88,
      93, 163, 165, 180, 183, 193
    danger in balancing, 72
  on Bill of Rights, 8–9, 18–19, 32,
    38–39, 136
    limits, 148
  Carpentier Lecture by, 176n
  on clear and present danger test, 52,
    82, 83, 84, 144
    user of, 97–98, 135
  on compelled testimony, 78
  on Congress, powers of, 38
  consistency of, 182–84

constitutional jurisprudence of, 9–10,
  11, 18, 19, 29, 62, 66, 73, 81, 188
  on constitutional jurisprudence,
    145, 149, 150, 151, 154, 155, 183
  historical interpretation of, 13, 28,
    29, 32, 34, 49, 59
  on importance of written constitu-
    tion, 34, 76, 126, 131, 133, 151,
    178
death of, 66, 182
direct/indirect dichotomy of, 22, 86,
  89, 92n, 157–58, 159–73, 182–83
dissent in *Dennis*, 111, 112
and due process clause, 17, 120, 126,
  128, 138
on electronic surveillance, 147
on Fifth Amendment, 17–18
on First Amendment, 6, 23, 54–55,
  60, 84, 90–91, 103, 111, 116, 117,
  129, 134, 135, 157, 188, 192
  literal reading of, 7, 13, 134
on Fourteenth Amendment, 48, 60,
  91, 120, 123, 126–27, 152
  incorporationist theory of, 60, 121,
    124, 125–26, 128, 129, 148
on Fourth Amendment, 16, 147
on freedom of assembly, 130, 135,
  173, 175–79, 184
  on use of streets, 89–90, 173–74,
    175, 176–77, 179–81
freedom of expression, 61
  limits of expression, 23–24
  symbolic expression, 148–49, 152–
    54, 180, 183, 190

[206]

Black, Hugo Lafayette (*cont.*)
  on freedom of petition, 129, 135, 174–75
  on freedom of the press, 96, 130, 135, 171–72, 191
  on freedom of religion, 130, 135, 136, 184–87
  on freedom of speech, 27–28, 58, 66, 130, 131, 134, 135, 157, 164, 173
  Gobitis, recanting of, 68, 73–74, 80
  on Hatch Act, 167–68
  James Madison Address of, 8, 13, 15–16, 71, 74, 82
  on judge-made law, 119, 126–28, 138, 182
  on libel and slander, 22–24, 27, 54–55, 61, 94, 96–97, 134–38, 156, 185, 191, 192
  literalism of, 19, 48
  on obscenity and pornography, 22–23, 27, 54–55, 61, 94, 96–97, 134, 137, 138, 156, 185
  practical nature of, 70
  on right to privacy, 146–47
  on search and seizure, 15, 16, 18
  on Sixth Amendment, 8, 181
  on slander. *See* libel and slander
  speech/conduct dichotomy of, 22, 86, 87, 93, 156–57, 159–73, 175, 176, 182
  on substantive due process, 138
  Swarthmore College Address by, 189–90
  on trial by jury, 8, 122, 187–88
  as United States senator, 120, 123–24
  Warren Court, reaction to, 66
Blackmun, Harry A., 75, 170
Blackstone, Sir William, 51, 52
Boorstin, Daniel J., 34, 35
Braden, George D., 122, 125
Brandeis, Louis D., 92n, 110
Brennan, William J., Jr., 174
Bridges, Harry, 83–84

Brown, Henry B., 35
  on Bill of Rights, 33
Burton, Harold Hitz, 17, 106
Butler, Pierce (d. 1822), 47

Cahn, Edmond, 5, 27–28, 82
  on Black's constitutional jurisprudence, 14
Cardozo, Benjamin N.
  on due process clause, 120
  on literalism, 12, 14–15
Chafee, Zechariah, Jr., 51, 54, 63, 97
  on historical interpretation of the Constitution, 50, 52, 53
Clark, Thomas C., 65, 102, 106, 174
  appointment of, 100
Clor, Harry M., 21, 56
Cohen, Felix: on jurisprudence, 172
Corwin, Edward S., 52, 53, 54, 58, 61
  on freedom of speech, 51
  on historical interpretation of First Amendment, 51
  on necessary and proper clause, 37

Dilliard, Irving, 69n, 112
Douglas, William O., 5, 17, 64, 76, 77, 84, 100, 102, 106, 114, 115, 116, 118
  absolutism of, 100, 116–17
  balancing, 175, 193
  on Classification Act (1879), 95
  on clear and present danger test, 86, 93, 110–11, 114
  dissent in *Dennis*, 110–11, 115, 135
  divisible divorce, 193
  on electronic surveillance, 150n
  on Fifth Amendment, 79
  on Fourth Amendment, 150n
  on freedom of speech, 92, 95, 99, 113, 135, 153
  Gobitis, recanting of, 69, 80
  libertarianism of, 86
  on right to petition, 174–75
Dunne, Gerald T., 72–73

Emerson, Thomas I., 2n
  on speech/conduct dichotomy of
    Black, 175

Fairman, Charles, 122
Feiner, Irving, 113
Fortas, Abe, 174
Francis, Willy, 17. *See also Louisiana ex
  rel. Francis* v. *Resweber*
Frank, John P., 61n, 145n
Frankfurter, Felix, 9, 20, 43, 65, 106,
    109, 118, 126, 142n
  on absolutism, 109, 156
  on authentic view, 33–34, 35
  on balancing, 108
    as balancer, 67, 72, 130
  on *Beauharnais*, 129
  on *Dennis*, 42, 108
  on due process clause, 109–10, 126
    defense of, 126
  on *Everson*, 43
  on First Amendment, 81
  on Fourteenth Amendment, 122
  on *Gobitis*, 67–68
  on judicial humility, 131n
  on *McCollum*, 43
  1957–58 switch of, 130, 132
  retirement of, 65, 144, 150
  on Smith Act, 109
  on treatment of minorities, 43
Frantz, Laurent B.
  on balancing, 14
  on Black, 10
  on freedom of speech, 23
  on Mendelson, 41
Freund, Paul A., 45, 88, 125, 133
  on direct/indirect dichotomy, 169
  on Fourteenth Amendment, 148
  on literalism, 178

Goldberg, Arthur J.: appointment, 65,
    144
Gregory, Dick, 152, 177
Griswold, Erwin N.
  on Black's jurisprudence, 9
  on Pentagon Papers Case, 25

Hamilton, Alexander, 37
  on Bill of Rights, 36, 40
  on freedom of the press, 49, 51
Hand, Learned, 4, 39, 48, 106, 107
  on judicial review, 45
Harlan, John Marshall (younger), 22, 65
  on *Cohen*, 170
  on due process, 126–27
  on freedom of speech, 130–31
  on *Street*, 169
  switch of 1957, 130, 132
Hart, Fred B.: on necessary and proper
    clause, 37–38
Henkin, Louis: on importance of writ-
    ten Constitution, 19
Holmes, Oliver Wendell, 2, 4, 92, 97,
    98, 110
  dissent in *Abrams*, 52, 110
  on First Amendment, 52
  on freedom of speech, 3
  on historical interpretation of Con-
    stitution, 49
Hook, Sidney, 18, 27
  on absolutism, 187
  on Black, 140, 154, 191
  on historical interpretation of Con-
    stitution, 50
Howard, A. E. Dick, 61, 62
  on Black, 61, 62, 153
Howard, J. Woodford: on *Thornhill*, 161
Howard, Jacob M.: sponsor of Four-
    teenth Amendment, 121, 123
Hughes, Charles Evans, 94

Jackson, Robert H., 64, 74, 80, 142
  on Bill of Rights, 38
  on *Dennis*, 107
  on dissent in *Kunz*, 113–14
  on divisible divorce, 193
  on freedom of speech, 113
  on *Korematsu*, 70, 106
  on symbolic expression, 155
Jefferson, Thomas, 59, 60
  on Bill of Rights, 45, 46
  on freedom of expression, 58

Jefferson, Thomas (*cont.*)
    on freedom of the press, 56
    letter to Abagail Adams, 56–58
    on libel, 56, 57
Jhering, Rudolf von, 172–73

Kalven, Harry, Jr., 5, 145n
    on Black, 5
    on First Amendment, 62–63
    on speech/conduct dichotomy, 159
Karst, Kenneth, 88
Knauer, Paul, 76

Lee, Richard Henry, 47
Levy, Leonard W., 53, 54, 61

McBride, Patrick
    on Black, 158, 175
    on speech/conduct dichotomy, 173
McCarthy, Joseph, 65, 98, 189
McCloskey, Robert G.
    on due process clause, 123
Madison, James, 37, 43, 57, 58, 59
    on American Revolution, 36–37
    on Bill of Rights, 38–39, 40, 46–47
    on freedom of the press, 48, 53, 56
    on judicial function, 46
    letter to Jefferson, 39–40
    on majority rule, 41, 43, 44
    on parchment barriers, 40, 44, 45
    on trial by jury, 48
Mason, Alpheus T., 46, 47
Meiklejohn, Alexander, 27, 54, 136
    on American Revolution, 35–36, 37
    on authentic view, 35–37
    on First Amendment, 26–28
    on freedom of speech, 23, 134–35
Mendelson, Wallace, 14, 21, 27, 43, 45,
        143, 145n
    on Black, 9, 11, 17n, 103, 141–42
    on Corwin, 54n
    on Frankfurter, 109–10n, 141–42
    on Madison, 39, 40, 46–48
    on majority rule, 41, 44
Meredith, James, 169

Minton, Sherman, 65, 102, 106, 113, 114
    appointment of, 100
Murphy, Frank, 17, 66, 76, 77, 82, 84
    death of, 64, 65, 99–100, 193
    on Fifth Amendment, 79
    on First Amendment, 103
    on Fourteenth Amendment, 94
    on free speech, 94
    Gobitis, recanting of, 69, 80
    libertarianism of, 84
    on *Thornhill*, 160–61, 162

Powell, Thomas Reed: criticism of
        Court (1920s–1930s), 11
Pritchett, C. Herman, 65

Reed, Stanley F., 64, 88–89, 106
    on freedom of the press, 95
    on preferred position, 85
Reich, Charles, 79, 82, 112
    on Black's absolutism, 79
Roberts, Owen J., 64, 87
    on balancing, 89
    on First Amendment, 24n, 185
    on freedom of assembly, 179
    on judicial function, 10
    on use of streets, 179
Roche, John P.: on intent of framers of
        Constitution, 30
Roosevelt, Franklin D.: appointment of
        Black, 5
Rostow, Eugene: on *Korematsu*, 70, 71
Rutledge, Wiley B., 17, 43n, 65, 76,
        77n, 79
    appointment of, 80
    on balancing, 91–92
    on clear and present danger test, 91
    death of, 64, 65, 99–100, 193
    libertarianism of, 84

Schubert, Glendon: on Black, 149–50,
        154
Shapiro, Martin, 43n
Sheppard, Sam, 187–88, 191

Stewart, Potter
  on right of assembly and petition, 173–74
  on right of privacy, 151
Stone, Harlan F., 64, 80, 162
  on *Gobitis*, 68
Swisher, Carl Brent: on Black, 71

Truman, Harry, 100

Vinson, Fred M., 102, 106, 108, 114
Warren, Earl, 71, 174, 177
White, G. Edward: on Black's jurisprudence, 190
Williams, Charlotte: on Black's judicial process, 119
Yarbrough, Tinsley: on Black, 158, 182, 183

Case Index

Abrams v. *United States*, 250 U.S. 616 (1919), 52, 92, 98n, 110n

Adamson v. *California*, 332 U.S. 46 (1947), 18n, 20n, 60n, 119, 121, 122, 124n, 125n, 126n, 128, 133n, 147, 148

Adderley v. *Florida*, 385 U.S. 39 (1966), 146n, 175n

Adkins v. *Children's Hospital*, 261 U.S. 525 (1923), 20n

Adler v. *Board of Education*, 342 U.S. 485 (1952), 159n

Afroyim v. *Rusk*, 387 U.S. 253 (1967), 75, 77

American Communications Association v. *Douds*, 339 U.S. 382 (1950), 101–3, 104, 106, 111, 112, 113, 116, 130, 133

American Federation of Labor v. *American Sash and Door Co.*, 335 U.S. 538 (1949), 131n

Anastaplo, In re, 336 U.S. 82 (1961), 58n, 65n, 132n, 146n

Arver v. *United States*, 245 U.S. 266 (1918), 31n

Associated Press v. *United States*, 326 U.S. 1 (1945), 92

Associated Press v. *Walker*, 388 U.S. 130 (1967), 96n

Bakery and Pastry Drivers v. *Wohl*, 315 U.S. 769 (1942), 92n

Barenblatt v. *United States*, 360 U.S. 109 (1959), 58n, 65n, 86n, 117n, 132n, 133n, 146n, 159n, 189n, 191–92

Barnette, see *West Virginia Board of Education* v. *Barnette*

Barron v. *Baltimore*, 7 Pet. 243 (1883), 120

Beauharnais v. *Illinois*, 343 U.S. 250 (1952), 20n, 97n, 105n, 116n, 129, 130, 131, 135n

Bell v. *Maryland*, 378 U.S. 226 (1964), 146n, 153n, 178n, 180n

Bellei, see *Rogers* v. *Bellei*

Betts v. *Brady*, 316 U.S. 455 (1942), 181n

Boddie v. *Connecticut*, 401 U.S. 371 (1971), 141n

Braden v. *United States*, 365 U.S. 431 (1961), 9n, 22n, 27, 49n, 94n, 134n

Breard v. *Alexandria*, 341 U.S. 622 (1951), 112n

Bridges v. *California*, 314 U.S. 252 (1941), 32n, 83, 85, 88, 89, 90, 91n, 93

Brown v. *Louisiana*, 383 U.S. 131 (1966), 146n, 153n

Butterfield v. *Zydok*, 342 U.S. 524 (1952), 117–18

Cantwell v. *Connecticut*, 310 U.S. 296 (1940), 92, 113n, 185n

Carlson v. *Landon*, 342 U.S. 524 (1952), 6n, 104n, 116, 117, 135

Carpenters Union v. *Ritter's Cafe*, 315 U.S. 722 (1942), 89–90, 91, 161n

Carroll v. *United States*, 267 U.S. 132 (1925), 147n

Chambers v. *Florida*, 309 U.S. 227 (1940), 189n

Chaplinsky v. *New Hampshire*, 315 U.S. 568 (1942), 94–95, 113

Coates v. *Cincinnati*, 402 U.S. 611 (1971), 158n

Cohen v. *California*, 403 U.S. 15 (1971), 169, 170–71

Communist Party v. *Subversive Activities Control Board*, 367 U.S. 1 (1961), 12n, 135n, 136n

Connecticut Birth Control Case, see *Griswold* v. *Connecticut*

Cox v. *Louisiana*, 379 U.S. 536 (1965), 87n, 158n, 176, 177n, 178n

Craig v. *Harney*, 331 U.S. 367 (1947), 85–86, 88, 89, 93

Curtis Publishing Co. v. *Butts*, 388 U.S. 130 (1967), 7n, 97n, 138n

Dayton v. *Dulles*, 357 U.S. 144 (1958), 130n

Dennis v. *United States*, 341 U.S. 494 (1951), 33, 42n, 43n, 105–11, 112, 113, 114, 115, 116, 118, 130, 135, 142, 145, 156n, 159n, 190

Donaldson v. *Read Magazine*, 333 U.S. 178 (1948), 23n, 96n

Duncan v. *Louisiana*, 391 U.S. 145 (1968), 123n, 127n, 128n

Dunne v. *United States*, 138 F. 2d 137 (8th Cir. 1943), *cert. denied*, 320 U.S. 790 (1943), 106n

Edwards v. *South Carolina*, 372 U.S. 229 (1963), 174n

Engel v. *Vitale*, 370 U.S. 421 (1962), 186n

Estin v. *Estin*, 334 U.S. 541 (1948), 193n

Everson v. *Board of Education*, 330 U.S. 1 (1947), 22n, 43n, 186n

Feiner v. *New York*, 340 U.S. 315 (1951), 7n, 113n, 114, 115, 116, 135, 152

Feldman v. *United States*, 322 U.S. 487 (1944), 77, 78

Fisher v. *Pace*, 336 U.S. 155 (1949), 93

Flag Salute Cases, see *Minersville School District* v. *Gobitis*, and *West Virginia Board of Education* v. *Barnette*

Follet v. *McCormick*, 321 U.S. 573 (1944), 24n

Giboney v. *Empire Storage and Ice Co.*, 336 U.S. 490 (1949), 162–66, 167, 171

Gideon v. *Wainwright*, 372 U.S. 335 (1963), 181n

Ginzburg v. *United States*, 383 U.S. 463 (1966), 138n

Gitlow v. *New York*, 268 U.S. 652 (1925), 3, 60, 92

Gobitis, see *Minersville School District* v. *Gobitis*

Green v. *United States*, 356 U.S. 165 (1958), 152n

Gregory v. *Chicago*, 394 U.S. 111 (1969), 135n, 153n, 158n, 159n, 173n, 177

Griswold v. *Connecticut*, 381 U.S. 479 (1965), 15n, 74n, 146–49, 151n, 178

Hague v. *Committee for Industrial Organization*, 307 U.S. 496 (1939), 179n

Haley v. *Ohio*, 332 U.S. 596 (1948), 126n

Hannegan v. *Esquire, Inc.*, 327 U.S. 146 (1946), 95n

Jackson, Ex parte, 96 U.S. 727 (1878), 95

Jamison v. *Texas*, 318 U.S. 413 (1943), 180n

Jones v. *Opelika*, 316 U.S. 584 (1942), 80n, 103–4, 185n

Katz v. *United States*, 389 U.S. 347 (1967), 15n, 147n

Kent v. *Dulles*, 357 U.S. 116 (1958), 130n

Kingsley Pictures Corp. v. *Board of Regents*, 360 U.S. 684 (1959), 137n, 138n, 172n

Knauer v. *United States*, 328 U.S. 654 (1946), 76, 77, 81

Konigsberg v. *State Bar of California*, 366 U.S. 36 (1961), 13n, 22n, 58n, 117n, 131, 132n, 133, 135n, 145n

Korematsu v. *United States*, 323 U.S. 214 (1944), 59n, 69–75, 78, 81, 97, 106

Kovacs v. *Cooper*, 336 U.S. 77 (1949), 80n, 81n

Kunz v. *New York*, 340 U.S. 290 (1951), 113, 114

Leary v. *United States*, 395 U.S. 6 (1969), 127n

Case Index

Lemon v. *Kurtzman*, 403 U.S. 602 (1971), 186n

Louisiana ex rel. Francis v. *Resweber*, 329 U.S. 459 (1947), 17n

Lovell v. *Griffin*, 303 U.S. 444 (1938), 94n

McCollum v. *Board of Education*, 333 U.S. 203 (1948), 43n, 109n, 110n

Marsh v. *Alabama*, 326 U.S. 501 (1946), 73, 89, 180n, 183, 187n

Martin v. *Struthers*, 319 U.S. 141 (1943), 64n, 80n, 157n, 185n

Milk Wagon Drivers Union v. *Meadowmoor Dairies*, 312 U.S. 287 (1941), 6n, 83n, 92, 117n, 157n

Minersville School District v. *Gobitis*, 310 U.S. 586 (1940), 42–43n, 67–68, 73, 80

Mishkin v. *New York*, 383 U.S. 502 (1966), 7n, 138n

Missouri v. *Holland*, 252 U.S. 416 (1920), 49n

Morehead v. *New York ex rel. Tipaldo*, 298 U.S. 587 (1936), 20

Murdock v. *Pennsylvania*, 319 U.S. 105 (1943), 24n, 80n, 113n, 115

New York Times Co. v. *Sullivan*, 376 U.S. 254 (1964), 28n, 83n, 94n, 137n

New York Times Co. v. *United States*, 403 U.S. 713 (1971), 25–26, 28, 135n, 168n, 171

Niemotko v. *Maryland*, 340 U.S. 268 (1951), 113

Olmstead v. *United States*, 277 U.S. 438 (1928), 147n

Paris Adult Theatre I v. *Slaton*, 413 U.S. 49 (1973), 28n

Pennekamp v. *Florida*, 328 U.S. 331 (1946), 85, 88, 89, 93, 96

Pentagon Papers Case, see *New York Times Co.* v. *United States*

Poulos v. *New Hampshire*, 345 U.S. 395 (1953), 153n

Reynolds v. *United States*, 98 U.S. 145 (1878), 186n

Robertson v. *Baldwin*, 165 U.S. 275 (1897), 33

Robinson v. *California*, 370 U.S. 660 (1962), 16

Rochin v. *California*, 342 U.S. 165 (1952), 18n, 20n, 126n

Roe v. *Wade*, 410 U.S. 113 (1973), 151n

Rogers v. *Bellei*, 401 U.S. 815 (1971), 75, 76, 77

Roth v. *United States*, 354 U.S. 476 (1957), 94n, 135

Saia v. *New York*, 334 U.S. 558 (1948), 113n

Schacht v. *United States*, 398 U.S. 58 (1970), 158n

Schaefer v. *United States*, 251 U.S. 466 (1920), 92n

Schenck v. *United States*, 249 U.S. 47 (1919), 92

Schneider v. *State*, 308 U.S. 147 (1939), 87, 89

Schneiderman v. *United States*, 320 U.S. 118 (1943), 77n

Sheppard v. *Maxwell*, 384 U.S. 333 (1966), 187–88, 191

Sherbert v. *Verner*, 374 U.S. 398 (1963), 186n

Smith v. *California*, 361 U.S. 147 (1959), 7n, 96n, 134n, 137n

Southern Pacific v. *Arizona*, 325 U.S. 761 (1945), 142n

Speiser v. *Randall*, 337 U.S. 513 (1958), 135

Spence v. *Washington*, 418 U.S. 405 (1974), 169n

State v. *Croswell* (N.Y. Sup. Ct. 1804), 51n

Street v. *New York*, 394 U.S. 576 (1969), 169, 171

Sweeney v. *Woodall*, 344 U.S. 86 (1952), 17n

Sweezy v. *New Hampshire*, 354 U.S. 234 (1957), 130, 132

Terminiello v. *Chicago*, 337 U.S. 1 (1949), 64n, 99, 115

Thomas v. *Collins*, 323 U.S. 516 (1945), 85n, 91–92

Thornhill v. *Alabama*, 310 U.S. 88 (1940), 82, 83, 90, 157n, 160–62, 164, 166, 167

Time, Inc. v. *Hill*, 385 U.S. 374 (1967), 14n, 83n, 138n

Tinker v. *Des Moines School District*, 393 U.S. 503 (1969), 125n, 146n, 153n, 159n

Trupiano v. *United States*, 334 U.S. 699 (1948), 147n

United Public Workers v. *Mitchell*, 330 U.S. 75 (1947), 167–68

United States v. *Ballard*, 322 U.S. 78 (1944), 142n, 185n

United States v. *Butler*, 297 U.S. 1 (1936), 10n

United States v. *Kahriger*, 345 U.S. 22 (1953), 42n

United States v. *Robel*, 389 U.S. 258 (1967), 145n

United States v. *White*, 401 U.S. 745 (1971), 151n

Uphaus v. *Wyman*, 360 U.S. 72 (1959), 132n

Valentine v. *Chrestensen*, 316 U.S. 52 (1942), 96n, 179n

Wade v. *Hunter*, 336 U.S. 684 (1949), 78–79, 81

West Virginia Board of Education v. *Barnette*, 319 U.S. 624 (1943), 38n, 42–43n, 69n, 73, 80n, 110n, 155n, 158n

Whitney v. *California*, 274 U.S. 357 (1927), 92n

Wieman v. *Updegraff*, 344 U.S. 183 (1952), 116n, 118n, 135, 159n

Wilkinson v. *United States*, 365 U.S. 399 (1961), 9n, 22n, 134n, 168n

Williams v. *North Carolina*, 325 U.S. 226 (1945), 120n

Winters v. *New York*, 333 U.S. 507 (1948), 95

Wisconsin v. *Yoder*, 406 U.S. 205 (1972), 185n, 186n

Yates v. *United States*, 354 U.S. 298 (1957), 7n, 130, 135, 159n